Unifying Force
Of Hinduism

UNIFYING FORCE OF HINDUISM

The Harekrsna Movement

HARIPADA ADHIKARY

authorHOUSE®

AuthorHouse™
1663 Liberty Drive
Bloomington, IN 47403
www.authorhouse.com
Phone: 1-800-839-8640

Published by AuthorHouse   04/23/2012

ISBN: 978-1-4685-0392-0 (sc)
ISBN: 978-1-4685-0393-7 (e)

DEDICATED TO
THE MEMORY OF MY LATE PARENTS

CONTENTS

PREFACE

Hindu religion is one of the oldest religion of the world started from the pre-historical era from what was known as 'Sanatana dharma'. The philosophy of the religion is very deeply rooted and complex, due to the assimilation and accommodation of many beliefs and thoughts of ancient India, within it. Hence there are so many variations in practices and existence of so many sects. The caste system although a social tradition, but is intimately linked with the practices of religion in India. Due to the existence of so many caste of different status higher and lower with their respective religious rights prescribed by the 'Law of Manu' and subsequently by the Brahmonical leaders, there were many divisions and subdivisions within the Hindu community.

No doubt these had weakened the society. There were religious and social reformers in the past who had recognized, the existence of unfair discrepancies in the religious practice due to the caste system and tried to rectify these with very limited success.

In these study the role of Hare Krsna movement introduced by Sri Caitanya to counter act the divisiveness of caste system, has been investigated. For the purpose of this study, many religious scriptures, including Vedas, Upanishads, Puranas, the epics, and many religious literature, particularly related to the Vaisnavas, Saktas and Saivas, have been consulted. Many old books, journals and lecture note books of the famous persons of nineteenth and early twentieth centuries, have also been consulted. For the purpose of field work many 'temples', 'religious' 'fairs', 'festivals', 'mahotsavas' and 'namyajnas' have been visited by myself or by my close associates.

Hundreds of religious leaders of various sects were interviewed and survey was carried out, to numerous people in different occasions in West Bengal and in U.K., to receive instant answers to few specific religious questionnaire to gather information. Besides these my forty years experiences as a keen observer of many events and the progress of the Hindu religion, have been added to it. For the purpose of description, it is worthwhile to mention few words or phrases here to avoid confusion. After the advent of Caitanya, the Hare Krsna movement, the movement of Caitanya or Vaisnavism have been used in different times in different places, but bear the same meaning.

Similarly Nama, Namakirtana, Namasankirtana or Caitanya kirtana, also bear the same meaning. In some scriptures although it has the same spelling 'Brahmana' has been meant as 'Paramatma' or God head, and in others 'Brahmana', means by caste. To avoid this confusion, in this study Brahmana always, is meant for Godhead and Brahmana by caste has been written as Brahmin.

During translation of many Bengali and Sanskrit words, I found very hard to select appropriate English words for the exact expression. I express my sincere apology if there is any error in it. Similarly in writing Sanskrit and Bengali words or certain Indian names, in English alphabets, to transpire the exact expression, some times a vowel or a letter has been omitted from the traditional spelling, such as Krishna as Krsna, Vrindavana, as Vrndavana, Chaitanya as Caitanya etc. For the purpose of this study to collect materials and information I have received helps and supports from many people. I like to express my gratitude to all of them.

I like to express my regards to all the scholars whose dedication and contribution, made the Vaisnava literature so rich and particularly to those whose names have been referred in this work. Among them few names I have got to mention here such as Mahatma Sisir Kumar Ghosh, Sahityaratna Dr. Hare Krishna Mukhopadhyay, Professor Sukumar Sen, Dr. Ramakanta Chakravorty and Mr. Nirmalnarayan Gupta, for not only to show my very deep regards and respects, but as this study is substantially based on many of their works.

I like to thank for constant guidance, to Dr. David Smith, Department of Religious Studies, Lancaster University, who encouraged me to be involved in this study. Lastly I like to acknowledge my gratitude to Mr. Bimal Dhur of Academic Publishers, Calcutta, for the publication of this book.

31st March 2012
Preston, U.K.

Haripada Adhikary

Abbreviations

ASB	Asiatic Society of Bengal.
BE	Bengali Era.
BG	Bhagavata Gita.
BSNS	Bhakisutras of Narada and Sandilyasutra.
BSPP	Bangiya Sahitya Parisat Patrika.
CBH	Caitanyabhagavata of Vrndavanadasa (Sahitya Akademi ed).
CCM	Caitanyacaritamrta (Sahitya Akademi ed.).
GGD	Gauraganoddesdipika.
GMV	General Mass Vaisnava.
GVM	Gaudiya Vaisnava Mandali.
GVA	Gauriya Vaisnava Abhidhana.
GVJ	Gaudiya Vaisnava Jivana
GVO	Gaudiya Vaisnava Organisation
GMV	General mass Vaisav
HKM	Hare Krsna Movement
ISKCON	International Society for Krsna Consciousness.
JASB	Journal of the Asiatic Society of Bengal.
JBORS	Journal of the Bihar and Orissa Research Society.
ODBL	Origin and Development of the Bengali Language.
PKT	Padakalpataru.
RM	Rasikamangala.
II	

CHAPTER I
Hindu Religion

Origin and Conception

Hinduism is unique among the great religions, in that it had no founder, but grew gradually from what was originally known as Sanatan Dharma, over a period from the prehistoric era, absorbing and assimilating all the ancient religious beliefs of India. Hence so much variations, exists in the practices, in various factions within the Hindu community.

The name of India in the Avesta (Oldest Persian Text), is Hindu, which like the old Persian Hi(n)du, is derived from the river Indus. In Sanskrit it is Sindu, the designation of the stream, transferred to the territory, adjacent to it and its tributaries. The inhabitants of these territories, were named as Indu initially by the IndoEuropean invader in about 2500 BC, which was later known as Hindu[1] and the land as Hindusthan[2].

The first chapter of the Avestan Vendidad contains an allusion to a portion of Northern India, describing sixteen lands or regions, created by Ahura Mazda and (Iranian deity) apparently, were regarded as under the Iranian sway. The fifteenth of these domains (according to Vendidad 1, 18)[3], was Hapta Hindu, 'Seven Rivers', a region of abnormal heat. Probably the region was identical with the territory of 'Sapta Sindhavas', 'Seven Rivers', mentioned in the Veda (Rigveda VIII, 24, 27).

---

[1] The Cambridge History of India by E.J. Rapson, 1921, p. 289.
[2] Patterns of Indian Thoughts by J.B. Chethimttam, 1971, p. 1, The Meaning and End of Religion by W.C. Smith, 1962, p. 64.
[3] Vendidad: Vol. Cho. 1 p 18; The Oxford History of Indian by V.A. Smith, 4th. Ed. p. 32.

1

The region was more comprehensive than the modern Punjab and must have included the lands watered in the north and northwest of Hindusthan by the river Indus and its affluents.

In historical time it is known that many tribes had passed into Asia from Europe. Among them were the Phygyans, the Mysians and the Bithynians.

The migratory unit who remained in Persia as an unbroken stock, was known as Ayrans.

The word Arya came from the sanskrit word Airya in Zend-Avesta (sacred book of ancient Persia), meaning good family.[1] It is the epithet that was used by the composers of the vedic hymns to distinguish their own stocks from that of their enemies, the dark skinned earlier inhabitants of India whom they called Dasas or Dasyas.

The Aryan who settled in Persia were later called Iranian and those who settled in India were called Indo-Aryan. They were distinct from the unrelated stocks of Dravidian and other original inhabitants of the Indian peninsula. So the Hindu religion of the present day, is the combined religion of the pre-Aryan Indians and the Indo-Aryans[2]

The oldest form of Indo-Aryan, the language of Rigveda, is distinguished from the oldest forms of Iranyan, the language of the Avesta, chiefly by the presence of a series of dental letters, the so-called cerebrals. The earlier forms of speech by which Indo-European, was modified in the various stages of its progress from the northwest, were predominantly Dravidian.

At the present time Dravidian languages are stable only in the countries of the south where they have developed great literature like Tamil, Malayalam, Kanarese and Telegu. The Indo-Aryan languages, the origins of which are from Sanskrit, have not extended very considerably to the south of Aryavarta, 'the Region of the Aryans,' defined by Manu, i.e. the country between the Himalayas and the Vindhyas (mountains) from the Bay of Bengal to the Arabian Sea. The chief representative of the midland languages of the area, is western Hindi. Immediately outside the languages of the midlands come those of the inner band Punjabi, Rajasthani and Gujarati on the west, Pahari on the north, and eastern Hindi on the east; and beyond them the languages of the outer band Bihari (mixed with eastern Hindi),

---

[1]   The Cambridge History of India by E.J. Rapson, p.p. 45, 63, 65.
[2]   The Wonder That Was India by A.L. Basham, 1985, p.p. 298, 302.

Bengali, Assamese and Oriya on the east, Kashmiri, Lahnda, Sindhi, and Kacchi on the west and Marathi on the south west.

Orthodox Brahmanism, as represented by Manu directed that all members of 'twice born' social orders, Brahmins, Kashtriyas, and Vaisyas, should resort to this region and enjoined that every man of these orders should be instructed in his religious and social duties by a Brahmin belonging to one of the people of Brahmarshidesa (Kurus, Matsyas, Panchalas and Surasenas)[1]. The oldest Indian documents are the Vedas. In chronological order from the oldest, they are Rigveda, Yajurveda, Samveda and Atharvaveda. The chronology based upon the linguistic and textual development of the vedic literature, is uncertain because of the absence of the documents or absolute dating. Nevertheless it is reasonable to believe that the major part of the Rigveda was prepared or at least refers to the events that took place, about 1500-1200 BC in the Punjab[2].

It is possible that the compilation of the Rigveda presupposes several centuries of the interactions of the Indo-Aryan with the local population and culture; so that some older, pre-Aryan ideology had become absorbed into it.

Vedic Gods and Goddesses

The principal vedia gods were Agni, Varuna, indra, Vayu, Surya, Mitra, Rudra, Swaraswati, Skanda, Vishnu etc. Later in the epic period (850 BC-200 AD)[3], the Vedic gods such as Indra, Mitra, and Varuna and Skanda were transformed into three divinities, Brahma, Vishnu, and Siva; and these in turn were conceived as but manifestations of the one Primival Spirit, the Lord adored by all, the one undecaying Brahmana.

There were many other gods of less importance worshipped in different parts of India. There were many mother goddesses who were also worshipped, such as Kali or Durga, (Sakti), Lakshmi, Swaraswati, Sitala, Manasha etc. Sakti is the one who became more popular. Including the

---

[1]   The Oxford History of India by V.A. Smith, 4th, Ed, p. 43-47.
[2]   Indian and Far Eastern Religious Traditions by R.D. Baird and A. Bloom, p. 10-15.
[3]   The Wonder That Was India by A.L. Basham, p. 298-320.

local deities there were numerous gods and goddesses, worshipped by the Hindus at some parts of the country.

The Hindu worship is not only confined to the propitiation of god and demigods, but also the whole nature was in some sense divine. Great and holy men were reverenced, both during their lives and for long after their death, for they contain a portion of god head. Thus the sixty three Nayanars of Tamil Saivism and the twelve Alvers of Tamil Vaisnavism still enjoy the status of demigods, as do their great religious teachers to their followers.

Not only men, but animals and plants were and still are holy, notably, the cow. According to one legend the cow Surabhi, the mother of all the cows, was one of the treasures churned from the cosmic ocean. The 'five products of the cow' (panchagavya) milk, curd, butter, urine and dung were all of great purifying potency, specially when combined in a single mixture.[1] The bull on the other hand, received honour largely as Nandi, the mount of Siva. The image of bull is found in most of the Saivite temples and honoured with occasional offerings. After the cow the snake was perhaps the most revered animal of ancient India and still is regularly worshipped in some parts.

The tree cults common, all over the world among the ancient people, were widespread in India, where many villages have their own sacred tree, usually the biggest one. 'Specially sacred were pipal (asatha) and banyan (vata). Among other trees asoka is notable to sometimes women pray for children. There were also sacred plants, such as tulsi (a type of basil). Two types of grass, kusha and durva, were also sacred from vedic times onwards

India primarily a Hindu country, the land dominated by the Brahmins, who have succeeded by means of peaceful penetration, not by the sword, in carrying their ideas to every corner of the country. The caste system, the characteristic of the Brahmin institution, nearly utterly unknown in Burma, Tibbet and other borderlands, dominates the whole of Hindu India and exercises no small influence over the powerful Muslim minority. Nearly all the Hindus, revere Brahmins.

Hardly there is any body who denies the authority of Vedas and other religious scriptures. The Sanskrit is the sacred language everywhere.

---

[1] Ibid. p. 319; Vishnu Purana, XXIII, 57-59.

Among the many gods and goddesses, Vishnu, Siva and Sakti (Kali), are recognized in all part of India.[1] The seven sacred cities include places such as Gaya, Kashi, Vrindavana, Mathura, Haridwara, Prayag and Puri in far south and as well as in north (known as Hindusthan). Similarly the cult of river is common to all Hindus. There are certain rivers such as Ganges, Yamuna, Sarasvati, Narmada, Godavari, Krisna and Kaveri are considered sacred. Every hill and mountain had some degree of sanctity and so also certain lakes specially Manasa in the high Himalayas and Puskara near Ajmer. All alike share in the affection felt about the tales of the great epics 'Mahabharata' and 'Ramayana'[2].

That civilization had been summed up in the terms Hinduism.

The Fundamentals of Hinduism

So the most fundamental understanding of Hinduism, rest upon the fact that the diverse people with their different belief of god and goddesses, had developed a similar type of social culture and civilization utterly different from any other parts of the world.

The Hindus in general are very dedicated in the name of religion and show respect to any kind of belief. They never disrespect to any faith. All in general are the believer of one Godhead with the Omnipotent power second to none. This power head could be Brahmana, Vishnu, Siva or female Godhead Kali according to belief. This power is invisible, but exists in all the elements of the Universe. These regards, respects or worshiping of numerous objects and elements are grossly interpreted as 330 million god and goddesses of the Hundu's

The common Hindus in general are not interested in the Theology or system of higher philosophy, but posses some sort of bhaki in their heart towards their object of worship and bhakti is the basis for Hindu philosophy.

---

[1] Oxford History of India by Vincent Smith, 4th. Ed. p 7.

[2] The Wonder That Was India by A.L. Basham, p. 320; Vedic Index, 11. p. 237, 298.

CHAPTER II

The Class System

The Origin of Class System and Varna

When the Aryans entered India there was already a class division in their tribal structure. The records of several other Indo-European peoples suggest that a tribal aristocracy was a feature of Indo-European society even before the tribes, migrated from their original home. As they settled among the darker aboriginals the Aryans seem to have laid greater stress than before, on the purity of their blood, and class divisions hardened, to exclude those Dasas who had found a lace in the fringes of Aryan society and those Aryans who had intermarried with the Dasas and adopted their ways.

Both these groups sank in the social scale. At the same time the priests, whose sacrificial lore was becoming more and more complicated, and who therefore required greater skill and training, were arrogating higher privileges to themselves. By the end of the Rig Vedic period (1400 BC), the society was divided into four great classes, and this fourfold division was given religious sanctions and looked on, as fundamental.

This is evident from one of the most important hymns of the collection, in which the four classes are said to have emanated from the dismembered primeval man, who was sacrificed by the gods at the beginning of the world[1].

The centre of the Aryan cult was sacrifice. By the end of the Rig Vedic period it was widely believed that the universe itself arose from a primeval sacrifice. There was no clearly defined creator-god in the main body of the Rig Veda. By the end of this period, however such a god had developed, it

---

[1]   The Wonder That Was India by A.L. Basham, p. 35.

is unknown whether wholly from the speculation of the brahmins or from non-Aryan influences.

The god was Prajapati, "the Lord of Beings", later called Brahma the masculine form of the neuter brahman. Prajapati was thought of as a primeval man (purusa), who existed before the foundation of the universe. The man was sacrificed presumably to himself, by the gods who were his children[1].

From the body of the divine victim the universe was produced.

The great "Hymn of the Primevalman" (Rigveda), in which the first cosmic sacrifice is described, bristles with obscurities, but its purport is quite clear.

> When they divided the man,
> into how many parts they divide him?
> What was his mouth, what were his arms,
> what were his thighs and his feet called?
> The brahman was his mouth,
> of his arm and was made the warrior,
> his thigh became the vaisya,
> of his feet the sudra was born[2].

The four classes, the priest (brahmin), warrior (kshatriya), trader (vaisya) and serf (sudra), were crystallizing throughout the period of Rig Veda. They have survived to the present day. The sanskrit word 'varna' was used for them, means colour and itself indicates their origin in the development of the old tribal class structure in contact with the people of different complexion and alien culture. The term varna does not mean caste and has never meant caste, by which convenient word it is often loosely translated[3].

Definition of a caste: A caste may be defined as a group of families internally united by peculiar rules for the observance of ceremonial purity, specially in the matters of diet and marriage. The same rules serve to fence it

---

[1] Ibid: p. 240-241.

[2] The Wonder That Was India, by A.L. Basham, p. 240-41.

[3] Ibid.: p. 35.

off from all other groups, each of which has its own set of rules. Admission to an established caste in along settled territory, can be obtained now a days by birth only and transitions from one caste to another which used to be feasible in ancient times are, no longer possible, except in frontier province like Manipur[1].

The families composing a caste may or may not have a tradition of descent from the same ancestor, and as a matter of fact, may or may not belong to one stock. Race, that is to say, descent by blood, has little concern with caste, in northern India, at all events, whatever may be the case in the south. The individual member of a caste may or may not be restricted to any particular occupation or occupations. The members may believe or disbelieve any creed or doctrine, religious or philosophical, ideas without affecting their caste position[2]. Each caste has its own dharma (religion) in addition to the common rules of morality as accepted by Hindus generally. The general Hindu dharma enforces among other things reverence to Brahmins, respect for sanctity for animal life in varying degrees, and specially veneration for the horned cattle, preeminently the cow. Every caste man is expected to observe accurately the rules of his own group and to refrain from doing violence to the feelings of the other groups concerning their rules.

The essential duty of a caste is to follow the custom of his group, more particularly in relation to diet or marriage. Violation of the rules on those subjects, if detected, usually involves unpleasant and costly social expiation and may result in expulsion from the caste, which means social ruin and inconveniences[3].

The Hindus have not any name for the caste institution, which seems to them part of the order of nature. It is almost impossible for a Hindu to regard himself otherwise than as a member of a particular caste or species of Hindu mankind. The proper sanskrit and vernacular term for a caste is jati (jat); although members of a jati may not be from a common ancestor. Their special caste rules make their community in effect a distinct species, whoever their ancestors might have been.

---

[1] The Oxford History of India, by V.A. Smith, 4th. Ed., p. 61.
[2] Ibid: p. 62.
[3] Origin and Growth of Caste in India: by N.K. Dutt, p. 149.

Distinction between Varna and Jati

Most of the misunderstanding on the subject has arisen from the persistent mistranslation of Manu's term varna as 'caste', whereas it should be rendered as 'class' or 'order' or by some equivalent term.

The compiler of the institutes of Manu was well aware of the distinction between varna and jati. While he mentions about fifty different castes, he lays much stress on the fact that there were only four varnas. The two terms are carelessly confused in one passage (x.31), but in that only. Separate caste existed from an early date. Their relation to one another remain, unaffected whether they are grouped theoretically under four occupational headings or not[1].

The Laws of Manu: In connection with the subject of the evolution of caste, the famous law book commonly called the Laws or Code or 'Institute of Manu' (Manavadharmasastra in Sanskrit) demands notice[2]. The treaties written in concise Sanskrit verse of the 'epic' type, comprises 2684 couplets (sloka) arranged in twelve chapters; and is the earliest of the metrical law books. It professes to be the composition of a sage named Bhrigu, who used the work of his predecessor[3]. The date of composition may lie between 200 BC and 200 AD. About one-tenth of the verses is found in Mahabharata[4].

The Laws of Manu form the foundation of the queer medley of the inconsistent system of jurisprudence administered by the High Courts of India under the name of Hindu Law. The prevalent error concerning the supposed 'original four castes' rests partly, as proved above, on erroneous interpretation of the text, and partly on fictitious explanation of the facts of caste offered by the author[5].

The early Sanskrits unduly exalted the authority of the Laws of Manu, which they regarded as veritable laws instead of mere rulings of a textbook

---

[1] The Oxford History of India by V.A. Smith, 4th. Ed, p. 64.
[2] Ibid: P. 68 70.
[3] The Vedic Age by R.C. Majumder, London, 1951, p. 21.
[4] History of Caste in India by S.V. Keikar, New York, 1909.
[5] Caste in India by Sir E. Denison Ross, London, 1930.

writer, which they actually are[1]. The fuller knowledge of the present day sees the book in truer perspective, but the old errors still exert a baneful influence in many directions[2].

In Bhagavad Gita, which is a part of Mahabharata compiled more or less in the same period (400 BC-400 AD) as that of Manu's Law, gave a bit more detail about the understanding of varna. In Gita Sri-Krsna said—

> Chaturvarnyam maya srastam
> guna karma vibhagasah
> tasya kartaram api mam
> viddhy akartarm avyayam[3].

It means, according to three modes (sattva, raja, tama) of material nature and the work associated with them, the four divisions of human society are created by me. Although I am the creator of this system, you should know that I am yet the nondoer, being unchangeable.

He the God is therefore the creator of the four divisions of the social order, beginning with the intelligent class of men, called brahmins, being situated in the mode of goodness (sattva). They were mainly responsible for the worshipping, teaching and advising the rulers. Next is the administrative class, called the kshatriyas due to them being situated in the mode of passion (raja).

The mercantile men called the vaisyas, are situated in the mixed mode of passion and ignorance. The sudras are the labour class, situated in the ignorant mode of material nature.

This division of class was based on the quality of a person but not according to his birth in a class. Accordingly not necessarily a descendant of a Brahmin would automatically would be a Brahmin

---

[1] Caste in India by J.H. Hutton, Cambridge, 1946. "Professor Hutton's work is of an anthropological study of great merit, in which he claims to find caste like features in the culture of primitive Indian tribes and traces the institution to pre-Aryan origins. The standard translation of Manu is that of 'Buhler' (The Law of Manu, S.B.E, VolXXV, Oxford, 1986.

[2] Oxford History of India by Smith, p. 70.

[3] The Bhagavad Gita 4/13.

On the other hand a descendant of a Sudra, if situated in the mode goodness (sattva), could be a Brahmin. Similarly descendant of a Brahmin, situated in the mode ignorance would be a Sudra[1].

This type of class division or four varnas, were adopted by the liberal Hindus and were strongly recommended by the social reformers, but were undermined and ignored by the Brahmonical administration.

Brahminical administration were more active for the safe guard of their descendant to adopt and support the caste system, depending on their birth rather than their qualities. The Brahmin class being the intelligent group, dominated the society, by controlling the administration and literature, introducing laws and regulations for the society, preserving the birth right of the caste system, denying the right of the lower class to read veda and other religious books etc.

As a result of these, over the centuries, people nearly forgot about the original basis of class division according to varna, rather suffered from the wrong interpretation of class system according to the caste and its disastrous effect in the Hindu society.

The Origin of the Word Caste and the system

It is clear that the four varnas existed since the time of Rigveda (1400 BC). It is also known that the class system which is later known as 'jati', existed before 300 BC, because the most obvious features of the institution are noticed by the Greek authors of ascertained date; and it is reasonable to believe that class (jati) separated from one another by rules of ceremonial purity, were in existence a few centuries earlier[2].

The word caste came from the Spanish 'caste' meaning breed, strain, or a complex of hereditary qualities. When Portuguese came to India in the 16th century, they found the Hindu community divided into many separate groups, which they called castas, meaning tribes, class or families[3]. The caste is the English and French adjustment of the original term. The name stuck, and became the usual word for the Hindu social group. In attempting

---

[1]   Ibid. 4/13.

[2]   The Oxford History of India by V.A. Smith, p. 64.

[3]   The Wonder That was India by A.L. Basham, p. 148.

to account for the remarkable proliferation of the caste in 18th and 19th century India, credulously accepted the traditional view that by a process of intermarriage and subdivision the 3,000 or more caste of modern India had evolved from the four primitive classes, and the term caste was applied indiscriminately to varna or class and jati or caste proper. This is a false terminology; castes rise and fall in the social scale, and old castes die out and the new ones are formed, but the four great classes are stable. They are never more or less than four, and for over 2,000 years their order to precedence has not altered. In the hierarchy, Brahmin is the highest caste, Kshatriya forming the second group, and the Vaisyas are the third. These three classes are called 'Dwijas' or twice born, once at their natural birth and again at their initiation, when they were invested with the sacred thread and received into the Aryan society. They have a higher status in the society. All others which form the fourth group, are called the Sudras[1].

They are the serving class, servants of the society, ie the three upper class. There is another class who are not included in this broad division, they are the untouchables situated at the very outer boundary of the periphery of Hinduism. To quote Dr. Ambedkar, they are the by product of the caste system.

To define a caste is harder than to explain the derivation of the term. It is easier to say what caste is not than what caste is. It is not the colour or complexion of the body, though the old pandits sometimes talk if they were. A Brahmin is no less Brahmin if he is born jet black; an untouchable is no less untouchable if he happened to be fair.

It is not Aryan or non-Aryan or conqueror and conquered. The Aryans never seemed to have penetrated to the East and South of India. The Brahmins of the South are the highest of the high caste men, but they are not in the record as having conquered by anybody. It is not occupation. Most artisanal occupations are overwhelmingly identified with particular castes, but the main occupation the agriculture is open to all and many castes have priests who are not Brahmins. There have been soldiers who are not Kshatriyas. Government servants have always been chosen from various castes. One does not have to be Vaisya to be a trader and sainthood is open to untouchable also. The average Hindu who observes the caste

---

[1] The Caste System by Dr. B.R. Ambedkar.

system, does so believe his religion wants him to do. Many attempts have been made to define caste, but due to its manifold aspects, variety of forms and elements, the attempted definitions, have ended up more or less in the line of descriptions and explanations.

According to Sir Edward Blunt, "It is an indigenous groups bearing a common name, membership of which is hereditary; imposing on its members certain restrictions in the matter of social intercourse; either following a common traditional occupation or claiming common origins and generally regarded as forming a single homogeneous community"[1].

Professor J.H. Hutton has interpreted caste system, "as an adaptation of one of the most primitive of social relationships, whereby a small clan, living in a comparative isolated village, would hold itself aloof from its neighbours by a complex system of taboos", and he has found embryonic caste features in the social structure of some of the wild tribes or present day India[2].

Senart gives a more descriptive definition. He states that a caste is a class of close cooperation, exclusive and in theory at any rate rigorously hereditary. It is equipped with certain traditional and independent organization, including a chief and a council; meeting on occasion in assembly endowed with more or less full authority. Often united with the celebration of certain festivals. It is further bound together by common occupation and the practice of common customs which relate particularly to marriage, food, and questions of ceremonial pollution.

Finally it rules its members by the exercise of a jurisdiction, the extent of which is fairly far and wide. By the sanctions of certain penalties, especially of exclusion, either absolute or revocal, from the group, succeeds in enforcing the community[3].

The system is so peculiar and complex that it is difficult to define it satisfactorily. It may be easier to elicit some of the features of the caste system which is noticeable even in present day and was very prominent in five hundred years ago.

The castes are group, with well developed group of their own, the membership of which is determined not by selection but by birth.

---

[1] Fundamentals of Sociology by P. Gisbert, 1973, pp. 377, 514.
[2] The Wonder That Was India by A.L. Basham, 1985, p. 149.
[3] Origin and Growth of Caste in India by N.K. Dutt, Vol. 1, 1968, p. 278.

The status of a person depends not on his wealth or his profession but on the traditional importance of his caste. A Brahmin officer and a non-Brahmin officer tough equal in status in office, belong to different status group in their private life and there could not be any social intercourse between them on equal terms.

Everywhere in India there was a definite scheme of social procedure amongst the caste with Brahmin at the top of the hierarchy and untouchables at the bottom. But in between so many castes it was not easy to distinguish the social procedure form one caste to another. However there was a system acknowledged largely by all. But the promotion and degradation could take place by the approval of the ruler and by the Brahmin.

There were simple rules as to what kind of food or drink could be accepted from which caste. But there was a great diversity in this matter in area to area. Certain types of foods were thought to be polluted by the touch of certain castes. The idea of pollution was so deep rooted in some places that not only touch but mere shadow of certain castes would have polluted certain food for some castes.

The segregation of individual castes or a group of castes in a village was the most obvious mark of civil privileges and had prevailed in more or less definite form all over India. Dominant caste used to occupy the privileged position and Sudras in less important position and the untouchables used to live at the outskirts or even outside the village.

Generally a caste or a group of allied castes used to consider some of the calling as their hereditary occupation. Thus a brahmin used to think that it was correct for him to be a priest, while a charmakar used to think, it was his duty to prepare shoes.

No caste would allow its member to take any calling which was thought to be degrading. Fisherman and washerman still only comes from these particular castes. None other than a Brahmin would be allowed to be a priest. It became the tradition that all the higher kind of jobs should be done by high caste people. All kind of manual and inferior jobs should be done by lower castes people.

The marriage was restricted by the social rule within there own castes. The principle of strict endogamy was such that it gave the impression that the essence of the caste system might have laid there. There was exception to these rules. As a result of intercastes marriage, the victims used to be outcaste and a new caste would be formed.

Discrepancies of Caste System

Having discussed the fourfold division of the Hindu society and the variations, it is important to note the most discriminatory features of the caste division, for which it has collected the bad reputation outside India, which is untouchability.

A group of the lowest castes, numbering about one-sixth of the total population, were thought to be untouchables (polluted) and their physical touch direct or indirect were avoided. They were outside the pale of varna system, though for the identification, at a later stage, known as fifth varna.

In general, intercaste marriage was forbidden, but the 'aunloma' marriage was recognized by the law givers. On the other hand the 'pratiloma' *ie* low caste man with high caste woman, was disapproved and severe punishment was prescribed for such an act.

The victims of such a union could not find a place in either of the laws in society. They were treated as an outcast. They remained, only at the bottom of the society. They were treated (despised), more or less like an animal. Like other castes they were also divided into hundreds of subcastes and endogamous as well.

It is worthwhile to note that a punishment imposed to a particular individual, sometimes would affect not only of his whole family, but also the community he belonged. Without going into details, some other factor that would cause a caste becoming outcasts are mentioned here such as, non-observance of the sacred rules, connected with uncleaned occupation, killing of animal as a profession, dealing with dead animals, eating beef, widow marriages and an offence committed by any of the members of the castes.

It is worthwhile also to know a bit more about what used to be considered as pollution or untouchable to have better idea about the extent of the social discrimination due to the caste system.

Castes reveal itself most obviously and most rigidly in everyday life, through the concept of pollution, a concept fundamental to the Hindu way of life. It is nothing to do with the physical cleanliness or with sin and is purely ritual.

The water of the Ganges is considered to be the most pure thing by the Hindus. To the orthodox, it is not only pure but it purifies every impure thing. It is to be noted that the water of Ganges itself is mixed up with many kinds of uncleaned material, including industrial wastes and dead bodies etc. By contrast water taken from a tube well, boiled and sealed up, in a sterilised bottle, carried by a physically clean untouchable by caste, used to be considered impure and its contact also used to be considered polluting. Pollution could be considered, wide range of things, such as to flay a dead animal is a polluting act, because it is an unclean occupation.

On the other side of the spectrum, a higher castes Hindu would be polluted if his shadow happened to be crossed by an untouchable. It is the taboo which produced instability, within the Hindu community, particularly in the more orthodox area of south. Sexual union is regarded as a polluting affair, if it involves people of different subcastes. It is a polluting act, even sometimes within a marriage with a partner of the same subcaste. During the period of menstruation, women are regarded as impure. Women of some castes are considered so impure that they are not allowed to enter the house during this period.

All sorts of excretion except that of the cow, are considered polluting agent. Eating beef is regarded as a sin for all the Hindus. Eating other types of meat and fish are polluting affair, to some castes. But these are very variable.

Religious Rights Based on Caste and its Effect

To elaborate the understanding, it will be of some help to study some of the references cited in the religious scriptures.

"If a King met a Brahmin on the road, the road belonged to Brahmin". The King used to be the master of all with the exception of the Brahmin.

A Brahmin, ignorant or learned, used to be a great divinity, just as also the fire, whether carried forth or not, used to be a great divinity[1]

It is declared in the Smritis that a Brahmin alone should be chosen as a teacher. At the time of distress a Brahmin may study under a Kshatriya or a Vaisya and during his pupilship he must walk behind such a teacher. Afterwards the Brahmin shall take precedence before the Kshatriya or Vaisya teacher[2]

Kings were not supposed to levy any tax on a Brahmin. Brahmins were exempted from taking oath in the witness box, in a court.

The punishment of a Brahmin if committed a crime such as killing somebody would have to give something for the expiation of his sin, which was thousand cows, for a Kshatriya, one hundred cows for a Vaisya and ten cows for a Sudra victim respectively.

Generally the punishment for murdering a Brahmin was execution except in the case of a Brahmin culprit, who was to be banished with a headless corpse branded on his forehead.

Vedas was not to be read in presence of a Sudra. A Brahmin must not give advice to a Sudra.

One must not eat food offered by an artisan, a physician, an usher, a washerman, an outcaste, a wine merchant, a spy, a hunter, a cobbler etc.

A Chandala was the foulest of man. It was sinful to touch, to speak, or to look at a Chandala. The penance for such touching was to take a bath, submerging the whole body.

If a funeral offering was looked at by a dog, Chandala or outcasts, it used to be blemished.

Without increasing the volume of examples, we can imagine the respective positions of different castes. The motive behind all these rules was not religious but worldly. The Brahmins tried to secure the unchallenged position in the society. They became blind with their selfishness. The pretension of the Brahmin was up to such a height that they glorified themselves and projected as omnipotent. Thus Manu says: "The whole world

---

[1]   Origin and Growth of Caste in India by N.K. Dutt, Vol. 1., 1968, p. 126.

[2]   Ibid. p. 129.

is under the power of Gods, the Gods are under the power of 'Mantras, and the Mantras are under the power of the Brahmin, the Brahmin is therefore our God"[1].

The theoretical aspect of the caste system as described in Hindu scriptures, was found in practice in the same degree. The Sudras were treated as the most degraded beings by all the Hindus, in every part of the Indian society. The vast majority of the Indian people remained illiterate, because they were not allowed to study. The Brahmins were the teachers who would never teach a Sudra. For the untouchables, it was even worse. To look at an untouchable, used to be considered polluting. So they were deprived of all the legitimate social and religious right[2].

Since the development of the caste system, the religious practices had shown some variations in different castes prescribed by the law makers. These law makers were the priests of the Brahmin caste. So all the laws and rules were designed to keep and preserve the benefit and domineering position of the Brahmins and depriving the other castes, the fair justice for the religious practices.

These practices had been going over the centuries and reached to a certain extent in the fifteenth and early sixteenth century, that it might have threatened the very existence of the Hindu community. A close up look at the situation of Bengal is analyzed here.

Navadvipa was the heart land of the Hindu culture and administration of India, as most of the learned panditas and law makers used to reside here. In this period the rightist force of the Hindu society, was represented by Smarta panditas, led by Raghunananda and Govindananda. Although the Hindu society was on the brink of disintegration, yet the Smarta panditas did not relax the so much stress that was already put on the distinction between the Brahmins and the other castes.

The Smartha Brahmins merely wanted to strengthen the social and economic positions of the Brahmins, which they thought could be achieved better, by defining the religious rights of the different castes. At that time the growth of the Kayestha intelligentsia and the appearance of big and

---

[1] Origin and Growth of Caste in India by N.K. Dutt, p. 57-59; The Wonder That Was India by A.L. Basham, 1985, p. 280.

[2] Ibid: Vol. 2, 1969, p. 163.

powerful landlords, had definitely enfeebled the social positions of the Brahmins. Raghunandana therefore wrote that there were only two castes, Brahmins and Sudras[1]. The Kayesthas were of course Sudras.

For the Sudras, Raghunandana and the contemporary Smriti writers prescribed only a few rights[2]. A Brahmin, according to Srikrisna Tarkalamkara, might even could commit adultery with a Sudra woman with unquestionable impunity.[3] But a Sudra was to be severely punished, if he married a Brahmin woman.

The Sudras including the Kayesthas and the Vaidyas, had no right to utter any vedic mantra[4]. They had only the duty to bow down to the feet of the Brahmin and 'serve' him (*"Tusnimeva hi Sudrasya Sanamangkarakam Matam . . . Pancyajne pi Sunrasya Dvijasasrusa Taya Jivanavan Bhavet . . . Iti Namaskaramatra Vidhanam"*)[5]. A Sudra including Kayestha and a Vaidya, could not be a Guru or preceptor.[6]

A Sudra could worship only Siva or Gopala[7]. In ordinary circumstances a Brahmin might not accept any gift from a Sudra or a Kayestha[8].

Under ordinary circumstances a Brahmin could not even act as priest of the Sudra including Kayestha[9]. Even Ramesh Chandra Dutta, ICS, a Kayestha of Rambagan, Calcutta, was severely taken to task by some Brahminical purists for his translation of the Rigveda into Bengali[10]. The Smartas imposed almost similar restrictions on woman belonging to all

[1] Astavimsatitattvani by Raghunandana, 'Sudranhikacaratattvam', Ed. by Benimadhav De, pp. 441, also 'Suddhitatta', p. 356.
[2] Kriyakandavaridhi by S.C. Mukhopadhyaya, Basumati Press, 2nd Ed. Vol. 1, pp. 67.
[3] Op. cit, by Bani Chakravorty, pp. 147-48; 249-51.
[4] Vaisnavism in Bengal by Dr. R. Chakraborty, p. 40.
[5] Sudranhikacaratattavm Raghunandana, op. cit., p. 504.
[6] Ibid. "Vaisnavacaraprakarana, pp. 527-28; "Saivacaraprakarana", p. 561.
[7] Ibid: "Vaisnavacaraprakarana", p. 527-528; "Saivacaraprakarana", p. 561.
[8] Ibid: "Prayascittavyavasthaprakarana", p. 654-655, 681, 691.
[9] Sudranhikacaratattavm Raghunandana, Vol. 111, PP. 696-697.
[10] The translation was regarded by Sasadhar Tarkacudamani as an "inconceivable desecration of the Vedas", Review article in Bangabasi 2, (Daily News paper), Bhadra (September) 7, 1885.

of the castes, including the Brahmins[1]. The apologists for the Smriti have utterly failed to explain, how such misanthropic writs, rules and injunctions, prepared by the Smartas, might have protected Hindu society from the Muhammedan impact.

These groups of people who used to control the administration of the Hindu society conservatively, were called as pasandi (cruel, philistine), by the Vaisnavas. They were mostly professors of Hindu Law, Sanskrit grammar and a philosophical system known as Navyanaya or New Logic. Navyanaya was first invented in Mithila by Udayanacarya in about 1326. It was further developed by nearly thirty scholars of Mithila between AD 1430 and 1500. The first Bengali scholar who achieved farflung fame as an exponent of various philosophical systems, including Navyanaya, was the celebrated scholar Vasudeva Sarvabhauma, who became a follower of Caitanya later on at Puri.

A.B. Keith described this logical system Navyanaya as "a vast mass of perverted ingenuity worthy of the most flourishing days of medieval scholasticism[2].

The Brahmins were in dominant position in the society, of which both the Radi and Vaidika Brahmins were the social leaders. The Varendra Brahmins do not seem to have been in a predominant position[3]. The majority of the people belonged to the non-Brahmonical castes and did not enjoy any social privilege. No liberal social philosophy could possibly evolve in a society which was dominated by a particular caste, such as the Brahmins.

Social relations were atrophied. The society itself was moribund, not because only of the political domination of the Muhammadans, but owing to the Brahmin monopoly of social power and privilege.

Regardless of caste, Hindu women were merely "scullery maids" and reproductive machines. Their individuality and independent position were

---

[1] Bani Chakravarti, op. cit. PP. 237f; S.C. Bandopadhyay, "Smritisastre Bengal" p. 181-182, 191-91. Austerities are prescribed by Ragunandana in "Suddhitattva", op. cit. pp. 345.

[2] Opinion quoted by Dinesh Chandra Bhattacharya, op. cit. p. 315.

[3] CBH.1 Ch. 2, pp. 9 18; 11, Ch. pp. 179-87.

not recognized in the Smritis[1]. They had no right to participate in many religious ceremonies. According to the Dayabhaga of Jimbutavahana, the Hindu widow had no right to sell, mortgage, and gift away her property. But she was entitled to Stridhana or a part of the property or wealth bequeathed by her father or husband[2]. Sati (widow burning) was not compulsory. Raghunandana's liberalism was mainly in his attempt to show that the practice of widow burning was not recognised as a 'regular' custom in the ancient Hindu scriptures[3]. But he prescribed brahmacarya or abstinence for the widow[4], which was tantamount to the practice of severe austerities.

The rigidity of the caste system, the cultural and the social alienation of large segments of the Hindu population by the shortsighted Brahmins, the utter selfishness of the Hindu aristocracy all these to some extent, favoured the conversion of low caste Hindus into Muslims. North and East Bengal fell an easy prey to Islam. The Tebet-Burmese tribes were probably converted by the Arab missionaries stationed at Chittagong[5]. The rigidity of the caste system made the lower castes extremely vulnerable to Muhammadan proselytisation. The hostility of the low caste to the inequities of the caste system is powerfully expressed in such writings as Niranjaner Usma or Wrath of Niranjana[6].

It must also be noted that the conversion of the Hindu into Muhammadanism was far more widespread in East Bengal than in other parts of Bengal mainly because the Hindu low castes and the Buddhists of East Bengal could no longer tolerate the Brahminical reaction. They were attracted by the liberal social philosophy of the Muhammadanism.

---

[1] Vaisnavism in Bengal by Dr. R. Chakravarty, 1985, p. 45.

[2] Smritisastre Bengali by S. C. Bandopadhyaya, pp. 181-82, 190-91.

[3] Astavimsatitattavani, "Suddhitatta" by Raghunandana, p. 345. 'Angiravacane'" Ya Nari Ityupadanat Sahamaranabhavopakso pi Sucitah".

[4] Ibid. p. 345, "Mrte Bhartari Tadanvrohanamveti Brahmacarya Maithunavarjanam Tambuladivarjanamca". He prescribed "Ekahara Gandhadravyarjana tarpans, etc."

[5] ODBL: pp. 208-09.

[6] Sunyapurana, pp. 332-33, Dharmapujavidhana, pp. 219-20. According to this legend Lord Niranjana and his cohorts persecuted the Hindus in the garb of predatory Muhammandans.

Another reason for their conversion was due to the misery and tyranny, they were experiencing during the proselytisations of the Muslim ruler Pir-Shah Jalal. Most of the conversions to Muhammadanism date from the reign of Shah Jalaluddin (1414-1430), who was possibly the only persecutor of the Hindus[1].

It is note worthy a few centuries earlier, Muslim religion was unknown in Bengal. But according to estimate in 1650 or thereabout, there were 8.6 million Hindus and 4.1 million Muslims[2].

---

[1] Bengal District Gazetteers: Mymensingh, E.A. Sachse, 1617, p. 36.

[2] Aspects of Bengali History and Society by Raechel Van M. Baumer, p. 10.

CHAPTER III

Bhakti The Basis Of Harekrsna Movement

Origin

Harekrishna movement is based on the belief of the bhakti cult. The origin of bhaki movement could be traced as early as 500 BC[1]. Some scholars would like to find the root of bhakti even earlier in 1200 BC, since the time of Rigveda in various types of prayers[2].

> *"To thee, O Agni, day by day,*
> *O thou illuminer of gloom,*
> *With thought we, bearing homage, come."*
> *"To thee the lord of sacrifice,*
> *The radiant guardian of the law,*
> *That growest in thine own abode.*
> *So, like a father to his son,*
> *Be easy of approach to us;*
> *Agni, for weal abide with us."*

Bhakti is a religious devotion to a personal deity. It is expressed by adoration as in meditation, chanting hymn, singing devotional songs, or by worshipping during puja on the theoretical level. The concrete expression is the offering of flowers, fruits, clothes, ornaments and other articles to the

---

[1] Indian and Far Eastern Religious Tradition by Robert D. Baired & Alfred Bloom, p. 48-49.

[2] Rigveda 1.1, from A.A. Macdonell, Hymns of the Rigveda, O U P, London, p. 72-73.

deity. While the supreme object of bhakti and puja is the deity itself, parents or elders, spiritual teachers, holy men and even the motherland, have been the object of devotion to some extent.

Perhaps the most concise and systemic account of bhakti theology are to be found in the Narada Bhakti Sutra and Sandilya Sutra.

These Bhaktisutras are not much older than twelfth cnetury[1]. For these Sutras Bhakti is neither knowledge, nor the following in a ritual acts, nor belief in a system. It is an affection and submission to a person. Bhakti is not preliminary to something else, but is an end in itself. It is surrender (propatti) to no earthy object, but to god only. Bhakti can be directed not only to Ghagavan but to any of his incarnations (avataras). Bhakti is higher than external observances and activities and is higher than philosophical meditation. Since it involves in submission in one's part, it also implies divine grace.

The ideology of bhakti was set against that of Karmakanda or rituals, the performance of purificatory rites, the utterance of mystic syllables and the observance of sacraments[2].

The vedic literature was probably as a whole after the entry of Aryans to India (1500 BC) and before the arrival of Buddha (563-483 BC), since some of the geographical locations, animal etc. mentioned in Rigveda are Indian. Although it is difficult to know the exact tijme, one might well follow the dating scheme of J.A.B. Van Buitenen. Rigveda 1400 BC, Yajurveda and Samveda 1400 100 BC, Atharva veda 1200 BC, Brahmanas 1000-800 BC, Aranyakas 800-600 BC. Oldest Upanishads (Brihadaranyaka, Chandogya, Taittiriya) 600-500 BC Early metrical Upanishads (Shvetashvatara, Katha) 500-300 BC Other upanishads rarely older than 300 BC[3].

The denigration of Karmakanda signified a direct attack on popular superstitions which had led to the multiplication of rituals and enabled the priests to maintain their ecclesiastical and social prominence. But though the importance of rituals is minimised in bhakti ideology, they are not totally relegated to the background.

---

[1] BSNS, 1, Sutras 25, 49: 11,1/2/13;

[2] BR,: 1/58, 1/68, 1/177, 2/50-56; 6/7 also 1/106-107.

[3] J.A.B. Van Buitenen, "Vedic Literature", in Civilisation of India Syllabus, Madison, Wis., University of Wisconsin Press, 1965.

According to the Bhaktiratnavali, the Kaliyuga is unfavourable for the observance of rites and ceremonies[1]. But even according to this work, "one may easily cross over the troublous sea of life" simply by correctly observing the rituals[2].

But correct observance of rituals is not possible in the Kaliage. Narada too did not totally discard the social customs and usages[3]. On the question of the expiation of sins there is a difference between Bhaktiratnavali and Sandilyasutra.

According to the former all sorts of sins swine bibbing, theft, murder of a woman, killing of kine, regicide and patricide, adultery with the preceptor's wife, are ipso facto expiated by the utterance of Visnu's sacred name[4]. The redemption of Ajamila, who committed the sin of living with a female slave outside wedlock, is cited as an instance of redemption simply by the utterance of the holy name Rama. Saktas used this concept[5]. This belief inspired many notorious robbers to worship the goddess Kali. Sandilya however holds a different view. According to him bhakti does not lead to the automatic expiation of sins and redemption[6]. After proper expiation, the former sinner finds redemption only in the practice of bhakti.

Bhakti is classified as lower or imperfect when it is motivated by worldly concerns such as sickness, danger, or the desire for some favour. The higher bhakti is completely selfless and involves single hearted attachment to God, all other affection having been destroyed[7].

The higher bhakti is considered far superior to yoga[8]. Yoga may be necessary for acquirement of knowledge and the practice of devotion. But the state of Samadhi, the eighth and the last stage of yoga in which thought

---

[1]   BR; 1/82-83.

[2]   BR; 1/106-107.

[3]   BSNS; 1 Sutras 13, 49.

[4]   BR; 5/525, 5/25: Ajamila was saved simply by uttering the name of Narayana one of his illegitimate children.

[5]   Ramkrishna (Paramahamsa) Kathamrita Vol. 1. pp. 45-46. This led many notorious robbers to worship the goddess Kali.

[6]   BSNS; 11, 2/220, 2/2/27.

[7]   BSNS: 1, Sutras 4, 35, 43, 46, 63, 64; BR:1/10-11,2/58-60;CCM; p 499.

[8]   Vaisnavism in Bengal by R. Chakravorty; p. 74.

is absorbed in the object of meditation, is considered inferior to Bhaki[1]. According to Jiva Gosvamin, bhakti is the best method of yoga in the form of the suppression of impulses[2]. Higher bhakti is not the result of human striving, but of pure grace. Such bhakti is not the means to liberation; it is liberation.

The bhakti-verses and aphorisms stress the need of cultivating moral and social virtues such as compassion, philanthropy, universal brotherhood regardless of friends and foes, nonviolence, truth and moral discipline[3].

According to Krsnadasa Kaviraja Chaitanya stated the following duties of a bhakta or devotee[4]:

"A bhaktavairagi should always sing God's name.
He should live by begging.
He should never be a glutton.
He should never utter or listen obscenties.
He should never eat well and dress well.
He should never be conceited.
He should be more tolerant than a tree.
He should be humbler than the grass.
He should pay everybody proper respect.
He should make up his mind to worship Krsna and
Radha in Vrindavana."

---

[1]   BSNS:1, 1/2/11.

[2]   Bhaktisamdarbha: p.70: (Sanskrit) Bhaktaiva Kryamanya Tadasaktatvena Sveta Eva Manonirodho 'pi Syaditi

[3]   BR: 2/29, 2/1014, 2/5860; BSNS: 1, Sutras, 64, 78.

[4]   CCM: pp 498-499. "*Vairagi Kariva Sada Namsamkirtana,*
Magiya Khayiya Kare Jivana Raksna.
*Sakapatraphalamule Udarabharana_*
Gramyakatha Na Sunive Gramya Katha Na Kahive.
Bhala Na Khayive Ara Bhala Na Parive.
Apan Manete Sada Krsnanama Lave,
Vraje Radhakrsna Seva Manasa Karive".

Vishnu Bhakti

The belief of many sects depend on bhakti such as Bhuddha bhakti, Shiva bhakti (Saiva), Kali bhakti (Sakta), Ram bhakti, Krsna bhakti etc. Vishnu, a solar deity who was of minimum significance in Rigveda, came into more prominence in the Brahmanas, during which time the cult of Vishnu, became known. The followers of Vishnu are known as Vaisnavas[1]. By the fourth century BC, it appears that the two most popular deities, were Vishnu and Shiva.

By the period of Puranas (AD 300-1200), Vishnu had expanded his scope and dominance, chiefly by reason of the doctrine of avataras, (incarnation or descent[2].

Theistic trends were commonly found to row outside the influence of Brahmins. When a local deity became sufficiently prominent, the Brahmins would attempt to bring such worship into their orbit of influence, either by indicating that the deity was really Vishnu under a different name or an avatara of Vishnu. The process has been called Brahmanization or Sanskritization, since it was a process whereby local deities were brought into the orbit of a widely accepted notion of orthodoxy[3]. In the Puranas although more than twenty avataras are mentioned to be ten of them seems prominent.

The traditional list of ten includes both human and animal forms. These are Matsya (the fish), Kurma (the Tortoise), Varaha (the Boar), Narasimha (the Man Lion), Vamana (the Dwarf Vamana), Parshurama (Rama with the Axe) Rama (of Ramayana), Krsna, Buddha, and Kalki (yet to come in future).

---

[1] A Study of Vaisnavism in Ancient and Mediaeval Bengal: by. Mukherji, pp. 41-42; The Spiritual Heritage of India by Swami Prabhavananda, p. 137

[2] Indian and Far Eastern Religious Tradition by R.D. Baird and Alfred Bloom., p. 58.

[3] "On the Archaism of the Bhagavata Purana." by J.A.B. Van Buitenen, in Milton Singer, ed., Krishna: Rites, Myths, and Rituals, Honolulu, East West Center Press. 1966, p. 35." Sanskritization, then refers to a process in Indian Civilization in which a person or a group consciously related himself or itself to an accepted notion of true and ancient ideology and conduct."

Along with Vishnu, the followers of his Avatara's, are also known as Vaishnavas. Although it is usually claimed that the Vaishnavas comprise the largest group of Indian devotees, in fact the largest number of such Vaishnavas are devotees of Krsna and Rama.

Rama Bhakti

Ramayana was one of the two Indian epics. It was substantially complete as early as 400 BC[1]. Devotion towards Rama developed since this period. In Ramayana Ram was presented as a great hero and was mentioned in most of the chapters. Most of the vedic gods were mentioned and Vishnu and Shiva hold position of prime importance. Surprisingly there was no mention of Krsna in this epic, although it was mentioned in other contemporary literature.

It was perhaps some time sin 200 BC Rama became embodies in the written tradition as an important incarnation of Vishnu[2]. Ramayana has so endeared itself to the hearts of numerous Indians that they not only worship Rama, but see Rama and sita as the ideal divine couple.

Ramananda lived in the fifteenth century and exerted considerable influence on the coarse of religious history in India[3]. A sect stemming form him was called Ramanandis. they had their faith in one personal god whom they called Rama. They also believed that bhakti consisted in perfect love toward god and all men were brothers.

Through Ramananda and his disciples the worship of Rama was spread throughout northern and central India. Kabir, one of the important figures in Ramananda's school objected to ceremonies. Believing that Rama was a spirit, Kabir concluded that he could not be worshiped in images but only through prayer.

Perhaps no one had been more influential in the worship of Rama than the poet Tulsi Das (1532-1623 AD). Tulsi Das in later life became a monk to go on pilgrimages throughout India, to settle in Banaras.

---

[1]   Indian and Far Eastern Religious Traditions by R.D. Baird and Alfred Bloom, pp. 55, 57.

[2]   The Oxford History of India by V.A. Smith, p. 59.

[3]   The Wonder That Was India by A.L. Basham, p. 151.

Out of more than twenty of his formal work, famous and influential one was his Ramcharitmanas ("The Lake of Rama's Deed"), based on standard Ramayana[1]

It had more popular appealin supporting devotion to Rama than Gita or the Bhagavata purana had had at that time. Tulsi Das laid great stress on the repetition of the name of Rama for the cultivation of bhakti. He urged the control of the senses and dedication of all action to God.

Krsna Bhakti

It is difficult to be certain about the origin of devotion to Krsna. Krsna is mentioned only a few times prior to the age of Mahabharat, an epic which was in the process of being written and edited from 400 BC, to 400 AD[2]. The Bhagavad Gita, which forms, only a small portion of that epic (which is three and one half times the length of the Christian Bible)[3], presents Krsna as the Supreme God, who if made the object of devotion would save men. This was elegantly shown, when Dussvasan brother of crown prince Durjadhana tried to unrobe Droupadi, the wife of five pandavas in front of the council and the blind King Dhritarastra. When pandavas could not come for her help, Droupadi prayed to Lord Krsna to save her from the embarrassment and Krsna provided her with an endless piece of garment[4]. Gita in fact is the summary of teachings, given by Lord Krsna to his beloved devotee Arjuna in the battle field of Kurukshetra. In these teachings all the emphasis on Bhakti are present. The climax of Gita is in chapter 11 where

---

[1]   Indian and Far Eastern Religious Tradition by R.D. Baird and Alfred Bloom, p. 57.
[2]   The Oxford History of India by V.A. Smith; p. 57.
[3]   Indian and Far Eastern Religious Tradition by R.D. Baired and R. Bloom; p. 52.
[4]   Kashidasi Mahabharat p. 335.
       "Sankate Paria Devi Na Dekhi Upay, Akul Haiya Krishna Smare
       JaduRay. Jhar Jhar Jhare Asru Jal Dunayane, Katarete Krishna
       Dake Dev Narayane," (Krishna is Droupadi's another name)
       Akash Marghete Raiye, Vividha Bashan Laiye, Droupadire Saghane Jogay"
       Jata Duswasan Kade, Tata Bashan Bade, Achchadhan Kari Sarbagaya.

the devotee Arjuna was given a mystical vision of Lord Krshna (Biswarupa darsana)[1]. Lord Krsna said "people who wants to fulfill their desire for various enjoyment of this material world, deviate from the main path of devotion and pray to different goddesses."[2].

In his concluding remark Lord Krsna said to Arjuna "abandon your all other religious commitments, just concentrate your all the devotion on myself, I will make you free from all the evils and will show the path of liberation[3]. While Krsna appears as Supreme God in Gita, some interpreters hold that Krsna is an incarnation of god Vishnu. The childhood and adolescent carrier of Krsna was more developed in fourth century (AD), in the addition to the Mahabharata, in the Harivansa and in the medieval Bhagavata Purana. In these literature mainly it was illustrated that the Supreme God Head came to the earth as human form as he is expected to come time to time as was the forecast in Gita.

It says "O descendant of Bharata, whenever and wherever there is a decline in religious practice and a predominant rise of irreligion I descend myself at that time. To save the pious and to annihilate the miscreants, as well as to reestablish the principles of religion, I advent myself millennium after millennium"[4].

The circumstances of his birth at Mathura in the prison of his uncle Kangsa[5], his safe journey to Gokul in Vrindavana with his father Vasudeva, under the protection of Vashaki nag, the pius snake, in the stormy night and miraculous activities such as, killing of demon Putana[6] by sucking her breast when he was a baby, killing of demon Kalia Nag[7], sheltering the people of Vrindabana by holding mount Gobardhana over their head during

---

[1] B.G. Chapter XI.

[2] B.G. 7/20. "*Kamai staistai hrita jnana pradyana devata*".

[3] B.G. 18/66: "*Sarva dharman parityajya mamekang sharanang braja, Ahang tang sarva papevovya mokshiashyami ma sucha.*"

[4] B.G. 4/78: "*Yada jadahidharmasyagianirbhavati bharata; Paritranaya sadhunang binashyacha duskritam; Dharma sangsthapanaya sambhamami yuge yuge*".

[5] Smt. Bh. by S.C. Mazumdar 10/3. p. 661.

[6] Ibid. 10/5. P. 668.

[7] Ibid. 10/16. P. 713.

the punishment given by Indra in the form of rain and thunder, killing of Kangsa and other activities.

This made many people believe that Krsna was in fact God head came as their saviour[1]. The friendly love of cowherd boys and cowherd girls (the gopies) and the affectionate love of the adults, to Krsna were regarded as a kind of devotion of Bhakti (sakhya and vatslya).

Worship of Krsna Prior to Sri Caitanya

From the sixth to the ninth centuries there was a series of twelve poet saints who significantly influenced South Indian religious life. They were called the Alvers or those who were immersed in God. They were more devotional than theological, and sang about the life of Krsna and Rama throughout south India. They interpreted Bhakti as the various types of love toward the deity, such as that between a father and a child, mutual friendship and between the lover and the beloved. The Alvers expressed their basic devotion to God in terms of friendly love (sakhya), a servant's devotion to his master (dasya), a mother's affection to her son (vatsalya), a son's respect for his father (pitribhakti) and also a women's love for her beloved (madhurya)[2]. The Alvers were followed by a series of theologians called Acharyas who provided a philosophical basis for bhakti and theism. Ramanuja was one in this succession[3].

Surrender to god or propatti is an aspect, as emphasized in the hymns of the Alvers. Propatti involves a sense of absolute humility and the willingness to give up any thing that is against the will of the God. It also involves faith that God will protect his devotees. In south India during the period of eleventh centuries, Nimbarka identified Krsna with Brahmana, the essence of the universe. Other bhakti philosopoher in south such as Ramanuja (1017-1137 AD) and Madhva (13th century), had been devoted to Krsna, but had placed little importance on cowherd element and had ignored Radha.

---

[1]   Ibid. 10/25. P. 789.

[2]   Ibid. 10/34. P. 840.

[3]   Indian and Far Eastern Religious Traditions by R.D. Baird and A. Blooms.
      p. 54.

Ramanuja was a believer of visistadvaita or qualified monoism[1] and Madhva taught dvaita or dualism[2]. For Nimberka, Radha was the eternal consort of Krsna and was an incarnation, like him at Vrindavana.

Nimberka was emphatic in his worship of Krsna and his consort Radha. His sect became popular in the north as well, and the success of bhakti movement there was dependent on him to a large extent.

In the fifteenth century, Vallabha founded a school which emphasized the grace of God coming through devotion as a cause of liberation. Vallabha and his descendants who headed this community were considered as incarnations of Krsna. Vallabha ultimately settled in Benares where he wrote commentary on the Bhagavata Purana.

After death of Vallaba his seven sons wondered throughout India gaining proselytes. Their sect attached itself to the adolescent Krsna, whose amorous sport with the gopis is the theme of the tenth chapter of the Bhagavata Purana. The guru of this sect was considered to be the manifestation of Krsna and union with Krsna was sought through intercourse with the guru. Husbands accepted this role of their wives and daughters.

From the fourth century AD. to the end of thirteenth century, Vaisnavism as a Brahmanical faith coexisted in Bengal with Buddhism, Jainism and along with the Saiva and Sakta workship[3]. Vaisnavism was an amorphous creed with a tendency towards heterogenicity. Vaisnavism was perhaps more popular in North and East Bengal than in West Bengal. Gaya in South Bihar was a notable centre of Avatara worship[4] The worship of Krsna, which became the basis of Gaudiya Vaisnava, was not particularly popular in early medieval Bengal. Krsna was merely regarded as an Avatara of Vishnu. But certain developments gradually led to the ascendancy of

---

[1] The History of Bengal: Hindu Period ed. by R.C. Majumder pp. 400, 401-404.

[2] A Study of Vaisnavism in Ancient and Medieval Bengal by S. Mukherji; pp. 41-42." The Gaya inscriptions on the Avatara concept afe the Krsnadvarika Temple Inscription, Sitala Temple Inscription, Nrsimha Temple Inscription and Ramgaya Dasavatara Temple Inscription."

[3] The Wonder That Was India by A.L. Basahan p. 332.

[4] Indian and Far Eastern Religious Traditions by R.D. Baird and A. Bloom p. 83. Madhv's views on dualism.

Krsna over the other Avatara of Vishnu[1]. In Bengal Vaishnavism assumed a tangible shape during the twelfth century which was the century of Sena rule. The early Sena rulers came to Bengal from Canara country of south[2]. Possibly with them came bhakti as a philosophical principle and as a way of life. A Vaishnava literature possibly developed in Bengal in the first quarter of the eighth century AD[3]. It is believed that this literature was mainly Apabhramsa (an underdeveloped literature). It is also believed that Gitagovinda composed by Joydeva (twelfth century) the great devotee of Krsna, followed the Apabhramsa tradition [4]. The Nimberka sect regards Joydeva as one of its guru[5]. Joydeva might have been influenced by the Krsna legend of the Brahmavaivartapurana[6] The bhakti element of Gitagovinda is concentrated in the concept of Krsna, an Avatara of Vishnu, as the lover of Radha[7] He regarded Radha as eternal consort of Krsna, even Radha element is superior than Krsna (the traditional believe still sang by the singer in Bengal every today. Field work)[8]. In the wake of the political revolution brought about by the Turko-Afgan conquest of Bengal in the beginning of the thirteenth century, some Buddhist propagated the idea of

---

[1] Vaisnavism in Bengal by R. Chakravorty. pp. 5.

[2] The Deopara Prasasti of Vijoyasena, Inscriptions of Bengal, III, p. 42; The Madhainagar Copper Plate of Laksmansena, Ibid, p. 106.

[3] Literary History of the Pala Period by Haraprasad Sastri; JBORS, V, 11, 1919 also ODBL, 1, p. 81.

[4] Joydeva has also be claimed for Mithila and Orissa. Vide, A Descriptive catalogue sanskrit manuscripts of Orissa in the collection of the Orissa State Museum, Bhubanesvara ed, Kedar Nath Mahapara, 1960, pp. WWW1.X1.

[5] Bangladese Nimvarka Sampradayera Vivarana by Dhananjayadasa Kathiyababa; Vol. 5, pp. 1539.

[6] Krsna in History and Legend by B.B. Majumder, Ch. 1, Appendix; Chs. III-IV.

[7] Gitgovinda and its Abhinaya, ed by Vasudev Sastri, Tanjore, Sarasvati Mahal Library, 1963; also Padavalikirtaner Itihas: by Svami Prajnananda, Vol. 1, Cho. 10 and 11.

[8] Numerous "Radhakrsna Temples" all over the World are the symbols of such a belief.

resisting the Muhammedans by forming against them in Hindu Buddhist united front[1].

This was the time possibly Vaisnavas had neutralized the Budhists by accepting Buddha as the incarnation of Visnu[2]. The Buddha incarnation is mentioned in Vadu Chandidasa's Srikrisnakirtana[3]

But this incarnation was sneered at by the Gaudiya Vaisnavas[4]. The Vaisnavas at this stage were two schools. The minorities, the tantric Vaisnavas with the ideal of Buddha, used to send their pray through meditation with chanting the name of Krsna in their heart[5] But the main stream Vaisnavas used to show their devotion through various devotional songs. This time many Bengali poets had written songs on Radha and Krsna. Govardhanacarya a poet, contemporary of Joydeva, was deeply acquainted with the Bhagavata legend of Krsna. The growing popularity of Radha worship was noted in his verse even in the twelfth century[6]. Vidyapati (fifteenth century) the court poet of Mithila wrote nine hundred thirty three songs-most of these were on love of Radha and Krsna[7]. Among hundreds of such a poet some prominents names who followed Vidyapati's style are Jnanadas, Gobindadasa Balaramdasa and Narottamadasa all of whom belonged to sixteenth century[8]

---

[1] Vaisanavism in Bengal by R. Chakravorty, pp. 18. also in, Conclusion of Suniti Kumar Chatterji; ODBL, 1 pp. 209-210.

[2] Vaisnavism in Bengal by R. Chakravorty; p. 9.

[3] Srikrisnakirtana by Vadu Chandidasa, p. 235, verse 4.

[4] Aryasaptasati, with the commentary of Ananta Pandita;

[5] Nirnayasagara press, Bombay, 1934, p. 204.

[6] Vaisnavism in Bengal by R. Chakravorty. p. 20.

[7] Vidyapatir Padavali by B.B. Majumdar, pp. 47-48, 56.

[8] Maithili Chyrestomathy by G.A. Grierson p. 34.

CHAPTER IV

Socio-Religious Context

Socio-Religious Background Prior to Sri Caitanya

Epigraphic and literary study makes it clear that the Vaisnavism gained considerable strength long before the advent of Sri-Caitanya. But it must be noted that the Tantras of various types too, had innumerable adherent in Bengal. With Kerala and Kashmir, Bengal was the third main centre of Tantrika culture in India. The Gaudasampradaya or the Bengal School of Tantra exercised its jurisction over a vast region extending from Nepal to Orissa. This region was known as Visnukranta circle. The term Visnukranta perhaps signified the Tantrika recognition of the popularity of the worship of Vishnu throughout the region.[1]. Kaulikarcanadipika left a Tantrika work on "circle-worship" suggests that the Tantra of the Gaudamarga was in vogue till eighteen centuries[2] Vrindavana Dasa[3] and K.C. Radi[4] also mentioned of various places in Navadvipa associated with Tantrika worship, of folk cult such as Vasuli, Manasa, Chandi and Dharma, last three being more popular. The rituals of other deities were also mentioned and sometimes influenced the worship. For instance, worship of Manasa included the worship of Mahadeva[5] and worship of Vasuli and Chandi, were deeply influenced by Saiva-Sakta rituals.

---

[1] "Tantras in Bengal" International Sanskrit Conference, ed. Raghavan, by G. Mukhopadhyaya, Vol. 1, 1975, pp. 80 87.

[2] Kaulikacaranadipika by R. Chattopadhyaya, p. 17.

[3] C. Bh. p. 12.

[4] Navadvipamahima by K.C. Radi.

[5] Manasapujapddhati by H.C. Sahityavinoda, pp. 43-44.

The worshippers of Manasa regarded the goddess, as a rival of Chandi. There was some cogency sometimes in the arguments that once Chandi, Manasa Lakshmi were a single goddess. Much later they acquired separate and antagonistic identities, owing mainly to priestly rivalry[1].

Chandi was worshipped as the deity mainly by the people who used to clear forests and who were engaged in trade and commerce[2]. Like Manasa, Chandi and Mangalchandi, were household goddesses.

The nature of Dharma cult was a subject of controversy. In Bankura Dharma was represented by a piece of stone. The cult-priests belonged to the untouchable caste of the Doms community. Dharma was a sort of local-folk, Buddha to Haraprasad Sastri, as Surya to S.C. Ray, as Kurma (Tortoise) to Suniti Kumar Chatterji, ancient Varuna to K.P. Chatterji and as a Sun-cult to Ashutosh Bhattacharya[3]. It is interesting to note that the known exponents of the Chandi worship, were all Brahmins[4].

The popularity of these cults signified the filtration of non-Vedic rituals into the Brahminic forms of worship. These popular cults did not endanger the caste based social order. The rightist forces in the Hindu society were represented by Smarta Panditas. So at least some of the Smartas accorded recognition to them. Raghunandana and Govindananda, recognized the validity of the worship of Manasa, Mangalchandi, Aranyasasthih, and vratas such as Kukkutimarkati and Piptaki[5].

It was believed that the Brahmins were compelled to recognize these non-Brahminical cult by the economic pressure, although the Saktas prohibited the Brahmins to act as a priest of the plebeian Sudras[6] (only

---

[1] Bangala Sahityer Itihas by Sukumar Sen, 1, 1, p. 226.

[2] Vaisnavism in Bengal by R. Chakravorty, p. 30.

[3] Brhaddharnnapurana, p. 210.

[4] West Bengal District Gazetteers, Bankura, Appendix A to Ch. III, Views discussed in pp. 207, 210-18.

[5] Vaisnavism in Bengal by R. Chakravorty, p. 31. (Raghunandana and Govindanada were contemporary of Sri-Chaitanya and were unquestionably the most representative Smarta of their time. Govindananda's father, Ganapati Bhatta, was a pascatya Vaidhika Brahmin of Midnapur, a neighbouring district of Navadvip).

[6] Hussain Shahi Bengal: by M.R. Tarafdar, p. 248.

the Dharma cult had priests from the lower castes). These cults did not challenge the social or the ritual supremacy of the Brahmins.

The recognition of some of the non-Vedic cults possibly reflected the popularity of the Smartas to some extent and also possibly it was an half-hearted attempt on the part of the Brahmins to establish some sort of social integration of the Hindu castes and sects. The Vasuli, Manasa and the Mangalachandi worshippers, sanskritised these goddesses by attributing to them the omnipotence of the Brahminical Durga[1]. Lastly some of these were apparently musical cults and powerful media of mass entertainment. To accord recognition to them was perhaps an unavoidable social necessity. But Smartas like Raghunandana felt that multiplication of such cults must be stopped and allowed the only rituals in their Nivandhas which had received their sanction.

The cult Tantrika Kaulacara, with its orgiasticism of wine and flesh, was a challenge to the moral fabric of the Hindu society. Some Vaisnavas felt the necessity of liberating Krsna worship from the clutches of the Tantras. Krsnananda and Agamavagisa (believed to be contemporary of Sri-Caitanya), wrote Tantrasara (a big Tantrika compendium) which is still in use. In these books verses were quoted from two Vaisnava Tantrika works named Brhatgautamiyatantra and Karmadipika, to prove the Tantrika nature of the worship of Visnu, and their consort.

It is indeed true that Raghunandana tried to make some of the Smarta regulation, prepared by his predecessor, flexible[2].

Both reformative measures and extra-Vedic rituals were introduced. But the attitude of the Smartas were incorrigibly ritualistic. There was no escape from the rituals, some of them were quite expensive. The rituals had become a trade with vested interests. They also bridled individual freedom of worship.

The singular fact was that the Muslim Ruler of Bengal did not interfere them. Because after performing so many rituals, the Hindus had very little time for creating any political trouble.

---

[1]   Brhat Tantrasastra Basumati Sahitya Mandir, pp. 164, 166, 190-91.

[2]   Vaisnavism in Bengal by R. Chakravorty, p. 31.

The predominance of the Hindu rituals and the continuance of the Muhammedan autocracy were perhaps complementary developments[1].

According to Krsnadasa Kaviraja there was a good deal of understanding between the conservative Hindus of Navadvipa and the Muhammedan Qazi of the town.[2].

The rituals and rites mentioned in Krtyatattva of Raghunandana and in Varsakriyakaumudi of Govindananda gradually multipled to an almost unmanageable extent. Many worshippers, with the rituals, did not like these multiplication at all. Some of the rituals such as Aryanyasasthi, Sarpapujana, Dyutapratipat, Madana trayodosi, Kukkutimarkativrata, Pipitakivrata, were non-Vedic in character. Raghunandana's emphasis on Sraddha was overwhelming. Sraddha in any form was a costly affair[3]. The Vaisnavas of Navadvipa felt the necessity of putting a briddle on the rituals. The alternative proposed by them was unritualistic and personalized bhakti for a personal god[4].

Here we must note that the profession of the Brahmin priest was highly technical and it could not be easily mastered. The factor of time limited the priest's scope for maintaining a large number of clients. But a guru who preached devotion and also denigrated the rituals, could easily build up a large practice and become affluent. Innumerable disciples from both sexes would receive Mantra or Name from him and remain be holden to him as long as they lived.

The Muhammedan conquest of Bengal had greatly disturbed the Hindu society.

Thousands upon thousands of Hindus had been converted into Muslims. This development possibly necessitated the compulsory

---

[1] Raghunandana's Indebtedness to His Predecessors by B. Bhattacharya, JASB, 1953, XIV, 2, pp. 176-76.

[2] CCM: (here after if no ed. is mentioned, refer to Sahitya Akadami-ed.), pp. 93-94; also CBH: p. 275.

[3] Vaisnavism in Bengal by R. Chakravorty, p. 34.

[4] In Chaitanyamangala, Adi 7, p. 9, Jayananda wrote that the advent of Chaitanya was necessary for the restoration of Bhahminical dharma "Dharmasamasthapana hetu yuga avatara"; In Adi 5, pp. 7-8, he described the effect of the Kaliage from the Smartha point of view.

obedience of all Hindus to the rituals and legal formations of the Smriti[1]. It is interesting to note that the Smartas did not set up any organization or make any arrangement, directed against Muhammedan proselytization. They merely emphasized suddhi or purification[2] They did not propagate the necessity of preaching Hinduism among those who belonged to the fringe of the Hindu society. The intelligent Brahmins who wrote the Smriti either lacked the courage to adapt an effective programme of Hindu proselytization or lacked the intellect, to think of it. Their whole programme was to catagorise, describe and multiply of rituals, of not much use[3].

There are some records of the oppression of the Hindus by the Muhammedans[4]. In Caitanyamangala of Jayananda gave some details of the tyranny and delinquency of the Muslims in Bengal[5]. The people in general suffered because of the tyrannical behaviour of the Hussain Shahi Government[6].

The Hindus of the upper castes of North and East Bengal were regularly embracing the Islam, to receive favour from the ruling Muhammedans[7]. The same book also recorded the fact that the Moorish slave-traders purchased Hindu boys. Mahuan, the Chinese traveller, mentioned the fact that the Hindus were in use in Bengal in the fifteenth century[8].

It also must be noted that the conversion of Hindu into Muslim was far more widespread in East Bengal, mainly because the Hindu low caste and the Buddhists of East Bengal could no longer tolerate the Brahminical reaction. They were attracted by the liberal social philosophy of the Islam.

Even after their conversion they remained mentally and culturally Hindu and carried on the native Bengali traditions, in literary and other

---

[1] Indo Muslim Relations by Debajyoti Burman, pp. 48 52. Prachin Bangla Sahitye Hindu Musalman by R.C. Bandopadhyaya, 1-10;

[2] Samayika Patre Banglar Samajcitra (editorial comment): Vol. II, p. 12.

[3] History of Bengali Literature by D.C. Sen, ed. 1954, pp. 208-09.

[4] Bangalaya Desividesi by B.K. Sarkar, pp. 21-22.

[5] Chaitanyamangala Nadiya ed. pp. 13 14.

[6] Manasamangala by Vijoya Gupta, pp. 54-62; Manasavijaya, pp. 63-82.

[7] The Book of Duate Barbosa Vol. II, pp. 147-48.

[8] Visvabharati Annals Mahuan's account, 1945, Vol. 1, p. 117; also in Sahitya Parisat Patrika B.E. 1981, 1, pp. 1-70.

matters[1]. There are some Muslims who thought of a Hindu-Muslim cultural synthesis. They felt the Islamic ideas combined with Hindu elements, would appeal to the minds of local Muhammedans to whom Hindu mythology was already known.

Muslim mystic poet such as Sayid Sultan was one of them who favored this kind of synthesis. The Avataravada, Yogic Tantrika ideas of Satchakra, were integral parts of his philosophy[2]. The Smartas possibly really did not desire the integration of Hindus; otherwise they would not have put so much stress on the distinction between the Brahmins and the other castes. There is not much evidence to suggest that Smartas and their patrons had put up a united front against the Muslim proselytization or the aforementioned popular caste, as they put up against the movement of Sri Caitanya.

Once the Smartas used to regard Tantric sects as non-Vedic and non-Brahminical. But the Upapuranas were deeply influenced by Tantra, and the Smartas were deeply influenced by the Upapuranas[3]. Raghunandana accepted the validity of Tantric diksa or initiation, and composed a tract on the Durgapuja ceremony.

It is interesting to note that Smartas like Raghunandana and Govindananda, were far more concerned with the specific rituals of Vaisnava worship than with the principle and the philosophy of that worship.

They do not show any clear evidence of their acquaintance with the doctrine of bhakti. Govindananda described the Gosthastami festival which was later accepted as ritual by the Gaudiya Vaisnavas[4]. He however mentioned many Tantrika Vaisnava ceremonies in Varsakriyakaumudi[5]. Bhakti was infused into the Vaisnava rituals described in Haribhaktivilasa.

The Smartas merely wanted to strengthen the social and economic position of the Brahmins. The formulation of the laws and rules were mainly for the benefit of the Brahmins. The Sudras and the common people did not matter to them at all. They were mainly written for the guidance of the

---

[1] ODBL by E.C. Dimcock, 1, pp. 208-09.
[2] Op. cit. by M.R. Tarafdar, p. 225.
[3] Studies in Puranic records on Hindu Rites and Customs by S.C. Hazra, p. 250.
[4] Varsakriyakaumudi by Govindananda, p. 478.
[5] Ibid. p. 102-04.

elite[1]. Since the time of Ganesa Jalal-ud-din (1414-1441), the Kayasthas had been steadily gaining a commanding in bureaucracy, economic affairs, and social relations[2]. They constituted the landed aristocracy in Bengal during the rule of Hussain Shahi dynasty.

In sixteenth century many of the Bengali zamindars were to be Kayasthas. The growth of the Kayastha intelligentia and the appearance of big and powerful Kayastha landlords must have enfeebled the social position of the Brahmins. Raghunandana, therefore wrote that there were only two castes, namely Brahmin and Sudra. The Kayasthas were of course, Sudras. For the Sudras Raghunandana and the contemporary Smriti writers prescribed only a very few rights[3]

A Brahmin might even commit adultery with a Sudra woman with unquestionable impunity[4]. But a Sudra was to be severely penalized if he married a Brahmin woman. The Sudras including the Kayasthas and the Vaidyas had no right to utter any Vedic mantra.

They had only the duty to bow down to the feet of the Brahmin[5]. A Sudra including a Kayastha and a Vaidya, could not be guru or preceptor.[6] A Sudra could worship only Siva and Gopal[7]. In ordinary circumstances a Brahmin could not accept a gift from a Sudra[8], nor he could act as priest of a Sudra[9]. The Smartas imposed almost similar restrictions on women belonging to all castes, including the Brahmins. According to Dayabhaga of Jimutvahana the Hindu widow had no right to sell, mortgage and gift away

---

[1] Vaisnovism in Bengal by R. Chakravarti, pp. 37-39. "J.P. Wise held the view that a great number of Hindus were converted during the reign of Jalaluddin (1414-1430). He attributed many of the conversions to avoid punishment for murder or caste offences and to the egalitarian appeal of Muhammedanism", Bengal District Gazetteers, Mymensingh, E.A. Sache, 1917, p. 17.

[2] Madhyayuger Bangia O Bangali by Sukumar Sen, pp. 15-16.

[3] Kriyakandavaridhi, ed. S.C. Mukhopadhyaya, Basumati Press, 2nd ed. Vol. 1. pp. 67.

[4] Op. cit., by Bani Chakravarty, pp. 147-48; 249-51.

[5] Op. cit., by Bani Chakravarty: pp. 147-48. also 504.

[6] "Diksaprakaran" in Kriyakandavaridhi, Vol. 1, pp. 6-7.

[7] Idib: "Vaisnavacaraprakarana", pp. 527-28, "Saivacaraprakarana, p. 561."

[8] Ibid: "Prayascittavyavasthaprakarana", pp. 654-55.

[9] Ibid: Vol. III, pp. 696-97.

her property. But she was entitled to Stridhana or a part of the property or wealth bequeathed by her father or husband[1]. Sati was not compulsory. But widow had to practice brahmacarya or abstinence which was tantamount to the practice of severe austerities[2]. This tradition and practices since then have been continuing, until today, amongst the middle class Hindus. Although the practices seem to have been waning away amongst the very lower and top social class Hindus who ignore it. It is interesting to note that the widowers do not have to practise any of these kind of austerities when their wives die. The Smriti have failed to explain how such a misanthropic writs, rules and injunctions prepared by the Smartas, might protect the Hindu society from the Muhammedan impact.

Vrindavana Dasa, Krisnadasa Kaviraja and the poets of the anthology titled Gaurangapadatarangini very often referred to a group of people as Pasandi (unkind, philistine), who were said to have organized a big opposition for the dissemination of bhakti. These so-called Pasandis were mostly professors of Hindu Law, Sanskrit grammar and a philosophical system known as Navyanyaya or New Logic[3].

Navyanyaya was first introduced in Mithila by Udayacarya in about 1326 AD. The first Bengali scholar who achieved fame of various philosophical system including Navyanyaya, was the scholar Vasudeva Sarvabhauma (who later became a follower of Caitanya Sri-Csaitanya at Puri). Science was a close book to the Navyanyaya scholars, many of whom were talented Brahmins.

Navyanyaya found no justification for emotional bhakti. But they evidently found justification for the Brahminical Smrti.

There is no evidence of their objection to the social and religious dominations of the Brahmins, which had been established by the Smrti. Moreover many professors of Navyanyaya also wrote Smrti-tracts[4]. It was also obvious that no pandita could write Smrtinivandha in a convincing

---

[1] Smrtisastre Bangali by S.C. Bandopadhyaya, pp. 181-82, 190-91.

[2] Astavimstitattvani, "Suddhitattva", p. 345; (Raghunandana prescribed Ekahara, Gandhadravyavarjana, Tarpana etc.)

[3] Vaisnavism in Bengal: by R. Chakravarty, p. 41.

[4] Op. cit. by D. C. Bhattacharya, pp. 264, 338-39.

manner if he had no idea of the logic of Navyanyaya. Both Smrti and Navyanyaya represented two related aspects of the Brahminical culture.

These were very obviously and bitterly felt by the lower castes, but were too decrepit and lacked the organization and leadership to protest against. The liberal minded Brahmins not particularly favoured these discriminatory outlook in the society, but were not bold enough to utter a word, rather had to watch the gradual disintegration of the Hindu society.

In late fifteenth and early sixteenth century Navadvipa was the greatest intellectual centre of Bengal. Saptagram was the principal riverport, almost adjacent to the "university town of Navadvipa[1].

Vrindavana Dasa gave some idea of the caste composition in the different parts of the town. These people were conchshell makers (Sankhari), sellers of grocery-goods (Gandhavanik), Flower-seller (Malakar), weaver (Tanti), milk traders (Goala) and beetlenut traders (Tambuli). There were men who belonged to the caste of Vadyakara or Drummers, the doctors who used to attend case for snake bite (Malovaidya), the Bhatts or panegyrists, the Vanik or merchants and the Muhammedans[2].

The Brahmmins were in a dominant position. The Vaidyas and the Kayasthas, although regarded as Sudra formed the moneyed class.

Only a handful of Brahmins were landlords or officials. Some poor Brahmins might make a living by trade. Marriage in Brahmin families was conditioned by Gotra, Mela and Gain. Both the Radi and Vaidika Brahmins were the social leaders. Varendra Brahmins were in comparatively lower position[3]. The wealth of the rich was lavishly spent in marriages and ceremonies[4]. Consequently priesthood was a good and lucrative trade. Incidentally some scoundrels such as Jagai and Madhai, belonged to the Brahmin class. In general many people had to be the victims of their nearly unopposed mischievous activities. This was also an additive elements, for the poor record of reputation of the Brahmins, morally and intellectually as a fair minded, top class, in the society at Navadvipa.

---

[1] Manasavijaya by Vipradasa, pp. 142-43 and Purchase His Pilgrims: by Ralph Fitch, X, p. 182.

[2] CBH. pp. 69-75, 92-93, 102-03, 93, 145.

[3] CBH, pp. 918, 179-87.

[4] CBH, pp. 36.

Superstition was considerably strengthened by the Smrtiwriters who prescribed various rituals like Santisvastayana against illluck and disease. It was also strengthened by the astrologers and practitioner of black magic. The rigidity of the caste system, the cultural and social alienation of a large segments of the Hindu population by the short sighted Brahmins and the utter selfishness of the Hindu aristocracy, to some extent favoured the conversion of the low caste Hindu into Muhammedan.

Raghunandana was contemporary of Caitanya and was unquestionably the leading representative of the Smarta of his time. There are different views about the actual time of Raghunandana's activities. P.V. Kane places him between 1490 and 1570[1], while M.M. Chakravartistated that Raghunandana was prominent between 1510 and 1565. According to Haraprasad Sastri, his 'Jyotisatattva' was completed in 1565[2]. He has been hailed as a liberal minded sociologist[3] inside and been depicted as the high priest of reaction on other side[4]. Another contemporary Smarta was Govindananda, author of Varsakriyakaumudi'. The works of Raghunandana and Govindanandana on rituals and rites show that they produced a paralysing effect in the society. The rituals were multiplying and the two Smartas, along with others, felt the necessary of cataloguing them for general information.

While there are many evidences to suggest that the Smartas were determined to maintain rigid caste rules and strict discipline within the Hindu community, there is no evidence to suggest that they had any definite policy or any positive programme to prevent Muhammadan proselytization. It is interesting to note that the Smartas did not even indirectly propose to set up any organisation or make any arrangement, directed against this proselytization. To them, the conversion from any other religion to Hindu community, was out of the question. To maintain their rigid rule, they emphasized on 'prayaschitta', suddhi or purification.

As a result Hindu society, gradually became ever eroding and feeble, without any positive programme to prevent or cure it. North and East

---

[1]   History of Dharmasastra by P.V. Kane, Vol. 1, p. 419.
[2]   Vaisnavism in Bengal by R. Chakravarty, p. 33.
[3]   The Positive Background of Hindu Sociology by B.K. Sarkar, p. 615.
[4]   Padavali Parichaya by Harekrishna Mukhopadhyaya, pp. 39-40.

Bengal fell an easy prey to Islam. The Tebet Burmese tribes, were probably converted by Arab missionaries stationed, at Chittagong[1].

There were some men in Navadvipa in fifteenth century who desired some religious and social reform or synthesis. To them the old conception of bhakti was possibly the only panacea.

Vrindavana Dasa often referred to the lack of bhakti in Hindu society. Sanskrit scholars and influencial Brahmins studied the Vaisnava mythology and the Gita. But they interpreted these works mainly from the ritualistic point of view[2]. These studied indifference to bhakti, being very painful to those who beloved it.

The Vaisnavas of Navadvipa at that time was led by Advaita Acarya, a Varendra Brahmin[3]. Advaita, a very learned man, who originally was from Sylhet in East Bengal, became the disciple of an ascetic named Madhavendra Puri who was apparently a member of the other founded by Sankaracarya, but really a preacher and theoriser of Krsnabhakti[4].

Sri-Caitanya's father Jagannatha Misra and brother Visvarupa, who later renounced the world and became an ascetic, had pronounced Vaisnava sympathies. In fact Vaisnava group in Navadvipa was constituted by men, most of whom originally came from sylhet[5]. It is believed that Advaita preached Vaisnavism in Sylhet before he came to Navadvipa. In this work advaita was helped by Isvara Puri, another disciple of Madhavendra Puri[6].

The Navadvipa Vaisnavas did not at first disobey the Smrti rules. There was a collection of songs in Gourapadatarangini which described the rituals of Caitanya's birth, Cudakarana, Upanayana and marriages[7]. The tremendous influence of Smartas was revealed in these songs.

But even the Vasinavas led by Advaita were prepared to compromise with Smrti. The Smartas were not prepared to accept bhakti as the final solution

---

[1] ODBL: pp. 208-09.

[2] CBH, p. 12.

[3] Madhyayeger Bangla Sahityer Tathya O Kalakarma by S. Mukhopadhyaya, p. 44. (Advaita Acarya, born in 1454 and died in 1550).

[4] CBH. p. 362; Bbaktiratnavali, Intro. p. 111.

[5] CBH. p. 10.

[6] Sir-Caitanyacariter Upadan by B. Majumdar, p. 626.

[7] Gourapadatarangini, Ch. 2, pp. 676.

of the spiritual and material problems. This rigid stand of the orthodox Brahmins made Advaitya very angry and he cursed these philistines[1].

It was later believed that Sri-Caitanya was the personification of Advaita's determination to flush out blasphemy and philistinism[2]. It is important to note that the Caitanya movement was sponsored mainly by the Brahmins. According to an estimate out of the first-four hundred ninety followers of Caitanya, two hundred thirty nine were Brahmins[3]. The fact certainly indicates that there was a great rift in the Brahminical society of Navadvipa and the adjoining area. It is interesting to note that in other parts of India some Brahmins supported the Vaisnava movements[4].

It should also be noted that the Brahmins who wanted a change, found a ready made ideology in bhakti (Sridhara Svamin's commentary on Bhagavatapurana)[5]. He was an ascetic of the Kevaladvaita order. He believed that bhakti is a form of disinterested work and is eternal. He stressed the importance of hymns and the singing of hymns.

It was possible that the Sufi mystics of the time influenced the development of Vaisnava emotionalism and the Vaisnava cult of love[6]. The Sufi saint Nuruddin Abdur Rahaman Zami (1414-1492), was a contemporary of Advaita. It is possible that Advaita was acquainted with the view points of Auls and Bauls who were undoubtedly influenced by the Sufi concept of the mystic love[7].

Hal (ecstasy), Dhikr (recitation of the name of God), and Sima (religious gatherings where hymns, are sung), the all fundamental Sufi concepts, might be regarded as the possible counterparts of Vaisnava Dasa (ecstasy), Namkirtan (recitation of the name of Krsna) and Mahotsava

---

[1]   CBH. p. 13.

[2]   CBH. p. 12.

[3]   Sri Caitanyacariter Upadan by B. Majumdar, p. 567. (There were 29 Kayasthas, 37 Vaidyas, 2 muslims and 16 women).

[4]   Hindu Caste and Sects. Second ed 1968, by J.N. Bhattacharya, pp. 37-39, 41-42, 45, 53, 57-65, 74, 78-79, 86.

[5]   Vaisnavism in Bengal: by R. Chakravorty, p. 50.

[6]   Bange Sufi Prabhava, 1935, by Enamul Huq. pp. 165-70, 171-78.7

[7]   CCM: Kalna ed. pp. 836-37 (Advaitya composed verses in the language of the Bauls).

(congressional singing of hymns). The Gaudiya Vaisnava emphasis on love divine and its liberal attitude towards caste might be attributed to Sufi influence. Muslim mystic poet like Sayid Sultan desired a cultural synthesis. Avataravada and Yogic Tantrika ideas of Satchakra were integral parts of his religious philosophy[1]. But there is no evidence of any direct link between Gaudiya Vaisnava philosopy and Sufi mysticism. As the region of Navadvipa, became the home land of the Brahminical Smrti had put up, a strong barrier between Hindus and the Muslims.

Comments and conclusion

On studying the socio-religious background, particularly in Bengal, it became very obvious that a reform of the religious practices, was overdue for the following reasons:

1. The Brahmins were in a dominant position. The majority of the people belonged to the non-Brahminical castes and did not enjoy the fair share of their rights for religious practices. Even the moneyed class such as the Kayesthas and the Vaidyas, were regarded as Sudras and were denied their rightful position in the social status.
2. The rigidity of the caste system, the cultural and social alientation of large section of the Hindu population by the short sighted Brahmins, the influence of the missionaries and the Mohammadan rulers, made the lower castes at the outer boundary of the Hindu society, extremely vulnerable to Muslim proselytization in a society, a major section of which had already been engulfed by the Buddhist religion.
3. Hindu society gradually became ever erodible and so feeble that the socio-religious reform, became a necessity for its very existence.
4. Regardless of castes, Hindu women were very subordinate. Their rights, individuality and independent position were not recognized in the society.
5. The Vaisnavas of Bengal led by Advaita Acarya were fatigued with the hardship of the Tantrikism and the multiplication of the Tantras. To them the only panacea left was to revive and stress on the old concept of bhakti.

---

[1] Muslim Bangla Sahitya, Dacca, 1957, by Enamul Hug. pp. 149-50.

CHAPTER V

Sri-Caitanya Legend

Chronology of incidents

Sri-Caitanya was born in Navadvipa in 1486 and died or disappeared in a mysterious circumstances in Puri, in 1533[1]. The life of Sri-Caitanya as narrated by his biographer, was very eventful and dominated the religious life for nearly half a century in India[2]. The historians of the Caitanya movement have derived their information chiefly from the biographical accounts of the close associates of him or of his movement just after him, such as Murari Gupta, Kavi Karnapura, Vrndavana Dasa, Krsnadasa Kaviraja. The accounts of Locana Dasa, Jayananda, and Cudamani Dasa contain some data and explanations which are not found in the more authoritative texts mentioned.

There was a considerable amount of information in the 1507 verses of the anthology titled Gaurapadatarangini[3]. Caitanya's father Jagannatha Misra was originally, from the Sylhet district of East Bengal. He was

---

[1] Chaitanyamangala, "Sesakhanda": by Jayananda, pp. 116-17 Sri Sri Caitanycaritamrter Bhamika by R. Nath, 4th ed., p. 63.

[2] Madhyayuger Bangla Sahityer Kalakram by S. Mukhopadhyaya, pp. 27-29. [Some important dates are: Birth: Feb. 1486; First marriage 1501-2, Second marriage: 1507; The beginnin gof the emotional stage for Krsna: 1905; Renunciation of the world: Jan. 25-26, 1510; Journey to Puri: Feb. 4, 1910; Commencement of the journey to the Deccan: April, 1510; Return to Puri: 1512; Journey from Puri to Vrindavana: 1515; Arrival at Allahabad: Jan. 1916; Arrival at Benaras: 1516; Return to Puri: May 1516; Death: June 1953].

[3] Vaisnavism in Bengal: by R. Chakravorty, p. 53.

described as a very religious person and had Vaisnava sympathy; but used to observe casterituals. His mother Sachi Devi was described as very religious too.

Jagannatha Misra had consecutive eight daughters: none of them survived. His other son, Visvarupa was ten years older than Bisvambara, Caitanya's earlier name. Visvarupa was very handsome and intelligent. In very young age he studied various aspect of Hindu religion. He was acquainted with Advaita Acarya and devoted to Vaisnavism.

He was later initiated into the worship of God by Madhavendra Puri a preaching monk of Sankara's "Bharati" order. His new name was Sankaranya Puri and at the age of sixteen he renunciated the world[1].

There were certain unusual and miraculous happenings surrounding the birth and in the later part of the carrier of Caitanya. His very handsome appearance, unusual body built, extraordinary talents of memory and intellect, made him convincingly distinct from other people. When he was due to be born, even after eleven months of gestation, he did not arrive. His father was really anxious and approached his astrologer, maternal grand father, Nilambara Chakravorty, who after calculating and judging the position of the stars, which influence the living beings, made a forecast that his daughter Sachi Devi would soon give birth to a genius, an extraordinary great man[2] His actual name was Visvambara. But as he was born under a tree named 'Nim' that was why his nick name was Nimai and he was unusually fair looking that was why all the neighbour used to call him as Gauranga.

As a baby Visvambara used to stop his natural cry on hearing name of Hari, Narayana or God. From the very childhood he was noted to be unusually sharp and intelligent, in compare to the other children. After the disappearance of Visvarupa, Caitanya's father thought that the excessive learning made his eldest son so eccentric that he had carelessly renounced

---

[1] Sri Amiya Nimai Charit by S.K. Ghosh, p. 58.
[2] Ibid. p. 36. quoted from CBH.
    "Choudda sata sat sake mash je phalgun
    pournamashi sandhyakale haila subhakshan.
    singha rashi singha lagna uccha grahagan,
    sharabarga astabarge sarvasubhakshan."

the world. So after a while he decided to keep the young Chaitnya away from the schools and the boy was allowed to be a real truant. Later on he was sent back to school again, only when he demanded his right of education[1].

Apart from general education, Caitanya acquired knowledge in Kalpa grammar and listened to lectures on subjects like rhetorics. He had that keenness of intellect which might have helped him to master some of the intricacies of Navyanyaya[2]. The biographers and the hymnologists, almost habitually described Caitanya as a brilliant scholar and master of the traditional learning. According to a current tradition in Navadvipa, Caitanya and the celebrated Naiyayika Raghunatha Siromani, were fellow students of Vasudeva Sarvabhauma[3]. But Raghunatha Siromani achieved fame as a scholar before the birth of Caitanya[4]. Others believed that Caitanya was a student of an institution run by Advaita Acarya. In that school he was awarded the appellation of Vidyasagara (Ocean of knowledge). In general he used to be called Nimai Pandita.

While he was a student, he wrote a small grammar book and a commentary on Nayasatra[5]. At a very unusually young age at sixteen, he started his own school which became the most popular one in Navadvipa within a very short spell of time. Caitanya's first marriage with Lakshmi Devi was held when he was an adolescent (16 years). Few months later after this event Caitanya went to East Bengal. During his sort stay in East Bengal, his wife died of a snake bite.[6].

---

[1] CBH: pp. 35-49.

[2] CBH: pp. 42-49. (Murari Gupta said that Caitanya studied in school of Visnu, Sudarsananda Gangadasa Pandita. Pandita op. cit. p. 22, Canto 9, verse 1.

[3] Advaitaprakasa: by Isana Nagara, Ch. 12, p. 118.

[4] Bangalir Sarasvat Avadan 1 by D.C. Bhattacharya, p. 94.

[5] Sri Amiya Nimai Charit: by S.K. Ghosh, p. 67, 69-70. (It is said that that his friend Raghunatha also wrote a commentary on the same subject and was very upset on hearing the context of Caitanya book which was of very high standard. Knowing this Caitanya destroyed his own commentary, so that his friend book would be popular); Op. cit.: by Isana Nagara, 126

[6] CBH: PP. 83-89; Op. cit. by Murari Gupta, p. 29, Canto 11, verses 11 16.

S.K. De, thinks first wife possibly held a unique place in his affection and the shock of her death might have something to do with his renunciation[1] His second marriage was with Visnupriya Devi, was when he was about twenty years. It was described in forty songs. After this about two years Sachi Devi, Caitanya's mother had a happy life with her son and daughter in law.

Visit to Gaya and the Start of Harekrsna Movement

At the age of twenty-two he departed on pilgrimage to Gaya, the site of a famous temple dedicated to Visnu. It was believed that there Lord Krsna had put his feet on the head of Gayasur and that markings were still there[2]. Incidentally there in Gaya centuries ago Buddha achieved Moksha under the Bodhi tree. There the young Caitanya, then known as Nimai Pandita, while worshiping at the feet of Visnu, received a sudden illumination that transformed his being. Tears rolled down his chicks and he lost himself in ecstasy[3].

Among the pilgrims was the monk Isvar Puri, a disciple of Madhava Puri a Sanyasin of the order of Sankara. Isvar Puri met Caitanya before at Navadvipa, had discussion with him about his writings.

At that time he knew Caitanya as a great scholar with a very unusual and extraordinary personality. Now as he witnessed his ecstatic condition, he recognized in him a great devotee. Caitanya asked for blessing from Isvarpuri, who then initiated him into the worship of Krsna[4]. Many Vaisnavas believes that Isvar Puri although initiated him, but accepted him as an Avatara of Krsna[5].

Caitanya returned to Navadvipa a changed man. The unrivalled, scholastic debater, the grammarian, the logician now disappeared. Instead there stood before men a serene, exalted person, continually chanting Hare Krsna, Hare Krsna. His former students gathered around him as had

---

[1]   Op. cit.: S.K. De, p. 75.
[2]   Sri Amiya Nimai Charit: by S.K. Ghosh, p. 93.
[3]   The Spiritual Heritage of India: by Swami Prabhavananda, p. 325.
[4]   Sri Amiya Nimai Charit: by S.K. Ghosh, CCM: p. 83.
[5]   CBH. P. 89.

been their custom, but he could no longer teach them. He addressed the students as brothers and said to them that he could no longer teach them any lesson.

Whenever he tried to explain anything to them, he saw the little boy Krsna before him playing upon his flute. So he gave up his teaching and devoted all of his time for the service of Krsna either by singing the name of Krsna, chanting or preaching. There upon he preached a kirtana (chant Hare Krsna,.)[1], which has come down to this day and is sung not only by the Vaisnavas of Bengal, but by the Vaisnavas of all over the world.

Before his departure to Gaya, Caitanya was known at Navadvip as a great scholar, but was not particularly known as a Vaisnava or its sympathizer. On the contrary this great debater was well known for his discussions and arguments on religious topics, mostly with the Vaisnavas and its associates, who were sceptical about his religious belief[2]. So the news of his devotion towards Krsna, was like a spark of enthusiasm to the Vaisnavas of Navadvipa. So all the Vaisnavites, the supporters of bhakti movement gathered around him. Among many associates, was Advaita. Acarya, Nityananda, Gadadhar and Srivasa, were the persons who helped tremendously to propagate the earlier phase of Caitanya movement or the so called are Hare Krsna Movement.

It is already mentioned (page 49) that the Vaisnavas of Navadvipa under the leadership of Advaita Acarya, were discontented with the hardship of Tantrikism. Advaita himself was a very learned man. It is said that Advaita studied the Vedas and the six systems of Indian Philosophy. In about 1452 1453 Advaita is said to have visited numerous holy places, including Mithila and met poet Vidyapati. He taught Yavana Haridasa Hindu philosophy and Bhagavtapurana[3].

According to Isana Nagara, even Caitanya's parents were his disciples[4]. He is said to have written bhakticommentaries on Gita and Yogavasista

---

[1]   The Spiritual Heritage of India: by Swami Prabhavananda, p. 325-26. [This chant is various names of Krsna, as "Hare Krsna Hare Hrsna Krsna Krsna Hare Hare Hare Ram Hare Ram Ram Ram Hare Hare!]

[2]   Sri Amiya Nimai Charit: by S.K. Ghosh, p. 67.

[3]   Vaisnavism in Bengal by R. Chakravorty, p. 123.

[4]   Advaitaprakasa: Ch. 10, p. 41.

Ramayana[1]. He blessed Nityananda just after his birth[2]. As a Varendra Brahmin he had to abide by the Brahminical conventions. The extreme aridness of the intellectual atmosphere of Navadvipa, was intolerable to him. He revolted against the Brahminical stereotype. He shouted imprecations against the philistines. The necessity of the Avatara of Narayana in Kaliage, was first propounded by Advaita before the advent of Sri Caitanya. The impending Caitanya avatara, he vigorously invoked against the Brahminical reaction[3]. This group of Vaisnavas led by Advaita Acharya, were delighted to accept Caitanya as their leader.

The other great helper of the Caitanya movement was Sri Nityananda. There had been a bit uncertainty about the early life of Nityananda and the caste he belonged. Nityananda was born in Birbhum. Birbhum a was tribal region inhabited by various types of castes, most of them were sudras. Birbhum was never a centre for Brahminical culture. In early age Nityananda visited many holy places, most of them were Saiva pilgrim centre[4]. In all probability Nityananda was Saiva Avadhuta converted into Vaisnavism by Madhavendra Puri and decided to live in Vrndavana[5]. Nityananda heard of Caitanya and came to stay at Navadvipa to join the movement. Cudamani Das gives a different account of Nityanandas career. According to him Nityananda renounced the world after meeting Caitanya at Navadvipa.

This meeteing was sought for and arranged by Nityananda himself[6]. Cudamani Das believed that Nityananda worshipped Caitanya, in his birth placaes Ekcaka, even before this meeting[7]. His career was predetermined by Madhavendra Puri[8].

So Caitanya became a great spiritual force in the city of Navadvipa and the lives of many unbelievers, were transformed by the love and touch of this God-intoxicated man. Some of his disciples in later years played an

---

[1] Ibid. Ch. 14, p. 59.

[2] Op. cit. by B. Majumdar, 443; Gaurangavijaya: by Cudamani Dasa, pp. 78.

[3] CBH. p. 13.

[4] CBH. pp. 49-50.

[5] Ibid. p. 56.

[6] CBH. p. 67.

[7] Ibid. pp. 2.

[8] Amiya Nimai Charit: by S.K. Ghosh, p. 256-68.

important part in the religious life of Bengal and India, by preaching his message of love and giving peace and consolation to many hungry souls.

At this time he began to preach the congregational chanting of the name of Krsna. By the advent of Caitanya and with the success of the Vaisnavas, some of the Brahmins were very envious. They created many hindrances on his path. They were so jealous that they finally took the matter before Kazi, the Muslim magistrate of Navadvipa. The magistrate took the complaints of the Brahmins seriously and first warned the followers of Caitanya not to chant loudly the name of Krsna. The Vasinavas disobeyed the order of Kazi and went on with their sankirtana (chanting) party as usual. The magistrate then sent constables who interrupted a sankirtana and broke some of the mridangas (drums). The magistrate also threatened to punish any body who would host the party of namsankirtana in his house. Caitanya quietly organized a mammoth, nonviolent mass demonstration, without breaking the law. He is the pioneer of the civil disobedience movement not only in India, but possibly in the world. He organized a procession of one hundred thousand men and thousands of mridangas and karatalas (hand cymbals). Caitanya explained to his followers, that they were banned from singing the name of Hari in the house, but were not banned singing in the streets. So this huge crowd passed over the roads of Navadvipa and finally reached the mansion of Kazi on chanting the name of Hari.

Conversion of Chand Kazi

Initially the Kazi hid inside the residence, on seeing the size of the crowd. However on getting assurances of the strictly nonviolent nature of the demonstration and invitation from Caitanya, Kazi appeared before the crowd to meet him. Soon they began discussion about the allegation against namsankirtana. The discussion was very polite and cordial with great logic and reasons. The Kazi was very impressed with the peaceful demonstration of the biggest crowd, the people of Navadvipa had ever witnessed, the atmosphere of the namsankirtana and with the conversation he had with Caitanya. Caitanya convinced the Kazi that the complaints against namsankirtana, were groundless. At the end of this dramatic discussion, Kazi Himself became a follower of the Hare Krsna Movement. This victory without any fight or bloodshed, by the cordial love and by the influence of bhakti brought by singing the name of Hari (God), raised the morale of the follower of Caitanya and many of them really believed that there must have been some spiritual force behind it[1]. The Kazi thenceforth declared that no one should hinder the sankirtana movement. Kazi's tomb still exists in the area of Navadvipa and Hindu pilgrims go there to show their respects[2].

After this incidence, Catianya began to preach and propagate his Hare Krsna movement more vigorously without much obstruction.

In the course of his preaching work, he used to send his followers in the different areas of the town to sing Hare Krsna.

Nityananda and Yaban Haridas, later known as Thakur Haridas were the chief of the preaching group locally. Nityananda was regarded as great enemy of the Brahminical order.

---

[1] Bhagavata "Golakera premadhana Harir nam sankirtana, rati na janmila kena tays ebe astra na dharila, prane kare na marila, chittosuddhi karila sabhar".

[2] Amiya Nimai Charit: by S.K. Ghosh, p. 266. (Kazi's descendants are residents, and they never objected to sankirtana, even during the days of Hindu Muslim riot).

With the help of Thakur Haridas, Nityanada converted at a great personal risk two notorious hooligans of Navadvipa named Jagai and Madhai[1].

These two drunken brothers physically assaulted Nityananda by throwing an earthen pot at him. But Nityananda was so kind, instead of counter-attacking, he politely requested the two brothers to chant the holy name of Lord Hari[2]. The two brothers were repentant later and became the followers of Caitanya. Their conversion gave a very big publicity for the movement.

Among many other miraculous activities, the cure of the two leprosy patients, Capala and Gopala[3] and bringing back life to the dead son of his associate Srivash, were well known to people[4]. Namasankirtan became daily routine among the Vaisnavas of Navadvipa, either in the house or in the street (nagar kirtana).

Very often during namesankirtana, Caitanya used to be seen in a state of ecstasy. During this state of many of his followers watched him to act in various ways as Krsna used to act in Vrindavana[5].

This sort of acts convinced his followers more and more that he was an incarnation of Krsna. But other non-Vaisnava people particularly students, teachers and Smartas, were very critical of this behaviouir. Some of them felt insulted with some of his behaviouir and wanted to embarrass, even punish him[6]. He was aware of this and planned his next move so that people would have more faith about his mission.

---

[1] Vaisnavism in Bengal: By R. Chakravorty, p. 63. [Jaban Haridas was a Muslim. He was attracted and the Hare Krsna movement and later known as Thakur Haridas. He became very close to Caitanya and was almost always with him till his death in Puri].

[2] CBH: pp. 204-11. (Merechha kalshir kana, tai bale ki prem devana).

[3] Srimad Bhagavatam: First Canto Part One; by A.C.B.S. Prabhupada, pp. 11.

[4] Amiya Nimai Charit: by S.K. Ghosh, pp., 289-300.

[5] Ibid: pp. 303-05.

[6] Srimad Bhaggavatam: First Canto part one; by A.C.B.S. Prabhupada, p. 14.

Renunciation of Caitanya

At the age of twenty-five two years after his conversion at Gaya, Caitanya was seized by a burning desire to forsake the wrold by renunciation, because people in general were inclined to show devotional loyalty to a sannyasin. He was initiated by Keshava Bharati, a Mayavadi sannyasin of Sankara order and a resident of Katowa in Bengal. Keshava Bharati received in his dream the Mahavakya the sacred words "Tat Tvam asi (That Thou Art)", which were revealed to the seers of the Upanisads[1]. Keshava Bharati, in initiating Gouranga into the mystery of the life of a monk, also initiated into the same Mahavakya and renamed him as Bhagavan Sri-Krsna Caitanya Bharati. It is interesting to note that Keshava Bharati himself, was not in the Vaisnava sampradaya.

His decision for the renunciation of the world had a tremendous impact in the Hindu society. There is hardly any parallel example in the history of religion. The heart breaking story of renunciation, when he left his aged mother, loving wife and his separation from the people of Navadvipa, soon spread in all directions and moved the people in a way that nothing else had done before in Bengal[2].

The story has since been carried to the furthest corners of the country through ballads, poetry, songs, dramas, and discourses. Yet even after five hundreds years, it has not lost, in the least, in its original pathos. There is no man or woman within the Hindu community, who even to this day hearing of Caitanya's renunciation, is not moved close to tears.

There could be few possibilities which had led to his renunciation[3]. Firstly, possibly he could not get over the death of his first wife Lakshmi Devi. Secondly, the attitude and behaviour of the non-Vaisnavas intelligent sects of Navadvipa, towards him, might have upset him very much. Thirdly, Keshav Bharati incidentally had visited Navadvipa at that moment and might have impressed him.

---

[1] Chandogya Upanisad: V1, Xiii, pp. 3.

[2] The Spiritual Heritage of India: By Swami Prabhavananda, p. 326.

[3] Jyotirmoy Sri caitanya: by Kalkut, p. 133. (Sannyasike sakalei namaskar kare, kew take apaman karena).

The fourth one, the one the Vaisnavas really believe in, was to teach the people of Kaliyuga, the process of self-realization, to achieve premabhakti, the highest stage of love towards God ("Apni achariye dharma jivke shikhay to teach people, he himself became the burning symbol as a devotee of God")[1]. He became a fullfledged preacher of the Bhagavatadharma. Although he was doing the same, in his life as a house holder, when he experienced some obstacles, he sacrificed the comfort of home life for the sake of the fallen souls.

After his initiation into the monastic order, he set out for Puri, the well known place for pilgrimage. There he resided for many years, with time to time departures for preaching or teaching. He visited various parts of India, worshipping in many temples and met numerous peoples, explaining the philosophy of the Hare Krsna movement. During these tour, he met many Hindu panditas and time to time tough resistance which he had overcome very successfully to make the movement very popular during that period.

He also visited Vrindavana, the holy seat of the Vaisnavas, where Krsna had engaged with his divine play with the cowherd boys and cowherd girls[2]. In his life as a house holder, his chief assistants, were Advaita Prabhu and Srivasa Thakura. But after he accepted the sannyasa, Nityananda Prabhu became his chief assistant who was deputised specifically to preach in Bengal and Six Goswamis were deputised to go to Vrindavana to excavate the present place of Pilgrimage. These six Goswamis were Rupa, Sanatana, Jiva, Gopala Bhatta, Raghunatha Dassa and Raghunath Bhatta, of which Rupa, Sanatana, were the head. The present city of Vrndavana owes much to Caitanya and his disciples for rescuing the holy place from oblivion.

During most of the last twelve years of his life, Caitanya lived in samadhi and in the state between samadhi and normal consciousness. In this state he was like an insane, in his love of Krsna consciousness.

In this state he was like mad in his love of Krsna, sometimes enjoying the sweetness of union with him, and sometimes suffering from the pangs of separation with him. The pangs were sweet too. The passing away of Caitanya is shredded in mystery, his biographers giving no certain accounts

---

[1]   Sri Sri Mahasankirtana: by Famous Vaisnava poet singer, T.K. Sarkar, p. 48.

[2]   Srimad Bhagvatam: First Cantopart one; by A.C.B.S. Prabhupada, p. 16.1. Sri Sri Mahasankirtana: by Famous Vaisnava poet

of it. Most of them, however, do state that at the age of forty eight, one day, he entered into the Jagannatha temple of Puri, and simply disappeared. Since then he was not seen to come out. His followers believe that in the image of God in the temple, Caitanya lives for eternity[1].

He travelled the length and breadth of the country, chanting the Hare Krsna mantra and spreading love of God. At many places crowds of hundreds of thousands of people would join his mission, in massive parties. Nevertheless, he also encountered opponents, the strongest of whom were the Mayabadis, an elite group of philosophers who were believer of monoism and held the view that God had no personality or form. These impersonalists also believed that the spiritual enlightenment could be obtained by a chosen few who knew sanskrit and arduously studied the Vedanta sutra. Throughout his travels Caitanya struggled against this group and succeeded in convincing many of them by the strength of his preaching force. One of the greatest philosophers of the Mayavada school, was Sharvabhauma Bhattacharya, the chief of the appointed panditas in the court of the King of Orissa, Maharaja Pratap Rudra and the state dean of faculty of Sanskrit literature. He met unconscious Caitanya, at his first visit to Jagannath temple, at Puri, in a state of transcendental ecstasy.

The Bhattacharya was attracted by the youthful lustre, with unusual body built, with very special features on it, very rarely ever exhibited. He realized such a transcendental trance was rarely exhibited and then only by the top most devotees[2]. He took Caitanya to his house for observation. A scholar like Bhattacharya who could detect an imposter easily, tested all the symptoms in the light of sastras.

Conversion of Sarvabhuma Bhattacharya

He also tested him as a scientist, rather than as a sentimentalist. He came to the conclusion that the unconscious state of Caitanya was genuine. Caitanya gained his consciousness after a very prolonged period when his other companion arrived there and chanted loudly the name of Lord Hari, as usual.

---

[1] The Spiritual Heritage of India: by Swami Prabhavananda, p. 327-28.

[2] CCM: p. 505-06.

Later it was disclosed that both the men were from Navadvipa.

Bhattacharya was the professor of many sannyasis, in the order of Sankaracharya Sampradaya, and he himself also belonged to that cult. Those who were followers of Sankara cult were known as Vedantists. As such Bhattacharya desired that the young sannyasi Caitanya should hear from him the teachings of Vedanta. Caitanya agreed and they sat together in the temple of Jagannatha. The Bhattacharya went on speaking continually for seven days, without any interruption from Caitanya, which raised some doubt in Bhattacharya's heart. In response to a query about this, Catianya answered, that without knowledge of Bhagavatam, it would be very hard for one to understand Vedanta. He thus explained to Bhattacharya, the Bhagavata dharma, the significance of namsankirtana and that the absolute personality of God head must be completely full of opulence, strength, fame, beauty, knowledge and renunciation. Yet the transcendental personality of Godhead is astonishingly ascertained as impersonal[1]. His this view is known as Achintavedavedbad. After hearing all these from Caitanya, the Bhattacharya was struck with wonder and regarded him in dead silence.

Then the Bhattacharya desired to listen to the explanation of the "atmarama" sloka from the Bhagavatam (1.7.10)[2].

At the request of Caitanya, first Bhattacharya himself scholarly explained the sloka in nine different ways chiefly based on logic because he was the most renowned scholar of logic of the time. Thus after hearing Bhattacharya, Caitanya explained the sloka in sixty four different ways without touching the nine explanations given by Bhattacharya. Some holds the view that Caitanya explained in eighteen different ways. On hearing these, Bhattacharya was convinced that such a scholarly presentation was impossible for an earthly creature.

---

[1] Srimad Bhagavatam: First Canto Part One; by A.C.B.S. Prabhupada, p. 22; CCM,

"*Sat din karen prabhu basiya sravan,*
Mayamay bad jaha pashandi bidhan."

[2] Ibid. p. 26.; CCM, "*Tabe prabhu sei sutra bakkhya arambila,*
shat prakar tar sadartha karila,
suni Bhattacharja tabe chamkia kahe,
iha ta samanya manusher sadhya nahe."

Bhattacharya was astounded by Caitanya's exposition of the Vedanta sutra and explanation of the atmarama sloka, he then surrendered unto him, repenting for his past dealing and not recognising him. Caitanya accepted him and manifested before him first as four armed Narayana and then as two handed lord Krsna with a flute in the hand[1]. Bhattacharya there after composed hundreds of celebrated slokas in the praise of Lord Caitanya[2].

Conversion of Prakasananda Sarasvati

The biggest confrontation with the Mayavadis was yet to come and it occurred at their very head quarters, for the centuries the capital of the Mayavadi school, the city of Benaras. When Caitanya came to Benaras with his devotee, continued his sankirtana movement, attracting crowds of thousands, wherever he went. He was very bitterly criticized by the Mayavadi leader Prakasananda Sarasvati, for singing and dancing with all sorts of ordinary people. He believed that a spiritualized should continually study abstract philosophy and engage in lengthy discussions about the Absolute Truth. He also thought that the chanting of Hare Krsna mantra did not have any spiritual significance and it was mere a sentiment. Caitanya's followers were extremely distressed about the Mayavadis constant criticism of him. So in order to pacify them, he accepted an invitation of a meeting with all the Mayavadi leaders[3]. After seating on the ground at the assembly, exhibiting his supreme mystic potency, manifested from his body a spiritual brilliant effulgence.

The Mayavadis were amazed and immediately stood up in respect.

The great Mayavadi sannyasi Prakasananda inquired from Caitanya the reasons for his preference of namsankirtana to the study of Vedantasutra and also the reasons that caused him to indulge in namsankirtana. Prakasananda believed that the duty of a sannyasi was to read the Vedantasutra. Caitanya replied that in this Kali yuga, it was not suitable for the numerous people to study Vedanta philosophy to attain the spiritual goal by acquiring the

---

[1] CCM: p. 505-06.

[2] Amiya Nimai Charit: by S.K. Ghost, p. 530. "*Tribhuvana pavana kripaya lesang tang pranamamicha Sri sachi tanayam*"

[3] Ibid: p. 835.

knowledge. Rather due to the short life span and due to the involvement with many other activities, it would be realistic to chant the holy name of the god with premabhakti, to make one free from material bondage.

He said that in this age of Kali there was no other religion but the glorification of the Lord by utterance of His holy name and that was the injunction of all the revealed scriptures. Then he uttered a sloka (from the Brhannaradiya Purana).

"Harer nama harer nama harer namaiva kevalam,
kalau nasty eva nasty eva nasty eva gatir anyatha."[1].

-In this age of Kali, there is no alternative, there is no alternative, there is no alternative, for spiritual progress other than the chanting of the holy name, chanting of the holy name, chanting of the holy name of the Lord.

The discussion went on for hours. Finally in one of the most astounding religious conversions of all time, Prakasananda Svarasvati, the Mayavadi's greatest scholar, along with all his followers, surrendered to Lord Caitanya and began to chant the holy name of Krsna with great enthusiasm[2].

As a result of this conversation, the people of the entire city of Benaras accepted, Caitanyas Hare Krsna movement. Prakasananda wrote himself about his feeling and thought of Caitanya during his converstion.

He could see an young sannyasi dancing, but he felt he was not a real monk but as imposter of a monk Sri Krsna himself was dancing and he could not hold his tears of joy[3]. After this incidence the movement did not encounter any other big resistance. In this way Lord Caitanya laid the foundation for a universal religion for mankind.

---

[1] Amiya Nimai Charit: by S.K. Ghosh, p. 839.
[2] Ibid: p. 849.
[3] Amiya Nimal Charit: by S.K. Ghosh, p. 849.
    "Bamantah madhurjai mrta nidhi kotiriva tanu,
    cchhatabhistangb bande harirmahaha sannyasa kapatam".

The Mist Around His Disappearance

The passing away of Caitanya is shrouded with misty. His biographers do not give certain accounts of it. Most of them, however, do state that in the last few years of his carrier, he had spent in the Jagannath temple of Puri, lived in samadhi or in a state between samadhi and consciousness. At the age of forty eight once he entered the temple and came out no more, simple disappearing in 1533. So there exists the belief that in the image of God in the temple, Caitanya lives for eternity. This is the most consentient view[1]. There are other opinions also.

In 'Caitanyamangal' (of Jayananda, p. 153), it is mentioned that when he was dancing during singing, in the Car Festival in the month of Asharh, his left big toe was suddenly pierced by a brick lying on the road. He developed temperature and whole body was swollen and died two days later, during the day of Akshay tritia. From this description, it appears that he died of gas gangrene. His body was buried within the temple in a place called 'Kaili Vaikuntha' according to the plan between Roy Ramananda and King Pratap Rudra and other few close advisers. The news was kept secret for a few reasons, the important one of which was to avoid the political tension between Bengal and Orissa. It was announced that the body of Caitanya blended with the shrine of Jagannatha[2].

Other view is that Caitanya was murdered by Vidyadhar who wanted to capture power from King Pratap Rudra. Vidyadhar realized the popularity of Caitanya and his loyalty to the King. So his plan would not be successful while Caitanya was alive.

According to this view Caitanya was killed within the temple by Vidyadhar and his close associates, body was buried there and for their own safety, they had to declare that Jagannatha himself was too pleased with his prayer and engulfed his body[3].

---

[1] The Spiritual Heritage of India: by Swami Prabhavananda, p. 328.
[2] Caitanya's Life and Teachings: by Jagannatha Sarkar, p. 239; Caitanyer Divyajivan O Ajnata Tirodhan Parba: by Madhav Pattanayak, p. 101.
[3] Sacha Jagannath Sri Krsna Caitanya: by Dr. Dipak Chandra, pp. 310-17.

CHAPTER VI

The Theology of Harekrsna Movement

The importance of the chanting of the name of Sri Hari was mentioned, before the advent of Caitanya. It was mentioned in Bhagavata (AD 300-1200) that the meditation on Lord Vishnu was the creed of the Satya Yuga (Golden Age), sacrifice was the creed of Treta Yuga (Silver age), worship was the creed of Dvapara Yuga (Copper age) and chanting of the name of Sri Hari was the creed for the age of Kali Yuga (present age)[1]. It was also said that the real religious Aryans welcomed the Kali age because by chanting the name of Hari, everything could be achieved that one would expect in Satya Yuga by meditation.[2].

In Kalisantran Upanishad (300 BC) first time, it was mentioned about repeating the name Hare Krsna and Hare Rama[3]. In Brhan-naradiya Purana, it was mentioned, in this black age of sin and sorrow, jealousy and hypocrisy, self-sufficiency and self-aggrandizement, there was no other means of redemption from the bondage of Maya than chanting the name

---

[1] Bhagavata: XII, 3, 52. *"Krte jaddhyaato Vishnu tretayang jajato makhahi, Dvapare paricharjyayang kalou taddharikirtanait"*.

[2] Bhagavata: XI, 5, 36. *"Kaling savajay-antarjya gunajna aravaginah, Jatra sankirtananaiva sarva sarthoh-vilavyate."*

[3] Commentary on CCM: Adilila, part 1, by A.C.B.S. Prabhupada, p. 140.
      "Hare Krsna Hare Krsna Krsna Krsna Hare Hare
      Hare Rama Hare Rama Rama Rama Hare Hare."

of Hari[1]. In Padma Purana it is mentioned also[2]. So what was already suggested in Vedic literature, Caitanya brougth that into light to convince people that there was no other way of transcendental liberation, but by the glorification of the Lord Hari by utterance of his holy name and that was the injuction of the revealed scriptures.

The advent of Caitanya and his role in the propagation of Hare Krsna movement seems very right fit in what was suggested by Karbhajan Muni (Saint) in Bhagavata Purana, few hundreds years earlier[3]. It said that, in the age of Kali God head would come down with fair complexion in the name of Caitanya as an avatara, to preach the name of Hari. Possibly keeping this forecast in mind when Keshav Bharati initiated Nimai Pandit, gave the name Bhagavan Sri Krsna Caitanya Bharati. Sri Caitanya preached the name of Hari as repeating the name Hare Krsna Hare Rama. Hara was one name of Radha. This was changed to Hare in the vocative. Radha was a part of Krsna or pleasure potency (Hladini sakti)[4]. Krsna was an avatara of Vishnu, so was Ram. So the words Hare Krsna or Rama bear the same meaning, the name of Hari or Vishnu. The words could be explained in other way also. The word Haro is the form of addressing the energy of the Lord, and the words Krsna and Rama are the forms of addressing the Lord Himself. Both Krsna and Rama mean "the supreme pleasure," and Haro is the supreme pleasure energy of the Lord, changed to Hare in the vocative. The supreme pleasure energy of the Lord helps people to reach the Lord[5].

---

[1] Srimad Bhagavatam: First Canto Part One; by A.C.B.S. Prabhupada, p. 35; CCM: by Sukamar Sen, p. 98, Adilila. *"Harer nama harer nama harer namaiva kevalam kalau nasty eva nasty eva nasty eva gatir anyatha".*

[2] Padma Puran: CCM Madhya / 17 / 133. *"Hari haraye Krsna Jadvaaya namah Jadavaya Madhavay Keshavaya namah."*

[3] Srimadbhagavatarn: 11, 5, 27. in CCM; Adilila, Chapter III, 40.
    "Kalijuge juga dharma namer prachar,
    Tathilagi, pitabarna Caitanya avatar".
   [Karbhajan was the foremost one of nine Saints who explained the King Nimi, the significance of the different avatar of God in different yuga].

[4] The Science of Self Realization: by A.C.B.S. Prabhupada, p. 344. [Interview with B.K. Sarkar, famous poet singer of Gengal with vast knowledge in Vaishnava sastra].

[5] Ibid: p. 167.

The material aatmosphere in which all the living beings are, is called Maya. The Maya is the material energy and is one of the multiple energies of the Lord. The living entities are also the energy of Lord, known as marginal energy. The marginal energy is described, as superior to material energy. When the superior energy is in contact with inferior energy an incompatible situation arises. But when the superior marginal energy is in contact with superior energy, Hara, it is established in its happy, normal condition[1]. These three words, Hare, Krsna and Rama, are considered as the transcendental seeds of the mahamantra. The chanting of this mantra is a spiritual call for the Lord and his energy, to give protection to the conditioned soul. This chanting is comparable exactly like the genuine cry of a child for his mother's presence. This genuine cry for Mother Hara with suddha bhakti, helps the devotee to achieve the Lord Father's grace. Lord reveals himself to the devotee when he is pleased with the suddha bhakri[2].

Caitanya's cultivation of bhakti and infinite love of God was best known from his teaching to one of his close disciple Rupa Goswami at Vrndavana. To make manifest this infinite love, according to him one must practice Vaidhi-bhakti or disciplinary devotion, by chanting the name of God, hearing and singing his praises, meditating upon the divine play and deeds of Krsna and engaging in the rites ceremonies of worship. He laid special stress on japa—repeating the name of God to the count of beads. Vaidhibhakti is the outward expression of Raganuga bhakti[3].

Patanjali, the father of Yoga philosophy, also approved the practice of japa as one of the methods of spiritual attainment for the name of God[4]. In chanting God's name one necessarily meditate upon his presence.

---

[1] The Science of Self Realization: by A.C.B.S. Prabhupada, p. 167.

[2] CCM: Adilila; Chapter 111, 14 and 19.
      "Chirakal nahi kari prembhakti dan
      Bhakti bina jagater nihi kona sthan".
      "Jugadharma prabataimu namsankirtan,
      Charibhava bhakti dia nachamu bhuvan".

[3] Srimad Bhagavatam First Canto Part One: by A.C.B.S. Prabhupada; p. 39 and CCM, p. 384-85.

[4] The Spiritual Heritage of India: by Swami Prabhavananda; p. 329.

Caitanya also emphasized the practice of ethical virtues, particularly humility and forbearance. By the conduct recommended one causes the divine love made manifest in the heart, the Raganuga bhakti, an almost unbearable thirst for the adored God. Of these manifestations there are five stages, corresponding to various expressions of love on the plane of human life[1].

The first one is known as santa, the peaceful stage in which one finds joy in the thought of God and the aspirant, attains poise and tranquility. He feels God near him, but still no definite relationship between two is established.

Then comes the second the dasya, the servant stage in which the aspirant feels that the God is the master or that he is the father or protector.

The third is sakhya, the stage of friendship. God is now realized as friend and playmate. He is felt to be nearer, as the sense of awe vanishes, and God of power and grandeur is forgotten. He is now not only the God, but a cherished friend.

The fourth is vatsalya, the child stage. Now the God of love is considered as a child and the devotee must take of him. This stage is thought of, as higher than the preceding stages because in human relationships a father or mother has more affection for a child than a child has for its parents.

The fifth and the last stage is madhura, the sweetest of the relationships, the relation between the lover and the beloved.

The strongest of the human ties, that between man and wife, finds its ultimate realization in the new tie between man and God, in which God is the beloved.

In this stage all elements of love admiration, comradeship, and communion are present. The highest expression of this type of love was to be found in the cowherd girls (gopies) in Vrndavana, particularly in Radha. When this kind of love possesses the heart, mystic union is attained. There

---

[1] Bhaktirasamrtasindhu: by Rupa Goswami; Translation: by A.C.B.S. Prabhupada, p. 335-45 and CCM, p. 386, "Dasa sakha pitradi preyasira Gana, ragamarge nija nija bhavera ganan."

is a definnite link between visvasa (faith) and bhakti. Insight born faith, strengthened by bhakti is far more fruitful than logic or rationalisation[1].

Caitanya gave little consideration to the theoretical knowledge of the problems of the God, the human soul and the universe. He was a God intoxicated man. His spiritual experiences transcended the realm of time, space and causation. His mind plunged into the domain where God is not an abstraction, but a reality in which dwell all joy, all sweetness, all love a reality situated deep in the loving heart of his devotees.

In Sankara's philosophy what was called as infinite knowledge, Caitanya called that infinite love[2].

God is known as Sat-chit-ananda, existence, knowledge and bliss and he is absolute, indefinable and inexpressible. He is the repository of infinite blessed attributes, the one the existence from the universe issued forth, in whom the universe at last dissolves the omnipresent, the omniscient and the omnipotent.

Such an account of the God head meant little to Caitanya. For him God was Krsna, the God of love enchantingly beautiful, eternally youthful and man was the eternal playmate, the eternal companion.

For him again the Krsna was not the one, who uttered the mighty spiritual discourses of Gita, the philosopher, the harmonizer and the avatara. For him he was the Krsna of Vrindavana, the great lover and the embodiment of love, divested of all the powers of the God head, the companion of the cowherd boys and cowherd girls (gop and gopies), playing upon his flute and drawing souls unto him by his compelling love.

He was the soul of souls eternally dwelling in Vrindavana, not a land one can point to in a map, but the heart of man, the Vrindavana that is beyond time and space. The Love divine, which is Krsna, is not to be acquired by man, for it is already existent in the soul., though covered by ignorance, by attachment to the world of the senses or Maya. When clouds of ignorance swept away, this forever existing love becomes manifest. Then does man realize himself.

---

[1] CCM: p. 194. *"Alsukika lila ei parama niguda,*
            visvase paiye tarke haya vahundura".
[2] The Spiritual Heritage of India: by Swami Prabhavananda, p. 328-39.

His philosophy of relation between atma (soul) and paramatma (God) is best known from his explanation of the atmarama verse of Bhagavata, given to Sharbabhouma Bhattacharya at Puri and later to his disciple Sanatana Goswami at Vrindavana and also from his teachings, to his disciple Rupa Goswami at Vrindavana.

Explanation of Atmarama verse of Bhagavata

Atmarama Verse which appears in Srimad-Bhagavatam as follows:

> *"Atmaramas ca munayo*
> *nigrantha apy urukrame*
> *kurvanty ahaitukim bhaktim*
> *itthambhuta guno harih."*

This verse indicates that those who are liberated souls and are fully self-satisfied, will eventually become devotee of the Lord.

This injunction is especially meant for the impersonalists, as they have no information of the Supreme personality of Godhead. They try to remain satisfied with the impersonal Brahman, but Krsna is so attractive and so strong that he attracts their minds. This is the purport of the verse.

Caitanya then went on to point out that there were eleven times in the Atmarama verse: 1 atmaramah, 2 ca, 3 munayah, 4 nigranthah, 5 apy, 7 urukrame, 8 kurvantyi, 9 ahaitukim, 10 ittambhutagunah, 11 harih. He then explained each and every one of these items. As far as the word atmarama is concerned, he explained that the word atma was to indicate: the 1 the Supreme Absolute Truth, 2 the body, 3 the mind, 4 endeavour, 5 conviction, 6 intelligence, and 7 nature.

The word atma means enjoyer. Therefore anyone who takes pleasure in the cultivation of knowledge of these seven items is known as atmarama. He then explained about the different kinds of atmaramas, or transcendentalists. As for the word munayah or muni, those who were great spiritual thinkers were called muni. Great sages, great austere persons, great mystics and learned scholars were also called munis. The word nigrantha indicates freedom from bondage of illusion. Nigrantha also means "one who has no connection with spiritual injunction". Grantha means revealed scriptures and nir is an affix which is used to mean no connection, constructing and also prohibiting. There were many instructions for spiritual realization, but persons who had no connection with such scriptural instructions were also known as nigrantha The word urukrama was to indicate a highly powerful person. The word krama was defined as an expert display of energies as well as stepping forward very quickly and the word urukrama, to indicate one who could step forward very far. (The greatest step forward was taken by Lord Vamunadeva, who covered the whole universe in two steps[1]). The word kurvanti was to indicate to work for others. But actually it meant when activities were performed for the satisfaction of the Supreme Lord. The word hetu was to indicate the reason or cause.

Generally people are engaged in transcendental activities for three reasons.

Some want material happiness, some want mystic perfection and some want liberation from material bondage. As far as material enjoyment is concerned, there are so many varieties that no one can enumerate them. As far as mystic power are concerned there are eighteen, and as far as types of liberation from material bondage is concerned there are five. The state of being where all these varieties are conspicuous by their absence is called ahetuki. The ahetuki qualification is especially mentioned because by the ahetuki service of the Lord, one can achieve the favour of the Lord.

The word bhakti can be used in ten different ways. Out of these ten one is sadhanbhakti or occupational devotional service. The other nine are called premabhakti, love of Godhead. those who are in the neutral position attain perfection up to love of Godhead. Similarly those who are situated in the relationship of master and servant, attain love of Godhead to the stage of attachment (dasya). Those who are related in friendship, attain love of God to the point of fraternity (sakya). Those who are in love with God as his parents (vatsalya), are elevated to the position of transcendental emotion. But only those who are related with the Supreme in conjugal love (madhura), can experience the highest of ecstasies. Thus there are different meanings of the word bhakti. The word itthambhuta indicate fully

---

[1] Srimad Bhagavatam: 2.7.40.

transcendental pleasure. In other words, derived by understanding Krsna as he is as the all attractive reservoir of all pleasures and reservoir of all pleasure giving tastes with all transcendental qualifications attracts one to become his devotee.

By virtue of such attraction, one can give up fruitive activities and endeavours for liberation and can even abandon the intense desire to achieve success in joga mystic power. The attraction of Krsna is so intense that one can lose respect for all other means of self-realization and simply surrender unto the Supreme Personality of Godhead. Caitanya also explained guna in all its different meanings. Guna indicate the unlimited transcendental blissful knowledge and eternity. He is fully perfect and his perfection is increased when he is controlled by the attention of his devotee. God is so kind and merciful that he can give himself in exchange for the devotional service of the devotee. His transcendental qualities are such that the perfection of his beauty, his perfect reciprocation of love between himself and his devotees and the flavour of his transcendental qualities attract different kinds of liberated souls.

The word Hari has different meanings of which two are foremost.

Hari means that he takes away all inauspicious things from the devotees life and that he attracts the mind of the devotee by awarding him transcendental love of God head.

Krsna is so attractive that anyone who can remember him in some way or another becomes freed from the four kinds of material miseries.

The Lord gives special attention to the devotee and banishes the devotee's various sinful activities, which are tumbling blocks for the advancement of devotional service. This is called routing the influence of ignorance. Simply by hearing about him, one develops love for him. That is the gift of the Lord. On one side he takes away inauspicious things and on the other side he awards the most auspicious things. That is the meaning of Hari.

When a person developed in love of Godhead, his body, mind and everything else are attracted by the transcendental qualities of the God. Such is the power of Krsna's merciful activities and transcendental qualities.

He is so attractive that out of transcendental attachment, a devotee will abandon all four principle aims of material life piety or religiosity (dharma), wealth or economic development (artha), love, fulfilment of desire or regulation of sense gratification (kama) and salvation of the soul (moksha).

The words api and ca are adverbs and can be used for virtually any purpose. The words ca or and can render seven different readings to the whole construction.

Caitanya thus established the importance of the eleven words in the Atmarama verse. Then he explained the each item as follows. The word brahman indicates the greatest in all respects. The God is the greatest in all opulences. No one can excel him in wealth, strength, fame, beauty, knowledge and renunciation. Thus the word brahman indicates the Supreme Personality of Godhead Krsna[1].

The Supreme Personality of Godhead is realized in three aspects, but they are all, one and the same. The Absolute Truth, the Supreme Personality, Krsna is everlasting. He existed before the manifestation of this cosmic world. He exists during its continuance and will continue to exist after its annihilation[2].

Therefore he is the soul of everything. He is pervading all, witnessing all and he is the Supreme form of everything.

There are three different kinds of transcendental processes mentioned in Vedic literature by which one can understand and achieve that Supreme perfection of the Absolute. They are called the process of knowledge (jnana joga), the process of mystic yoga (karma yoga) and the process of devotional service (bhakti yoga). The followers of these three processes realize the Absolute Truth in three different aspects.

Those who follow the process of knowledge, realize him as impersonal Brahmana; those who follow the process of yoga, realize him as the localized Supersoul (paramatma); those who follow the devotional service, realize him as the Supreme Personality of God head, Sri Krsna. In other words although the word Brahmana indicate Krsna and nothing else,

---

[1]   Vishnu Purana: 1.12.57.
[2]   Srimad-Bhagavatam: 2.9.33.

still according to the process that is followed, the God is realized in three different perceptions.

As far as devotional service is concerned, there are two divisions. In the beginning there is vaidhi bhakti, or devotional service with regulative principles. In the higher stage there is raganuga-bhakti or devotional service in pure love.

The Supreme Personality of Godhead is the Absolute Truth, but he is manifested by the expansions of his different energies also.

Those who follow the regulative principles of devotional service ultimately attain the Vaikuntha planets in the spiritual world, but one who follows the principles of love in devotional service, attains to the supreme abode, the highest planet in the spiritual world known as Krsnaloka or Goloka Vrndavana.

Transcendentalists can also be divided into three categories. The word akama refers to one who does not have any material desires. Moksakama refers to one who seeks liberation from material miseries, and sarvakama refers to one has the material desire to enjoy. The intelligent transcendentalist gives up all other processes and engage himself in the devotional service of the God, even though he may have many desires. It is not by any kind of transcendental activity—neither fruitive action, nor the cultivation of knowledge, nor cultivation of mystic yoga that a person can achieve the highest perfection, without adding a tinge of devotional service.

Caitanya then explained the word projjhita means desire for liberation. Somehow or other, if one comes to Krsna and begin to sing or hear about him, Krsna is so kind that he awards him the consciousness, and the devotee gradually forgets everything and engages himself in the devotional service of the God.

When one comes to Lords in devotional service or in full Krsna consciousness, the reward is the Krsna himself. The method of devotional service, the service itself, association of pure devotee and the causeless mercy of Krsna, all act so wonderfully that one can easily give up all other desire and become absorbed in the thought of Krsna, even if he is distressed, in want of material possessions, inquisitive or is actually an wiseman cultivating knowledge.

In summary Caitanya said Krsna is the meaning of all the words in the Atmarama verse. Up to this point Caitanya gave the introduction of Atmarama verse. Then he explained the real inner meaning of it. In the cultivation of knowledge there are two kinds of transcendentalists. One of them worship the impersonal Brahmana, and the other desire of liberation. Since monoists or advaitavadis worship the impersonal features of Brahmana, they are therefore called worshippers of Brahmana (Mayavadis). These worshippers of Brahmana are further divided into three categories: the neophyte, one who is absorbed in the realization of Brahmana and the one who has actually realized himself as Brahmana. Accoding to Caitanya if devotional service is added, the knower of Brahmana can then become liberated; otherwise there is no possibility of liberation. Anyone who is fully engaged in devotional service in Krsna consciousness is understood to be already realized in Brahmana. He believed "the devotional service is so strong, one is attracted to Krsna even from the platform of Brahmana worship and with the rewards from the Lord, he eternally engages in the service of Krsna.

There are two kinds of liberated souls having material bodies: the soul liberated by devotional service and soul liberated by the cultivation of knowledge.

The liberated souls simply by cultivation of knowledge without devotion, fall due to their many offences and the liberated soul in devotional service, attracted by the transcendental qualities of Krsna, become more and more elevated. In other words, those who attain self-realization by the execution of devotional service, attain a transcendental body, and being attracted to transcendental qualities of Krsna, engage fully in pure devotional service.

Anyone who is not attracted to Krsna is understood to be still under the spell of the illusory energy (maya), but one who is attempting to be liberated by the process of devotional service is actually liberated from the spell of maya.

Sankara (eighth century A.D.) was the one who wrote commentary on Vedanta. He was the believer of advaitabad or monoism. He believed in Brahmana who was impersonal and infinite and also believed in complete union with Brahmana. According to him Vedantic knowledge was the only means for this complete union[1].

According to Bhaskara, in the state of bondage that is ignorance, the individual souls are different from God; and in the state of liberation that is knowledge, they become one with him and all consciousness of separation is dissolved. This union is possible only after death, never in any time during life. In this respect the philosophy of Bhaskara differs from the other systems we have studied[2].

Yamuna in tenth century and Ramanuja in eleventh century, promoted the idea of visistha advaitabad or qualified non-dualism. God is the Supreme being. He is the whole of which individual souls are parts and are related to him, as are the waves of the ocean to ocean. The universe is a transformation of God. God is its soul and the visible world is his body[3].

Ramanuja did not take into consideration knowledge that was self-luminous and absolute. Knowledge, he declared, was always relative and in it there was always a distinction between subject and object.

In short Ramanuja did not admit nirvikalpa samadhi, the unitary consciousness, the experience of the Self as one with Brahmana. He is at the heart of a bhakta, a devotee, who preserved his distinction from Brahmana in order to enjoy the bliss of divine love[4].

Nimberka approached the fundamental problem of the God, the universe, and the soul, believing that infinite was the God and infinite were the ways to apprehend and comprehend him. According to Nimberka's philosophy of bhedabheda or dualism in non-dualims, Brahmana has two aspects, the absolute and the relatives, or in other words, the impersonal and the personal. Thus there exists almost an identity between the philosophy of Nimberka and that of Bhaskara with the important difference that according to Bhaskara the individual soul is a part of Brahmana only

---

[1]   The Spiritual Heritage of India: by Swami Prabhavananda, p. 285.

[2]   Ibid: p. 300.

[3]   Ibid: p. 303.

[4]   Ibid: p. 307.

so long it remains in ignorance that in knowledge and emancipation it becomes one with him; whereas Nimberka declares that the soul is a part of Brahmana and is also one with him, both in the state of ignorance and that in knowledge and emancipation and that it realizes itself as living both in union with Brahmana and separate from him[1].

Madhva (thirteenth century) founded the Vaisnava sects known as Brahma or Sad Vaisnava. Madhva's philosophy of dvaitabad, is based upon the idea of difference or distinction. The distinctions are known to be five in number: God is distinct from individual souls. God is distinct from non-living matter. One individual soul is distinct from every other. Individual souls are distinct from matter. In matter, when it is divided, the parts are distinct from one another[2].

Achintabhedabhedbad

Sri-Caitanya believed in Achintabhedabhedbad[3]. As a first step he believed in to awaken the jiva soul[4]. The constant chanting of the holy name of Krsna without offence, awakens the real nature of the soul of the chanter. When the soul awakens, he sees by the light of pure knowledge, the real nature of Sri Krsna, His form, qualities, deeds and realms. By the grace of the supreme lord Krsna and repeated chanting of his holy name, the real nature of the chanter awakens in his heart of hearts. He who sees the jivasouls and the world separate from the oversoul Paramatma, the partial immanent aspect of Krsna, is liable to fall a victim to Maya—His deluding potency. But he who visualizes that the Jivasouls and the universe emanate from the all pervading supreme soul Paramatma, existing in him and inseparably connected with him but are not identical with him, is liberated from Maya. Like the bubbles, sense-percepts of the senses and words of the vedas are

---

[1]   The Spiritual Heritage of India: p. 318.

[2]   Ibid: p. 320.

[3]   CCM: Adilila / 6 / 37 38.
      "Mahavishnur maha angasha advaita guna dham,
      Isvare abhed haite advaita purna nam".

[4]   The Teaching and Philosophy of Lord Caitanya: by Srimad B.P. Tirtha Maharaj (1967).

inseparably linked with the source; so also the whole universe including the Jivasouls exist in the all pervading oversoul Pramatma, is inseparably connected with him but is not one and the same with him. This is known as the docrine of Achinta Bhedabheda, *ie* inconceivable simultaneous existence of distinction and non-distinction, between the Supreme Lord, the Jiva-souls and the universe. Be it remembered that this knowledge of self and Paramatma cannot be realized by dissertations, philosophical discussions, or by dry intellectualism. But he who approaches the Supreme Lord with unconditional self-surrender, is the only recipient of his and to him alone, and the Lord reveal himself in all his aspects in unalloyed existence.

Deification and personality of Caitanya

Both in the Caitanyabhagavata and Caitanyacaritamrta, Advaita Acarya has been described, as a senior, scholarly and highly respectable leader of the Vaisnavas of Navadvipa. Very often Vrndavana Dasa describes Advaita as the prophet of the Caitanya movement.

It is important to mention that the necessity of the Avatara of Narayana, specially suited to the spiritual needs of the kali yuga, was first propounded by Advaita Acharya before the advent of Caitanya. The impending Caitanya Avatara he vigorously invoked against Brahminical reaction. He had the idea that of a forearmed Visnu, reincarnated with the mission of flushing out the infidels and the philistines[1]. There is however a view that Advaita initially supported the philosophical concepts of Sankara Acarya[2]. Supposedly that this view is correct, one may yet say that his original idea must have been thoroughly changed due to the close contact with Madhvendra Puri, who was his guru (teacher). Even before Caitanya had renounced the world, Advaita, Srivasa, Murari Gupta and other Vaisnavas worshipped him as Narayana[3]. The great importance of Advaita in the Caitanya movement

---

[1] CBH: p. 13. *"Prakasiye cari bhuja cakra laimu hate.*
      Pasandire katya karimu skandha nasa.
      Tabe Krsna prabhu mora muin tara dasa".

[2] Advaita Siddhi: ed. Rajendranath Ghosh, Vol. 1, pp. 141-43, 1931.

[3] CBH: II, Ch. 2, pp. 129 141, Ch. 6, pp. 156-62.

consisted in the fact that it was he who boldly proclaimed at Puri that Caitanya, as supreme God, was the quintessence of the avataras[1]. Such a proclamation in a great pilgrim centre like Puri had certainly had a great bearing on the propagation of the Caitanya Vaisnava faith.

At Puri Advaita also sang a hymn on Caitanya Narayana[2]. Vrndavana Dasa however informed us that Caitanya's 'mood' was always that of a 'servant'[3]. None therefore had the courage to inform him that he was the veritable Narayana or Krsna. But Advaita was bold enough to proclaim Caitanya's divinity in Caitanya's presence. According to Vrndavana Dasa Caitanya felt ashamed when he heard of this proclamation[4]. He also told Srivasa that he did not understand why people were lionizing him and neglecting Krsnanama[5]. Both Sanatana and Rupa were present at Puri when Advaita made this significant proclamation of Caitany's divinity. They also worshipped Caitanya as a God. Caitanya advised them to learn love mixed with devotion (premabhakti) from Advaita whom he described as the 'storekeeper of bhakti'. Advaita blessed the two brothers[6]. Caitanya advised two learned brothers to spread bhakti among the Hindi-speaking pascimas or Upper/Western Indians[7]. Later in a trance Caitanya confessed

---

[1]   CBH: III, Ch. 9, p. 414: *"Aji ara kona Avatara gaoya nai,*
                Sava Avataramaya Caitanyagosain".

[2]   CBH: p. 414: The song: *"Sricaitanya Narayana karunasagara,*
                Dindukhitera bandhu more daya kara".

[3]   CBH: p. 415, *"Niravadhi dasyabhave prabhura vihara,*
                mui Krsnadasa bai na bolaye ara".
      also, p. 175: *"Dasyabhave nace prabhu Gaurangasundara",* p. 223: *"Nimai Pandita satya Srikrsnera dasa".*

[4]   CBH: p. 415: *"Ksaneka thakiya prabhu stmstuti suni,*
                Lajja yena paite lagila nyasamani".

[5]   CBH: p. 416: *"Chadiya Krsna nama Krsna kirtana,*
                Ki gayila amare ta bujhaha ekhana".

[6]   CBH: p. 418.

[7]   CBH: p. 418. *"Tomra sabha yata rajasa tamasa,*
                Pascima sabhare giya deha bhaktirassa".

that he was really an Avatara and that his advent as an Avatara had been caused by Advaita Acharya[1].

The reasons for the Vaisnabas, accepting him as an Avatara

A. Various forecasts in the religious scriptures:
These books were written or compiled quite a few centuries, prior to the advent of Caitanya.

(1) The forecast in Bhagavata (11/5/32). This is a quotation from the 'Saint Karbhajan', the leader of the nine top Saints named 'Nabayogendra', who explained the Great devotee, King' Nimi, the different significance, of the Godhead in different Yuga[2].

"Krsnavarnang Tvisakrsnang Sangopangastra Parshadham,
Yajnai Sankirtana Prayeerjajanti Hi Sumedhasa."

It means—who always utters the name of Krsna, but his complexion, is not dark (the word krsna means dark), associated with all the companions (pancahatattva, the five together-the God himself, his companion Nityananda, Advaita, Gadadhar, and Srivash who represent respectivly, Balaram, Siva, Radha and other male companion in Dvapara yuga), would be regarded in Kali yuga as God head, and intelligent people would worship him by chanting his name through sankirtana and if possible by distribution of prasadam (a portion of food sacrificed for God).

---

[1] CBH: p. 418. Here Caitanya is saying Advaita Acarya:
"Sutiya achilu mui Ksirasagarbhitare
Nidrabhanga haila mor tomaro hunkare"
It means Caitanya is saying that as Visnu while he was retiring at Kshirodesagar, on the support of Ananta Naga, he was awaken up by a call from Advaita who brought him to Nadia.
[2] Bhagavata: 11/5/32.

(2) In Bhagavata Saint Garga said when he christened Srikrsna in Dvapara yuga although the baby was dark in complexion but would possess (10/8/13).

> *"Sukla, Rakta, Pita Varna Aye Tin Dyuti,*
> *Satya, Treta, Kalikale Dharen Sripati"*[1]

It means God would possess white, red, and yellow complexion respectively in Satya, Treta and Kali yuga.

(3) Saint Garga also said

> *"Kaliyuge Yuga Dharma Namer Prachar,*
> *Tathilagi Pitavarna Caitanya Avatar*[2]*".*

It means in Kali age it would the religion to chant the name of Hari (God) and for this purpose Godhead would incarnate as an Avatara name Caitanya (literary means consciousness). It is worthwhile to mention that when Bhrarati initiated Gauranga into monostary, he gave this name to him.

(4) The great king Prahlad is well known for his devotion. One of his quotation as mentioned in Bhagavata[3], is like this:

> *Dharmang Mahapurusha Pashi Yuganubrttang,*
> Chhannam Kalou Jadbhava Striyugohoata Sa Tvam"

Oh God, sometimes you incarnate yourself in disguise, in Kali Yuga. That is why your another name is Triyuga. The followers of Caitanya, believe this statement is true in case of Caitanya.

---

[1] Bhgavata: 10/8/13.
[2] Ibid: 11/5/27.
[3] Ibid: 7/9/38.

(5) It was mentioned in 'Krsna Jamal', Godhead said:

> *"Punna Kshetre Navadvipe Bhavishami Sachi suta"*
> *It means in Navadevipa, I would incarnate as a son of Sachi Devi.*

(6) It is mentioned in 'Bayu Puran':

> *"Kalou Sankirtanarambhe Bhavishami Sachi Suta".*

It means in 'Kali Yuga' I would incarnate as a son of Sachi Devi, at the beginning of the 'Namsankirtana Movement'.

(7) It was recorded in 'Brahma-Jamal' that

> *"Athabahang Dharadhame Bhutva Madbhakta Rupadhrk,*
> *Mayayang Cha Bhavishami Kalou Sankirtanagame".*

It means some times I would incarnate as my own devotee particularly in 'Kali Yuga' as son of Sachi Devi.

(8) It was mentioned in 'Ananta Sanhita' that—

"Ja Eba Bhagavan Krsno Radhika Pranaballavam"—The Maheshvari, who is the most intimate with Radharani, the cause, means and effect of all the creations, the Omnipotent sometimes incarnate in this world with unparallel yellow complexion. The followers of Caitanya believe the statement was true in case 'Gauranga Mahaprabhu'[1].

(9) The same forecast was also made in 'Agama Puran'[2].

---

[1] Catianya Caritamrta: by Krsnadas Kaviraj, Commentaries by A.C. Bhaktivedanta Swami Prabhupada, Vol. 1, p. 82-83.

[2] CCM: Adikhanda, Ch. 3 / 13.

B. Incidences during his appearance:

(1) Caitanya was born after more than eleven months of gestation. After ten months when the baby did not arrive, his father Jagannath Misra became very worried and consulted his father in law Mr. Nilambar Chakravorty who himself was a great astrologer. He had a good look of Sachi Devi and after judging all the aspects, he made the forecast that soon she would deliver a baby, who was likely to be of a very unusually great personality[1].

(2) It is said that during his birth there was unusual co-incidences of few good things. The full moon of the month of 'Falgun' (a month of spring) revealed itself. An eclipse hid the moon, and at once the joyous music of chanting the name of 'Hari' was resounded, all over the Navadvipa city. Many people rushed to bathe in the Ganges chanting 'Hari bol! Hari bol!'. Such was the moment the very baby Gauranga was born[2]. The astrologers counted that, as very significant. They feel whenever there had been any incarnation, always that was marked with unusual change of nature like this.

(3) The time of his appearance and the positions of the stars as judged by the astrologers quoted from CCM:

"Singha Rashi Singgha Lagna Uchcha Grahagana,
Sada Barga Asta Barga Sarva Subhakshan[3]."

These very special positions of stars and planets, during his arrival was very unusual combination, as judged and forecast was made by his astrologer maternal grand father 'Nilambar Chakravorty', who was a very prominent astrologer based on 'Hora-sastra'. These special positions of stars and planets, had been analyzed and judged by many other prominent astrologers who came to the

---

[1] Amiya Nimai Charit: by Mahatma S.K. Ghosh. p. 36.
[2] AmiyaNimai Charit: p. 36; CCM: Adikhanda, Ch. 13 / 3637.
[3] CCM: Adikhanda, Ch. 13 / 90.

conclusion that anybody born at that moment would likely to be supernatural.

(4) The complexion, appearance, the physical built and the body features of Caitanya, were significantly different from the average Bengalis at that time. According to 'Samudrik-sastra's supernatural man should have some thirty two special body features which are described like these:

"Pancha-dirgha Panchasuksham Sapta-rakta Sada-unnata
Tri-hrasva-Prithu Gambhiro Dvatringasha Lakshano Mahan"[1].

This means the thirty two features likely present in the body of a supernatural man would be like these, five organ tall, five sharp, seven red, six prominent, three short, three broad and three deep seated. According to 'Samudrika-sastra a bit detail of these organs are like these. The five tall prominent or elongated organs are, nose, arm, chin, eyes and knee. Five sharp organs are, skin, fingertip, teeth, body hair and scalp hair. Seven red or red shot organs are eyes, sole, palm, tongue, palate, nailbed, mouth and lips. The six prominent organs are, chest, shoulder, nail, nose, waist and mouth. The three short organs are neck, leg, and the pelvic region. The three broad organs are forehead, chest and waist.[2].

These features of the supernatural person, were present in the body of Caitanya, as mentioned in CCM:

"Batrish Lakshan Mahapurush Bhusan
Aye Sishu Ange Dekhi Se Sava Lakshana.
Narayaner Chinya Jukta Srihasta Charan,
Aye Shishu Sarva Loker Karibe Taran"[3].

---

[1] CCM: Adikhanda Ch. 13 / 90.

[2] Commentary on CCM: by A.C. Bhaktivedanta Swani Prabhupada, Vol. 2, p. 287.

[3] CCM: Adikhanda, Ch. 14 / 14; Ch. 14 / 16.

This means, this baby has the thirty two features that are likely to be present in a supernatural person. This baby has got the signs of 'Narayana' in his hand and feet. He would emancipate all the people. With this understanding he was named as 'Vishwambhar' the supporter of the universe like Vishnu himself.

C. Other incidences in his carrier that could be mentioned which were believed by his followers as supernatural. There are many incidences of these kind; only some of them are mentioned here.

(1) Whenever the baby used to cry, would stop immediately on hearing the name of 'Hari'.

(2) One day two thieves saw him wondering lost through the city, brilliant ornament on and they planned to kidnap him and thus they carried him towards their den. But in a mysterious way the kidnappers lost their way and at the end they appeared in Jagannath Mishra's house.

(3) The very successful non-violent mass movement of Hare Krshna which became very popular within a short spell of time. The influencial persons such as Chand Kaji, the local administrator became the followers of Caitanya[1]; so also was the notorious drunkards such as Jagai and Madhai were convinced and joined the movement.

(4) The India famous greatest Sanskrit Pandit Keshab Kashmiri was defeated by Caitanya in argument on religious matters and was despondent at night while mother Goddess Sarasvati advised him in his dream that Gauranga was the supreme God Himself

> *"Sarasvati sapne tare upadesh kaila,*
> *Sakshat Isvar kari prabhure janila"*[2]

---

[1]   Ibid., Ch.-17 / 322.

[2]   CCM., Ch. / 6 / 164.

(5) It was believed that Caitanya revealed himself as Vishnu with six arms to some of his very close associates such as Nityananda, Advaitaya, Srivash[1] and later on Sarvabhouma Bhattacharya and Rupa and Sanatana Goswami.

> "Pratham sadabhuj tare dakhaila Isvar,
> Sankha chakra gada padma sarnga benudhar".

(6) Once during the performance of namsankirtana at the residence of Srivash, his son died. Although he himself did not express condolence his wife did. Caitanya made his dead son speaking advising his mother not to be upset, as this is the ultimate fate of all the living souls

> "Srivash putrer tatha haila paraloke,
> Tavo Srivasher chitte najanmila soke.
> Mrita balak mukhe kaila jnan kathan,
> Apne dui bhai haila Srivash nandana"[2].

(7) The then very learned man such as Keshaba Kashmiri, Rupa, Sanatana, Sarvabhouma Bhattacharya[3] and Prakashananda[4], were convinced that Caitanya was the incarnation of Godhead. This news was good enough to convince the other followers, to accept it.

(8) The mysterious way of his disappearance.

The Personality of Caitanya to non-Vasinava Hindus

(1) In general people were very convinced that Caitanya was a genius. People did not have any doubt about his extraordinary talent, knowledge in

---

[1] Ibid., Ch. / 17 / 21.

[2] Ibid., Ch. / 17 / 441 444.

[3] CCM: Madhyakhanda, Ch. / 6 / 461.

[4] Ibid: Ch. / 25 / 131.

general and in Vedanta sashtra. So to listen to his advice, was more sensible than an average religious leader.

(2) Many low castes Hindus who were at the outer edge of the society, were about to leave the Hindu religion due to the social and religious restrictions, imposed upon them (mentioned previously), found some confidence and very strong assurances from Caitanya to stay in.

(3) The other Hindus those who did not have any strong religious conviction toward any particular sects, were attracted by his very strong personality, the rationality and the depth of his arguments and his very simple approach of religious practice. The people were impressed by his forward vision, broadness of his thought and fairness of his outlook for equal right for everybody irrespective of their social status. These qualities gave the assurances to all castes and sects to form the base of a large society rather than a section.

(4) His commitment and practices of non-violence proved the genuineness of his approach. The way he mobilized the mass, conquered the heart of the mass without holding any weapon, just with namasankirtana, particularly the conversion of Chand Kaji influenced other people[1]. People found very strong leadership within Caitanya and under his leadership they could foresee a better future for the Hindu community.

(5) His dedication and sacrifice of all the enjoyment of the material world by accepting the hard life of a monk, leaving his old mother and young loving wife, not only impressed his friend and enemy alike, but the news became the heart breaking one. With this personal sacrifice, nobody had any doubt about his sincerity of his heart. Even after five hundred years later, this incidence did not loose its original pathos, and still many people eagerly listen and sing the Kirtana of Nimai sannyas.

These scale of personal sacrifice had influenced the general mass in the past still influence

---

[1]   CCM: Adikhanda / 17 / 433-36.

CHAPTER VII

Impact Of Harekrsna Movement On Caste System And Community

Before the advent of Caitanya there were other influencial bhaktibadi Vaisnava leaders such as Ramanuja, Nimberka and Madhva who preached the importance of Bhakti, but all maintained strict caste system. Ramanuja did not permit right to study Veda to the women and the lower caste. So also did not Madhva[1].

So Caitanya was the first spiritual leader, denounced the caste system to create a castless society. He invited and received people from any caste, who wanted to participate. This was obvious from the beginning of the movement. People of the lower caste got some sort of assurance and felt confident to stay within the Hindu community as a part of it, rather than to accept other religion. Liberal minded Brahmins who did not like strict principles of caste system and ritualistic religious bindings of the Smartas, and the lower castes who were deprived of the social justice, joined the movement with the hope to form a uniform society for all. Thus hundreds of thousands of people, all over the country, responded to the call of love, by joining the movement. Initially liberal minded Brahmins, with the leadership of Advaita, Nityananda, Gadadhara and Srivasa, participated in large numbers which gave the movement a morale boost. Out of his first 490 disciples, were 239 Brahmins, 37 Vaidya, 29 Kayestha and the remaining other caste[2].

---

[1] Bharatia Sahitye Caitanya; by Nirmal Gupta, p. 241.
[2] Caitanya Charchar Pachsha Bachhar: by D. Bandopadhyay, p. 10.

In the atmosphere of uncertainty, amidst of social insecurity, when Caitanya deva brought the word of hope through premabhakti to the nation, to the lower class, the bhakibad became the only belief to hold on. From within the ancient religious framework, when Caitanya and his followers were preaching village to village, the words of love towards God, new enthusiasm evolved, and the people enjoyed the pleasure of their religious aspiration through the new movement of premabhakti[1].

Caitanya himself wanted to give respect to the people of lower class and to bring the untouchables, up to the equal level of status. This gave him matchless popularity. People of the lower class were the real power of Caitanya movement and they were the majority of the community[2]. His Achintabhedavebad made the Vaisnavas separated from the other belief and put them to the higher level. Rich and poor were equally attracted. Subarna banik sampradaya (class), a rich business community, did not have much social status during the rule of King Ballal Sen. This community at large joined the Harekrsna movement[3].

In sixteenth and seventeenth century this Harekrsna movement of bhakti increased the social status of many non-Brahmin Hindus. Even sometimes non-Brahmins became the guru (religious teacher) not only of Khatriya, Vaiysa or Sudra, but of Brahmins also, which was unthinkable before this movement. Narahari Sarkar of Srikhanda was a Vaidya. He had many Brahmin disciples. Narottam Thakur was Kayestha. He had Brahmin disciples such as prominent Ganganarayan Chakravorty, Ramkrishna Chakravorty and Dwija Basanta. Caitanya's south Indian disciple Gopal Bhatta mentioned in his book "Haribhakibilasha", quoting from Skandha Puran, the right of Khatriya, Vaisya, Sudra and the women, to pray with the sacred stone Salagram Seela. Sanatan Goswami also had the same opinion[4].

Caitanya's views about women were very liberal. He declared about the women's right in the male-dominated society. This approach attracted many women disciples and they joined the movement in large number.

---

1   Ibid: p. 20.
2   Ibid: p. 11
3   Ibid: p. 9.
4   Ibid: p. 4.

Harekrsna movement started as a religious movement. But in the social and political atmosphere of Bengal and in India, in practical term, it brought an unparalleled social reform, declaring equal right for every body[1].

Caitanya's influence extended up to the top level of administration of Bengal, ruled by Hussain Shah. His chief minister, Sakar Malik (original name Amar) and brother of the finance minister known as Dabir Khas (original name Santosh), were convinced by Caitanya and his Harekrsna movement to such an extent that they gave up their ministerial job and actively joined the movement. These two ministers were brothers. After initiation, Caitanya gave them the name Sanatana and Rupa respectively. Their participation helped the movement in many ways. Participation of highly intellectual and influencial personality of their stature, gave a very good publicity for the movement. More over the administrative ability and experience of Sanatana and Rupa made the organizing structure of the movement very firm. They were sent to Vrndavana, the birth place of Krsna and were later known as Sanatana Goswami and Rupa Goswami, respectively. The name Vrndavana was hardly mentioned in the literature before. As mentioned earlier, Caitanya was more devoted towards the Vrndavana Lila of Krsna. At that time the site of Vrndavana was merely a dense forest. Along with Sanatana and Rupa, other four people such as Jiva, raghunath Das and Raghunath Bhatta, known as six Gowarmi's, were deputized to revive Vrndavana, which they did successfully. Today Vrndavana is one of the most popular place of pilgrimages in India with thousands of temple on the bank of river Jamuna, extending across thirty two square miles of land[2]. It can be said that Vrndavana is the discovery of Caitanya.

In Bengal this time Harekrsna movement brought a new life to the Hindu society. Muslim proselytisation had been stopped. Many Hindus who had apathy towards the religion, actively participated and joined the movement. In Navadvipa itself 95% of the population became the follower of Caitanya and joined the movement.

Nityananda was made incharge along with other helper such as Advaita, Srivash and Sridhar to preach the philosophy in Bengal.

---

[1] Caitanya Charchar Pachsha Bachhar: by D. Bandopadhyay: p. 90.

[2] Documentary Vedeo Film: by The Investigator.

Nityananda performed this task very successfully. He was responsible for the conversion of Jagai and Madhai, the two notorious representative of the provincial administrator, in to the folds of the movement who later became great helper of the movement. This incidence and the news of the conversion of the local administrator, Chand Kazi, helped to make up the mind of the almost rest of the people of Navadvipa, irrespective of their caste to join the movement.

Nityananda started his mass movement in a place called Panihati. It was Nityananda who set a glorious record of mass contact by organizing a big feast and festival at Panihati. In Vaisnava chronicles this festival is called Chidamahotsava or Dandamahotsava[1]. Its cost was borne by Ragunatha Dasa, an affluent non-Brahmin supporter of Nityananda. The news of the feast spread far and wide. Innumerable people, including top class Brahmin and very lower class non-Brahmin, ate together in a same place which was unthinkable at that time. The food was prepared by mixing Cida (husk free parboiled flat rice), thickly boiled milk, curd, banana paste, sugar butter etc. It was continuously served to innumerable people by sixty men for the whole day. Differences of the caste were not observed during the feast[2].

Nityananda lived in Panihati for three months. The Gopala system presumably evolved during this period mainly by him. In Saptagram he converted Uddharana Datta, a leading merchant, of the Suvaranavanik caste.

His conversion led to the conversion of the entire Vanik community of Saptagram, where Nityananda used kirtana as an effective mass medium[3]. Dimock holds that Nityananda was responsible for the creation of Vaisnava Sahajya school.

He also believed that Nityananda was responsible for the conversion of two thousands five hundred Buddhist monks and nuns, into the fold of the Harekrsna movement[4]. Considerable importance must be attached to Nityananda's fraternization with God. Worship of Krsna as a servant or brother could easily be practised by householders. Fraternization with

---

[1] CCM: 486-92.

[2] Sri-Caitanyadeva O Tanhar Parsadgana: by G. Roychaudhuri, pp. 91-92.

[3] CBH: 382.

[4] Vaisnavism in Bengal: by H. Chakravarti, p. 154.

God might easily strengthen the brotherhood of men in a plural society. In pursuit of this idea Nityananda disregarded caste rules and lived with the Sudras. Historian such as Girijasankar Raychaudhuri said that Nityananda was responsible for the slackening of the caste rules in Bengal. All credit goes to him for the gradual evolution of a liberal Vaisnava society in Bengal which did not observe caste distinctions. Raychaudhuri quotes the opinion of Brajendranath Sil, the eminent scholar and professor of philosophy, to the effect that Nityananda was the greatest democrat in the history of Bengal[1]. In the absence of a political theory of liberalism, the spiritual idea of fraternization with God was definitely a source of social liberalism in a caste-based society. Dimmok opines that Nityananda might have been responsible for whatever egalitarian tendencies, the Vaisnava movement had shown[2].

The followers of Nityananda took the first step towards spreading the cult among the tribal population of Bengal. They spread the cult among the Hajongs of the Garo Hills, bordering on Mymensing. Vaisnavas of Nityananda school were active among the tribal community of Tripura also[3].

Since Vaisnava movement was proliferating very rapidly, and too many leading Vaisnavas were taking active part in preaching, there were some minor differences among the various groups and also it was felt that the efficient coordination was necessary. The idea of a central cultural coordinating body with sixty four Mohanta (head of a group), twelve Gopals, and their disciples and subdisciples, were mainly his plan[4].

After the death of Nityananda, Advaita and Srivash, Srinivash Acharya, Narrottam Thakur and Shyamananda took the responsibility of the movement of Namasankirtana. Nityananda's wife, Jahnaba Devi and son Birchandra took the leading role of the followers of Nityananda.

They together organised the famous Mahotsava of Namsankiratana in the house of King Santosh Datta of Khetari in the district of Rajsahi, in the eighth decade of sixteenth century. It was in the month of Phalgun on the

---

[1] SriChaitanyadeva O Tahar Parsadagana: by G. Rarychaudhuri, p. 990, 96.

[2] Dimock, op. cit. p. 51.

[3] GVA: pp. 1859 1860. See "Garo Pahar".

[4] Dvadasa Gopala: by Amulayadhan roybhatta, pp. 19-23.

birthday of Caitanya. This was very important for a few reasons. This is the first time a new style of Kirtan was introduced by Narottam Das named garanhati Kirtan, with 108 rythm in it. This was the first time the statue of Gauranga along with Vishnupriya, Vallabikanta, Srikrsna, Brajamohan, Radhamohan, and Radhakanta, were established. In other words this was the first time the statue of Caitanya was worshipped formally as Krsna[1].

Khetari festival and Kirtan both were directed by Jahnava Devi.

She travelled far and wide both in Bengal and in Vrindavana along with her disciples, preaching the thought of Nityananda among all the castes. Nityananda's son, Virachandra also had very important role at this stage. While some Vaisnava acharyas were presenting themselves as an incarnation, Virachandra opposed them.

His main credit was conversion of more than thousand people believed to be Buddhist, into the fold of Vaisnavism. According to the historian Haroprasad Sastri, in this region of Bengal, there was Buddhist acharya known as Nada Pandit was the leader of the Sahajiya section of the Buddhist. These peoples were the followers of Nada Pandit, that's why they were known as Nada, Nedi. They were very free community and very liberal in their sexual life. This was the main reason they were regarded as very lower class of people and were more or less abandoned in the society. Virachandra brought them back to the main stream current of the society. These people are known as Vaisnava Sahajiya. Ayul, Baul, Sai and Darbesh belong to Nada, Nedi group of people.

These group of people are believed to be originally Hindu. Due to prejudicial treatment and social injustice, these people were forced to take up Buddhism, among which there was no caste prejudice. Since there was no caste bar in the Vaisnava religion of Caitanya, these people were easily attracted[2].

Like Jahnaba Devi, Advaita's wife Sitathakurani and son Achyutananda, were faithful followers of Caitanya and played a leading part in the Harekrsna movement, after the death of Advaita. The followers of Sita Devi and Achyuta consolidated their hold in Santipur.

---

1   Caitanya Charchar Pachsho Bachhar: by D. Bandopadhyay, p. 38.
2   Caitanya Charchar Pachsho Bachhar: by D. Bandopadhyay: p. 39.

Santipur was a noted centre for the Sakta worship. The local Brahmins were very dominating. Harekrsna movement led by Adavaita, later by his descendants, although managed to create a Vaisnava society, failed to curb the Brahmins. It was with the help of the local weavers that the Santipur goswamins were able to transform the town into a Vaisnava holy place. The local Chaudhuri non-Brahmin zamindars patronized the Krsna cult. They built the fabulous Syamchand temple of Santipur[1]. They initiated the Rasayatra festival in the middle of seventeenth century. This is really a famous festival of Bengal, in which thousands of people participate, take part in various activities, eat together the same food irrespective of their caste[2].

Progress of the movement

The progress of any movement depends on its foundation, its appeal to the general mass, the organizational integrity, along with the supportive literature, which is ultimately responsible for the continuous publicity and for the documents of authenticity. The appeal of the Harekrsna movement is very universal, widely spread, and well liked.

From the early stage of the movement people from all the sections of the community had participated in large number, irrespective of their castes. The movement started at Navadvipa, a district in Bengal, but in the course of time, brought social reform not only in Bengal, but all over India and attracted people of all the category of social status and professions. These include influencial religious personalities, politicians, historians writers, poets and singers. As a result of the involvement of these intellectuals and their activities in the respective fields, they have propagated more and more publicity, which in turn have been attracting more and more people. The important religious figures utilized the spirit of the movement, to bring unanimity in the Hindu religion. The politicians and the social reformers utilized the spirit of the movement to inspire the community for social reform and to abolish the caste system. The most important expedient to

---

[1] Late Medieval Temples of Bengal: by D.J. McCutchion, p. 33.
[2] Santipur Paricaya: by K. Bhattacharya, pp. 243-52. Progress of the Movement p. 101

influence the community, is the vastness of the Vaisnava literature. Since the advent of the Caitanya movement, the Vrndavana activities of Krsna with the cowherd boys and girls particularly with Radha, has become well known. In fact hardly Radha was known, or mentioned in the literature before the Caitanya era. The principle reasons for the gaining popularity of the Radha-Krsna activities at Vrndavana (Radha-Krsna lila), are the production of enormous amount of literature of various kinds of compositions, of writings of drama, poetry and songs, by the numerous disciples, followers and admirers of Caitanya. They have not only produced the literature on Radha and Krsna but also on the life history and the activities of Caitanya himself.

In Calcutta University, which is one of the biggest in India, there is a special department of Vaisnava Padavali. In Bengali literature the Vaisnava padavali is the most important component. The vast Bengali compositions of Rabindranath Tagore, particularly his numerous songs were greatly influenced by the Vaisnava literature[1]. What we understand as a English textbook today, in that sense "Caitanya charitamrita of Krsnadas Kaviraj" was the first Bengali textbook[2]

In late nineteenth century and first half of this century, the two prominent unparallel personalities dominated the religious thought all over India, Sri-Ramkrsna paramhamsha and his disciple Swami Vivekananda. It is note worthy to analyze their views, about the religious concept of Caitanya and its impact in the society.

Ramkrsna, a priest of an endowed temple at Dakshineswar who had deviated significantly from his expected role as a pujari (brahmin ritualist). He behaved as a sannyasi; even though he was married to Saradamani Devi, the marriage was consummated. Years of practices of various sadhanas (spiritual disciplines) led him to teach that all the religions were essentially true. He taught that the God of each sect whether Vaisnava, Sakta, Christian, or Muslim, was the same and could be worshipped according to one's inherent preference for the type of religious practice.

---

[1] Interview with Mr. Nisit Sadhu, Composer and Music Director in Bengali Film; Valsnavism in Bengal: by Dr. R. Chakravorty, pp. 449-50.

[2] Caitanya Charitamrita: by Sukumar Sen, p. v.

He demonstrated exceptional spiritual powers (siddhis), being able to go into prolonged trance states such as 'nirvikalpa samadhi' or induce altered states of consciousness in others.

The message of Ramkrsna centered on the realization of God and the renunciation of "woman and wealth". His mystical experience and the devotional experience of the Grace of Sakti form a mystical unity of opposites. Brahmana, the impersonal absolute, and Sakti, the personal Godhead, were the same. Jnana and bhakti may lead to the goal.

Ramkrsna realized that even the philosophies of advaita, visistaadvaita, and dvaita (monoism, qualified monoism and dualism) were different because of the varying spiritual tendencies, within the individual, but that they ultimately resolved themselves as different ways of expressing the same truth. Ramkrsna taught that he could know this because he was an 'isvarakoti', one who could merge with the Absolute and return. By the implication of these teachings his followers believe that he was an avatara, not different from Ram and Krsna[1].

Ramkrsna appears to have instructed his disciples in two ways, regarding renunciation. For the householders he taught the mental renunciation of the "Gita", but for those who never touched women, he taught that they also renounce "in actuality".

His requirement was to renounce the wealth, set them against the world of material goods and left only with mendicancy. The monastic order which bears his name did not solely come form his message or his practice. He initiated no one as a sannyasi in his life time. He entitled no one as swami, nor set a rule for them. He did ask his favourite disciple, Narendranath Datta, the future Vivekananda, to keep his boys together and to teach them. Ramkrsna's universalism was total. His liberal religion in the 1880s has taught that religion based on reasons, could get rid of the world of superstition and the social ills which weighted down the men and women. However Ramkrsna never travelled outside to his local territory to preach his view. His message was carrired by Vivekananda far and wide. This liberal religious view of Ramkrsna was translated by Vivekananda, as the principles for social reform and were supported by humantarian

---

[1] Caitanya Charimrita Vol. III, p. 265-67; Relligion in Modern India: by R.D. Baired, 1989, pp. 58-59.

commitments. This liberal view towards all mankind was very common with Caitanya and possibly the continuation of the approach what Caitanya started four century earlier. This is proved by the view of these two leaders had about Caitanya.

Sri Ramakrsna Paramhamsa (1836-1886)

Ramakrsna belonged to bhakti cult, was a votary of Kali (Sakti). He himself did not do any study at school or college. His religious knowledge mainly came from his own perception through his devotion to Kali. After Caitanya he was the greatest religious personality in India. He learnt Vedanta from a wondering ascetic named Tota Puri and later preached syncretism.

His veneration for both Christ and Kali was quite deep and His respects for Caitanya was also very great. Ramkrsna's mind was full with the thought of Caitanya. He participated in Vaisnava festivals in many occasions. In numerous time he mentioned his name, and cited his approach and dedication, during conversation. Sometimes Caitanya's namsankirtana, watching drama about him, even sometimes thought about him used to bring samadhi (ectasy) to him. He himself was also an expert Akhariya or singer of the Padavalikirtana who knew how to add Akhara sentences to the original wording of Padavali. He came into contact with the Kartabhaja sects of the Vaisnavas and knew of their secrets.

It is said that Ramakrsna Paramhamsa was regarded as the best of the Vaisnavas by Bhagavan Das Babaji of Kalna who acted as a sort of general superintendent of the Gaudiya Vaisnava order in Bengal[1]. It is also said that the celebrated Paramhamsa experienced the indescribable ecstasy of the milkmaids of Vrndavana, and that he regarded himself as one of them[2]. In the words of Swami Nivedananda, one of his biographers," the curtain suddenly rose, Sri-Krsna with his soulenthralling grace appeared, walked up to him and merged in his person"[3] These are the examples of thought of Ramakrsna towards Caitanya and Srikrsna.

---

[1]   Sajjanatosani: Vol. 2, 1885, pp. 111-13.

[2]   Vaisanvism in Bengal: by Dr. R. Chakravorty, p. 433.

[3]   The Cultural Heritage of India: Vol. 3, p. 259.

Ramakrsna's View on Sri-Caitanya

"By renouncing the enjoyment of the material world of everyday life, as poison, to modulate the life, by teaching the devotee to stand in the place of Krsnapriya (Radha) in love and by preaching the significance of the namasankirtana, Lord Caitanya endeavoured to prevent the abominable practices and amelioration of the country at that time. As a result of his influence, thought and teachings, by showing the way to the deviated one, by bringing back the outcast to the bindings of the new society, by including the outsiders within the caste of the devotee of God and by setting an unparallel example of a pure and very high ideals of dedication and renunciation in front of all the class of people, he executed an unprecedented benefit of the mankind. Not only that, by the supernatural adaptation in the life of Caitanya, it had been proved beyond doubt that the eight type of mental and physical enjoyment, evolved from the love and union of the ordinary hero and heroine, could be presented in the intense thought of God, of a pure hearted devotee. This expression was preached by the Vaisnavas as 'Madhurabhava' (love to God as a beloved) which helped tremendously to the society, by the inclusion of many general terminology into the spiritual literature and by the explanation that the enjoyment of the natural desire could be achieved by the undiluted pure and intense thought of God[1]."

Swami Vivekananda's view on Sri-Caitanya[2]

"Mahaprabhu Caitanya was the greatest among all the incarnation of Gods. Great philosopher Sankaracarya came and showed that there were not much difference between the Buddhist religion and the core substances of Vedanta. Then came bright intellectual Ramanuja who opened the staircase of the spiritual prayer up to the highest level, in front of all from Brahmin to Paria (lower caste). The Influence of Ramanuja extended in Northern India also. Many big religious leaders accepted his thought. But sometimes

---

[1] Sri Sri Ramakrsna Lila Prasanga: by Swami Saradananda, p. 131.
[2] Complete Works of Swami Vivekananda Centenary Vol. VI p. 320.

later, relatively in modern age, during the period of Muslim rule, appeared in Northern India, Caitanya the brightest of all the incarnations[1].

In modern India the Hindu sampradayas (sects) could be divided into mainly two categories; Dvaitavadi (Duelist) and Advaitavadi (Monoist). Ramanuja is the ideal of one and Sankaracarya is of another. All the Dvaitavadi sects have followed Ramanuja the initiator of Dvaitavad philosophy, such as religious teacher Saint Madva of South India. Caitanya accepted the philosophy of Madhvacharya and preached in Bengal[2]. This was the only one time Bengal got rid of the religious idleness and weariness, and united herself with the religious life of whole India. The influence of Caitanya exists all over India. In every place, where there is a bhakti sect, prevails the deep appreciation of the activities of his life, with discussion and prayer. Most of his so called disciples in Bengal do not know how his power is still working all over India. It is my firm belief that the whole Vallavacharya sect is a branch of the followers of Caitanya[3]".

"The love insanity of the gopies (cowherd girl) was immensely evident in the life of this great saint of Northern India. He himself was a Brahmin, being born in a Brahmin family, himself a professor of 'naya sastra', and was an unparallel debater, because from the childhood he had learnt to know, that the knowledge was the greatest of all. Whereas by the blessings of some pious man (satya drasta), his whole life style became completely changed.

By giving up the fight of argument and the teaching of naya, he became an insane, a bhaktivadi teacher, the greatest of all. The spirit of his flow of bhakti flooded the whole Bengal and assured each and every individual. His intensity of love was boundless. Pious or sinner, Hindu or Muslim, pure or impure minded and prostitute or wanderer, all were the recipient of his blessings. Still today his religious sect gives shelter to those who are poor, subjects of tyranny, weak and out cast and those who are not accepted in the conservative society[4].

It is notable although Gauranga after taking initiation from a guru of Bharati order, became a Bharati, the uprise of his religious genius started

---

[1]   Complete Works of Swami Vivekananda Centenary Vo III. P. 265-67
[2]   Ibid Vol. III, p. 324-25.
[3]   Ibid Vol. I V, p. 337; Bharatiya Sahitye Caitanya: by N.N. Gupta, 1986, p. 1.
[4]   Ibid Vol. III, p. 265-67.

from the contact of Isvara Puri. It seems these Puries have an important role in spiritual uprise of Bengal. Incidentally to mention Sri-Ramkrsna recieved his initiation from Tota Puri.

Bengal is a country of bhakti and bhakta (devotee). In the Jagannath temple the stone where Caitanya used to stand to watch Jagannath, possibly was eroded due to flow of tears of his premabhakti. When he took initiation, he succeeded in his examination of efficiency, by keeping a lump of sugar on his tongue and not let it be melted by controlling the secretion of saliva. By the help of his inner sight he rescued Vrndavana and he achieved this through the strength of bhakti[1].

Rational judgement of the Bengalis

It is believed that the Bengali rational judgement gained ascendency during the nineteenth century. Rammohan ray initiated the Brahma Samaj movement with a view of leveling the angularities. The 'young Bengali, educated in the Hindu College of Calcutta, initially preached iconoclasm. Social and religious reformation became the creed of a good number of Bengalis educated in the institution set up by the British. Rammohun ray (1774-1833) propagated total reformation. He preached pantheism, the necessity for the repudiation of the caste system and the suppression of such harmful superstitions as the widowburning.

It should be noted that the position of Vaisnavism was unassailable. It had a vast social base. W. Ward wrote in 1811:

"Two persons in ten, of the whole Hindu population of Bengal are supposed to be the followers of Caitanya[2] In 1880 Walton Hamilton described Vaisnavism as one of the principal religions of Bengal[3]. Bholanauth Chunder wrote in 1869. One fifth of the population of Bengal are now followers of Caitanya. Nearly all of the opulent families of Calcutta belong to this sect"[4]

---

[1]   Ibid Vol. VI, p. 123.
[2]   Ward Account: Vol. 3, p. 262.
[3]   Description of Hindusthan: W. Hamilton. Vol. 1, p. 208.
[4]   The Travels of a Hindu: by B.N. Chunder, Vol. 1, pp. 35-36.

The census figures corroborate these statements. According to the census 1881, 5,68,052 people of Bengal, belonged to the Vaisnava caste[1]. Word noted the remarkable opulence and social importance of the Vaisnava gosvamins. They were patronized by many rich landlords. Krsnaram Basu, a kayastha landlord bore the huge expense of the construction of the chariot of Mahesh. Nearly all prostitutes of the growing Calcutta metropolis professed the religion of Caitanya before their death, that they may be entitled to some sort of funeral rites[2].

A large number of people became Bairagis (Vaisnava mendicants) to avoid worldly troubles, unpleasant connections and debts. Some people became Vaisnava beggars to evade stringent caste rules. The simplicity was the strength of Vaisnavism. The theory and practice of bhakti had been accepted even by the caste conscious Brahmins. Caitanya was respected as a great saint by all castes mainly because he renounced the world. Vaisnavism had also strengthened the eclectic ideals by which it was itself very deeply influenced. Vaisnavism was quite compatible with polytheistic worship. But the chief reason behind its growing popularity was its liberal attitude towards caste[3].

The eclectic tendency resulted in the construction of hundreds of Vaisnava, Saiva and Sakta temples by people belonging to both high and low castes. The Saktas had been affected by the soft, mellow spirit of Vaisnavism, kirtan songs and poetry. Although Sakta poet like Ramprasad Sen and Kamalakanta Bhattacharya preached Kali-Krsna nonduality in their simple passion-laden songs, but Sakta popularity never came up to the level to match up the popularity of the Harekrsna movement.

During eighteenth century tantra was popular among a powerful section of the Bengali Zaminders. Sizable segments of the upper castes also observed tantrika kulachar. The steady growth of the Calcutta metropolis as the city of the Bengali new rich, and the tragic waning of the late medieval estates after the introduction of the Permanent Settlement (a new Law for the settlement of the land) in 1793, resulted in the pauperisation of the Kali-worshipping Rajas, who once retained bands of club wielding

---

[1] Report of the Census of Bengal: by A. Boudillion.
[2] Ward op. cit. Vol. p. 262.
[3] Valsnavism in Bengal: by Dr. R. Chakravorty, p. 386.

bodyguards recruited from the scheduled castes. These people were once associated with plunder and murder in the name of worshipping Kali (Sakti). Professional robbers also used to worship Kali (possibly still do), praying for their success in robbery[1]

The tradition of intoxication of the participants by the influence of alcohol, gaza, charas and bhang (Indian hempm, canabis, mariona and Hasish), during celebration, still exists.

But the new rich men of Calcutta very soon developed a different way of life. They were staunch supporters of British Law and Order from which they derived immense benefit. Most of them professed or patronized Harekrsna movement. One may say that the popularity of Vaisnavism towards the end of eighteenth century and the beginning of the nineteenth century was an indirect effect of the consolidation of British power in Bengal, which gradually put an end to plunder and murder in the name of religon[2]. All old zaminders, however, did not give up their Sakta faith. The Rajas of Krsnanagar, for instance, were unflinching Saktas, though they did not disrespect the Vaisnavas. The Navadvipa Gosvamins had very little influence over them. Siddha Caitanya dasa of Navadvipa once publicly described, one Raja of Krsnanagar as an incarnation of Ravana, there by implying that Caitanya was the incarnation of Rama. But almost all among the new rich of the later half of the eighteenth century were Vaisnava. Among them prominent were Ganganarayan Sinha, the Raja of Cossimbazar, Maharaja Nanda Kumar, the Raja of Posta and the Rajas of Sobhabazar. Raja Sukhamaya Rayabahadur of Posta, spent huge sums during one of his pilgrimages to Puri. Lala Babu, a very rich Zamindar, ultimately became a mendicant. Other prominent new rich to mention who professed Vaisnavism or patronised the Vaisnavas were, Govinda Mitra, the notorious black zamindar of Calcutta, the millionaire Rajas of Sobhabazar, Motilal Mullick of Pathuria ghata, Jayanarayana Ghosal of Bhukailash and the Tagore families of Pathuriaghata and Jorasanko and the majority of the Suvarnavanik landlords of Calcutta. The most of the temples built by the new rich, were the Harekrsna temples. Suvarnavanik millionaire Matilal

---

[1] Ibid: p. 387.
[2] Vaisnavism in Bengal: by Dr. R. Chakrovorty: p. 387.

Sil and the trustees of his vast estate, for instance, built eight Vaisnava temples[1].

The nine towered temple Radhakanta, located in Tollyganj, built by the local mondal zaminder (1809) and the Syamsundara temple in Baharu (1821-1825) village were very well known. In these temples there were statues and paintings of the activities of Caitanya were well preserved.

The Vaisnava fair and festivals were extremely popular in the nineteenth century. In 1802 Gauranga fair in Navadvipa was a famous event. The people did not have to observe caste rules, as long as they were present in the fair. The festvals for the Harekrsna movement were held regularly in Calcutta and in many other districts. In the festival, singing of Harekrsna by the mass of the participant, happened to be an important aspect.

In the fair apart from the house hold followers of Caitanya many mendicants used to participate. Generally the Vaisnava mendicants preferred seclusion and they used to live in Akhdas or Monasteries. These Akhdas were set up throughout Bengal.

The populous ones of them were located, at Simulia, Navadvipa, Kalna, Jiaganj, Kenduli, Maynadol, Ramkeli, Gayeshpur and Kambuliyatola[2].

The Harekrsna movement still did not develop any central organisation. For a long time the Akhdas of Navadvipa and Kalna kept some sort of control over the followers of the movement. The Vaisnava tradition was kept alive by the secular organisation of the house holding Vaisnavas. Possibly the earliest association of the lay member of the movement was the Haribhaktipradayini Sabha of Behala at South Calcutta (1852). This Sabha published a journal also named *Samvadapatra* (1856)[3]. Another similar association was organized at Kolutola, Central Calcutta, in 1861. This one was named as Sri-Caitanya Sabha and its journal was called as *Sri-Caitanyakirtikaumadi Patrika*[4]. In 1898 or thereabout Calcutta and suburban areas had as many as twenty-nine Harisabhas or associations with a pronounced commitment or sympathy for the Harersna movement. These associations constituted a powerful Vaisnava milieu in the

---

[1] Ibid: p. 388, 389.
[2] Gaudiya Vaisnava Jivana: Vol. 2, pp. 133, 205-06.
[3] Bangla Samayika Patra: by B. Bandopaddhyaya, Vol. 1, p. 141.
[4] Ibid. p. 172.

urban-industrial surroundings. The main reason behind the multiplication of these associations in 1898, was the outbreak of the bubonic plague in Calcutta, in an epidemic form.

It was believed that the devastating plague would disappear, if the citizen chanted the name of Hari and Caitanya Mahaprabhu. even Muhammadans and Christians sang kirtana[1]. All these Harisabhas strengthened the position of the Harekrsna movement.

The plague revealed the fact that the urban culture of Calcutta had an imperishable link with what a sociologist described as "the traditional matrix of sacred culture". In Calcutta and to a considerable extent in the city of Madras, the traditional cultural media "not only continue to survive but have also been incorporated in novel ways into an emerging popular and classical culture. Much of the urban popular culture is seen as an extension of the path of devotion (bhaktimarga), more accessible to modern man than the paths of ritual observance (Karmamargh), or the path of sacred knowledge (jnanamarga)"[2].

Publications for the Harekrsna Movement

The supporters of the Harekrsna movement felt the need of disseminating their views on a wide scale. The Vaisnava biographies, 'Narottamavilasa' and 'Jagadisacaritravijaya' were published by Bengali publishers in 1815. The publication of Gaudiya Vaisnava classics, such as CCM, Bhaktirasamritasindhu, and Haribhaktivilasa was advertised in the Samacaradarpana between 1818 and 1829[3].

Later the responsibility for publishing Vaisnava and Sahajiya manuscripts was shouldered by a group of printers and publishers of North Calcutta, who were known as 'Batatala' publishers. Batatala publishers were keenly aware of the great demand for the Vaisnava books in rural areas.

---

[1] Charitasudha: by Ramdasa Babaji, Vol. 2, pp. 171-74, also Sangitakosa, pp. 751-800 (the collected devotional songs by these clubs)

[2] Anthropology of Folk Religion: by Milton Singer, Ed. Charles Leslie "The Great Tradition of Hinduism in the City of Madras", p. 158.

[3] Samvadpatre Sekaler Katha: Vol. I, pp. 75-76, 90-91.

They published good number of original Vaisnava works and numerous ordinary prints for the publicity of the Harekrsna movement.

Between 1815 and 1899, nearly fifty important Vaisnava works were published in Calcutta. Most of these works were written in Bengali verse and prose. This shows that the Vaisnavas were conscious of the value of the publicity through the press.

The supporters of the movement felt that although the publication of Batatala, was adequate for the general mass of supporter, that might have not met the demand for the sophisticated Vaisnavas. To satisfy this requirement, there were quite a few other sophisticated publications, were made. In 1845 Muktarama Vidyavagisa edited, printed and published, at his own cost an authentic edition of Gopala Bhatta Goswamis 'Haribhaktivilasa. In 1854 Rajendra Mitra edited Karnapura's 'Caitanyacandradaya' with a very interesting introduction. Later on Ramanarayan Vidyaratna of Murshidabad, brilliantly fulfilled the task of bringing out the reliable editions of the Vrindavana tests, Vaisnava biography and the Padavalis. He was also associated with a project of Vaisnava publications financed by Radharamana Ghose, Bhagavatabhusana who was the private secretary of the king of Tripura state. Radharamana set up 'Radharamana' press at Baharampur, from which an authentic edition of the 'Bhagavatapurana' with four Sanskrit commentaries and Bengali translation was brought out at a cost of a million rupees in those days[1].

The earliest Vaisnava weekly 'Bhagavata Samacara' which was edited by Brajamohan Chakravorty in 1831. Another contemporary Vaisnava weekly was 'Bhaktisuchaka' (1835). Between 1846 and 1861 at least four other journal for the Harekrsna movement was published.

These are 'Nityadharmanuranjika' (1846), 'Samvatsarikasambadpatra' (1856), 'Advaitatattapradarsaka, Patrika' (1856) and 'Sri-Caitanyakirtikaumadi Patrika' in 1861[2]

The journalism for the Harekrsna movement and the Gaudiya Vaisnava organization in Bengal really became meaningful under the guidance of a dynamic Vaisnava Deputy Magistrate named Kedarnath Datta, Bhaktivinoda (1838-1914).

---

[1] Samvadpatre Sekaler Katha: Vol. 2, p. 124.

[2] Bangla Samayika Patra: Vol. 1, pp. 54-86, 141, 148-72.

In his youth he came in close contact with Dvijendranath Tagore (1840-1926), brother of Rabindranath Tagore, and together with him, he studied Western Philosophy and History[1]. Kedarnath first publishsed the famous Vaisnava journal, 'Sajjanatosani', in 1884.

In 1885 he founded Vaisnavasociety named 'Vaisnava Sabha'. The Vaisnava Sabha appointed three Vaisnava preachers for West Bengal[2].

The Movement at Dacca and Balasore publishesd two journals, titled, 'Ratnakara' and 'Haribhaktipradayini', respectively[3]. The other short lived journals appeared in Calcutta in the same year; these were 'Vaisnava', 'Navamanjari', and Tattvamanjari'[4].

In 1894 Manmathanath Mitra organised in Burdwan town an association for the movement, called 'Vardhamana Vaisnavadharma Uddhipani Sabha'[5]. Tripura too had a Vaisnava club known as 'Aggartala Haribhaktipradayini Sabha' (1895)[6] This association was organised by King Viracandra Manikya.

An association at Mushidabad, organised a popular Mahotsava at Dakshinakhanda in 1884[7]. A Gaudiya Vaisnava named Premananda Bharati (1857-1914), preached in Europe and U.S.A.[8]. A 'Caitanyasamaja' was established in the U.S.A. in about 1897 by an American convert named Professor Osman[9]. In about 1899 the orthodox Gaudiya Vaisnavas of Calcutta established a new Vaisnava society in Calcutta which was known as 'Gaurangasamaja'[10].

This society was founded by an eminent journalist Sisir Kumar Ghose (1840-1911). A Vaisnava journal named 'Vaisnava pratibha' appeared

---

[1] Sri Bhaktivinode Thakurer Svalikhita Jivani pp. 112-14.
[2] Sajjanatosani: 1885, Vol. 2. p. 3.
[3] Ibid: p. 217.
[4] Ibid: p. 217.
[5] Ibid. Vol. 6, 1894, pp. 74-75.
[6] Sajjanatosani: Vol. 7, 1895, pp. 289-91.
[7] Ibid. Vol. 8, 1896, pp. 111-13.
[8] Charitasudha: by Ramadasa Babaji, Vol. 1, pp. 270-98.
[9] Sajjanatosani: 1897, Vol. 9, p. 3.
[10] Sahitya Sadhaka Charitamila: Sisir Kumar Ghose, by Bandopadhyaya, 86, p. 49.

in Calcutta in 1899-1900[1]. S.K. Ghose created an excitation in the intellectual circle of Calcutta, by publishing the first volume of the book 'Amiyanimaicarita' in 1892. With the help of Bhaktivinode and Radhikanath Goswami, S.K. Ghose published a fortnightly journal, 'Sri-Sri-Visnupriya Patrika' in 1890. It was later amalgamated with the famous weekly 'Anandabazar Patrika'. In 1901 another journal called 'Sri-Sri-Gauranga Patrika,' was published. A society named 'Gaudesvara Vaisnava' was established in Vrndavana. Its journal was also named as 'Gaudesvara'. The Bengali Vaisnavas of Vrindavana established an association, in 1892 or there about which was called 'Sricaitanyamatavodhini Sabha'. Its journal was 'Sricaitanyamatavodhini'. Shortly after there was another Vaisnava society formed, named 'Vaisnavadharmapracarini Sabha'. This society awarded titles to thirty-four outstanding Gaudiya Vaisnavas, including Sisir Kumar Ghose[2]

The leading Gaudiya Vaisnavas had quite different political opinions. Sisir Kumar Ghose was renowned for his long and bitter struggles against the indigoplanters and the tyrannical bureaucrats. He used the 'Amritabazar Patrika' in defence of the right for his country man. He believed that the basic interests of the Indians and the Englishmen were never identical. He said "We are we and they are they"[3]. Kedarnath Datta, on the other hand preached loyalty to the Raj in Sajjanatosani[4] and believed that the British and the Bengalis were brothers, because they belonged to the Aryan race[5].

Kedarnath also realized that it would take a long time to abolish the caste system completely from the Hindu society, due to the existing influence from the Zamindars and Brahminical cult. So to restructure, the caste system according to the classification of 'Varna', mentioned in Veda, he made some suggestions. These suggestions came through 'Sajjanatosani,' and possibly represented the social philosophy of the enlightened Gaudiya Vaisnavas. These were as follows[6]:

---

[1] Sajjantosani: Vol. 12, 1900-1901, p. 1.

[2] Ibid. Vol. 4, 1892, pp. 68-69.

[3] Mahatma Sisir Kumar Ghose: by A.N. Basu, ed, 1976, p. 2.

[4] Sajjanatosani: Vol. 4, 1892, p. 1.

[5] Ibid. Vol. 2, 1885, p. 78.

[6] Ibid. Vol. 2, 1885, pp. 123-24.

(1) Birth should never be a factor in the determination of caste, Caste should be determined according to the svabhava or nature of a man and his parents.

(2) A man's caste should not be considered at all before he attains the age of fifteen.

(3) Once fixed, the caste of a man should be preserved and protected from the assaults of the so-called Samajpatis by the zamindars and the government.

In 1886, Bhakti Vinode (originally Kedarnath Dutta) founded the 'Visvavaisnava Sabha' (Vaisnava Society of the World). It was the combination of the two societies, called 'Harisadhana Samaja' and 'Vaisnava Sabha'. It was claimed that the 'Visva Vaisnava Sabha', had originally been founded by Rupa Goswamin and Jiva Goswamin. Later the Sabha was transformed into the Gaudiya Mission. The mission established branches in different parts of India. Both celibrate monks and householders were its member. The monks lived in the monasteries established by the Mission.

The Gaudiya Mission preached the following concepts[1]:

(1) Absolute truth was self-evident as Krsna.

(2) Krsna, the God was equipped with transcendental personality and attributes.

(3) One could worship God only at his pleasure.

(4) The 'guru' was the medium through which God's grace reached man.

(5) The concept of incomprehensible duality in nonduality was faultless.

(6) Without 'bhakti' none could hope to be a true spiritualist.

(7) Love for Krsna had to be both very deep and dynamic.

(8) The Universe was not an illusion. It was real, as it had a vital link with Krsna.

(9) The 'Holy Name' (Hari, Krsna or Rama) is of supreme importance in the Kali age.

---

[1] Vaisnavism in Bengal: by Dr. R. Chakravorty, p. 397-98. Summarized from 'Outlines of Gaudiya Mission', published by Calcutta Gaudiya Mission.

Gaudiya Mission had ostensibly no social aim. It did not pretend that it was an organization with a social mission. But it did set up schools, libraries, research centres and free hospitals. These however had secondary importance. Its primary object was to preach mysticism.

Some Vaisnavas felt that the Vaisnavism should have a programme of social work among the weaker sections of the society. Three very prominent Vaisnava missionaries worked hard to spread the faith among the untouchables. They were Prabhu Jagatbandhu (1871-1921), Atulcandra Campati (d. 1925) and Haribolananda Thakur, in early twentieth century. Prabhu Jagatbandhu worked among the Doms (very low caste), of North Calcutta and the Namasudras of Faridpur and Jessore. Later he founded a sect himself known as 'Mohanta sects[1].

His disciples founded the 'Uddharana Matha' of Maniktala, Calcutta. Atulcandra Campati, a former Headmaster of a school, worked very hard for the welfare of the untouchables and the prostitutes of Calcutta.

Haribolananda Thakur roamed about in Calcutta, asking everybody, including children and the Europeans to chant the name of God.

He was the leading organizer of the many of the Harisabhas mentioned before, which were financed by his rich Suvarnavanik disciple, Kshetra Mallik. He too worked among the untouchables of Calcutta for many years.

His disciples regarded him as the incarnation of Advaita Acarya[2]. The chief proponent of the Nityanada in Bengal and Orrisa, was the Gaudiya Vaisnava mendicant Radharamana Charana Dasa Deva (b. 1853). He established two powerful centres in Puri and Navadvipa respectively. He asked Bengalis to give up their narrow provincial outlook and respect all Indians as their brothers. He said that Caitanya had abandoned Bengal because he could not tolerate the meanness of the Bengalis[3].

The activities of Radharamana was best described in his biography written by Ramadasa Babaji, who himself was a great Vaisnava and kirtan singer and the founder of a Vaisnava museum and liberty in Baranager (1933). Radharamana attached great importance to Nityananda. He never

---

[1]   Religious Movements in Modern Bengal: by B.G. Roy, p. 95.
[2]   Gaudiya Vaisnava Jivana: Vol. 2, pp. 273-80.
[3]   Charitasudha: by Ramadasa Babaji, Vol. I. 180-82.

advised, the householders to renounce, the world. His ideal was the ideal of disinterested service to everybody, including parents, children, wife, brothers, sisters, and servants[1]. His view was that caste better should be forgotten in social relations. To him caste was utterly meaningless. What mattered most, was humanity as a totality of human relations[2]. He recognised Jessus Christ as a very important Avatara of God[3]. Radharamana was of the opinion that every type of relation with Krsna was psychic. Nobody could establish with Him any relation with physical sense of term[4].

Harekrsna movement and the Bengali Renaissance

The nineteenth century witnessed the ascendancy of rational judgement over blind faith among the upper castes Hindus of Bengal.

Both the conservative and liberal Hindus welcomed the spread of English education and adopted many Western concepts. But this English education and the Western concepts could not weaken the Hinduism at all in Bengal. Krsna, Siva, Durga, Kali and many other lesser gods and goddesses, were quite popular. The priests enjoyed great authority in town and villages. The middle class Hindus in the urban areas observed, all sorts sacraments and rituals[5].

The educated Bengalis felt the necessity for the modernisation of Hinduism. Rammohun ray propagated total reformation. He repudiated caste system. Later Isvarcandra Vidyasagar (1820-1891) started a movement for the marriage of widows and prevention of polygamy. As a reformer Vidyasagar belonged to the class of Rammohun. But unlike rammohun he said nothing about religion.

A second group of upper caste Bengali Hindus thought of fastening a liberal interpretation on the myths and the philosophical system of the Hindus. They spoke of the reformation of the Hindu spirit, without disturbing the forms and outward symbols of Hinduism. These Bengali

---

[1]   Charitasudha: by Ramadasa Babaji, Vol. II. p. 68.

[2]   Ibid, pp. 287-94.

[3]   Ibid, pp. 396-97.

[4]   Ibid, Vol. 6, p. 81.

[5]   Vaisnavism in Bengal: by Dr. R. Chakravoty, p. 402.

Hindus did not support those who propagated drastic reforms. Their spokesman was Bankimchandra Chattopadhyaya (1838-1894), the Ex-Deputy magistrate and the great novelist. Ramakrsna Paramhamsa (1836-1886) preached that it was not essential for the Hindus to observe the caste system and rituals. The spirit of Hinduism was, according to him, one of tolerance, pursuit of truth, and service to mankind. If one practised Hinduism with those ideals, one would gradually rise above caste and superstitions.

A third group which was rather amorphous, began to prophess an 'Aryan' revival in near future. The Indian Hindus, regardless of caste, clime and colour, were regarded by them as degenerated Aryans. This group was headed by Brahma leaders like Rajnarayan Basu (1826-1899).

Various aspects of Hinduism and Hindu society were discussed and debated upon in such famous cultural associations as the Society for the Acquisition of General Knowledge (1838), the Bethune Society (1851-1869) and the Burrabazar Family Library Club (1870-1882). The tremendous strength of Hinduism was described by Akshayakumar Dutta in 'Bharatvarsiya Upasaka Sampradaya' (1870-1882). The word revival was used, in a special sense in connection with Hinduism[1].

Roughly speaking the ward had two meanings. According to Bankimchandra Hindu revival meant nationalist awakening. According to Ramakrsna, it meant universal religious and ethical uplift. The approach of the former was intensely intellectual. The approach of the later was intuitive, nonintellectual and devotional.

These two interpretations became the starting points of parallel revivalist movement after 1880, when the Brahma movement grew weaker owing to sectarian divisions. These two movements could not ignore Harekrsna movement and Sri-Caitanya.

During 1870 and 1900 the Hindu itelligentsia of Bengal felt a deep urge to rediscover the Harekrsna movement and the associated culture of Bengal. They unearthed a great mass of material hitherto unknown. They found that the Harekrsna movement was integrally connected with the growth and development of the Bengali literature. The main emphasis of the research was, of course, laid on the Bengali phase of the Catianya

---

[1] Ibid p. 402-03.

movement. Some of the leading scholars who worked for the discovery of the material or the conclusion they came to, are listed here:

(1) Ramagati Nyayaratna (1831-1894):
    In 'Banglabhasa O Sahityavisyaka Prastava' (1872)
    He sketched out a history of the Vaisnava literature of Bengal.
    He came to the conclusion that the Vaisnavas created the Bengali. He also gave some biographical data[1]

(2) Akshayachandra Sarkar (1846-1917): With Saradacharan Mitra and Baradakanta Mitra, he edited, 'Pracinakavyasagraha' and published it in parts. In 1884 the work was published in two volumes. The Kavyas (poetry), published in it, were the Padavali of Vidyapati, Chandidasa, Govindadasa and the Mangala-kavyas of Ramesvara and Mukundarama. Aksayacandra himself was a strict vagetarian. The Padavali was edited with great care in a critical manner[2].

(3) Ramadasa Sen (1845-1887). In an essay in his 'Aitihasika Rahasya', he dealt with the biographies and principal works of the Gaudiya Vaisnava Acaryas. This essay was written on Vaisnava ideals also from historical point of view[3].

(4) Rajakrsna Mukhopadhyaya (1846-1886). His 'Nanapravandha' (1885) certain biographical sketch of Vidyapati and an analysis of the themes of his songs and also many other kirtana of the later dates.[4]

(5) Rajanikanta Gupta (1849-1900). Among his many works on the activities of the Vaisnavas of various time, the work on Jayadeva was prominent. He wrote a biography of Jayadeva entitled 'Jayadevacaritra' (1873). It was written as a prize essay. The author was awarded a cash prize of Rs.50 by Maharaja Saurindramohan Tagore of Pathuriaghata,

---

[1] Vaisnavism in Bengal: by Dr. R. Chakravoty, p. 404.

[2] Vaisnava Padavali Part 1: Vidyapati, pp. 2831; chandidasa, pp. 31-34; Brajabhakha, pp. 34-43; Caitanya, pp. 51-54.

[3] Gaudiya Vaisnavacaryavrnder Granthavalir Vivaran': in The work Dr. Ramdas Sen, 1, 3rd ed. 1902, pp. 85-101.

[4] Nanapravandha: 3rd ed. (1937), 'Vidyapati' pp. 11-33.

Calcutta. The work had a musical notations of the Kirtana songs prepared by Ksetramohan Goswani[1].

(6) Aghoranath Chattopadhyaya, a Brahma author, wrote 'Bhaktacaritamala' and 'Haridasa Thakura' in 1896[2]. Biographical sketches of Sanatana Gosvamin, Rupa Gosvamin, and Jiva Gosvamin, were given in the first part of his work. In 1894 he wrote a biography of raghunatha Dasa Gosvamin entitled 'Srimadraghunatha Dasa Gosvamira Jivanacarita'[3].

(7) The celebrated Indologist Haraprasad Sastri (1853-1931). He emphasized the necessity of discovering the Vaisnava lore in Bengal in a lecture delivered in 1891 at a meeting of the Kambuliyatola Reading Club (Calcutta). The subject of his lecture was 'Vernacular Literature of Bengal before the Introduction of English Education'. This lecture of 16 pages published in 1891. He also delivered the learned lectures on Joyadeva and Vidyapati in the 'Vangiya Sahitya Parisad', established in 1894[4]. Besides these two lectures he has many other activities on Harekrsna movement. His view would be elaborated a bit more later on.

(8) A famous journalist, Nagendranath Gupta (1861-1904). Among his many activities on Vaisnavism, it is worthwhile to mention that he edited the songs of Vidyapati in 'Vidyapati Thakurer Padavali' in 1909. He also delivered lectures on the Vaisnava literary tradition of Mithila and Govindadasa[5].

(9) Nagendranath Basu (1866-1938). He edited the first complete Bengalil encyclopaedia entitled Visvakosa, which is a variable mine of information. Numerous Vaisnava celebrities, rituals and places associated with the Hare-krsna movement are discussed in the encylopaedic volumes. Nagendranath also edited Jayananda's Caitanyamangala[6].

---

[1] Vaisnavism in Bengal: by Dr. R. Chakravorty, p. 404.

[2] Bhaktacharitamala: published by Gurudasa Chattopadhyaya (1896).

[3] The works were reviewed in Sajjanatosani: 1894, Vol. 6, pp. 37-39.

[4] Sahitya Sadhaka Charitamala: by H.P. Sastri, Vol. 7, p. 45.

[5] Ibid: Vol. 6, p. 71; Govindadasa Kaviraja: by Sukumar Sen, pp. 72-90.

[6] Valsnavism in Bengal: by Dr. R. Chakravorty, p. 405.

(10) Jagatbandhu Bhadra (b. 1841). He edited with detailed notes and biographical sketches, 'Gaurapadatarangini' which was published by the Vangiya Sahitya Parisad in 1903. Bhadra's biographical sketches and notes were used by Satish Chandra Ray in his edition of the 'Padakalpataru' anthology. In many respects, 'Gaurapadatarangini' represented a pioneering effort[1].

(11) The linguistic aspect of 'Padavali' literature were analyzed by G.A. Grierson (Calcutta 1889), in The Modern Vernacular Literature of Hindustan[2].

(12) Yogendranath Vidyabhusan (1845-1904). His research was aimed on various activities of Caitanya. He wrote a biography of Caitanya[3].

(13) Hemchandra Bandopadhyaya (1838-1903). The poet, based on his research, prepared a comparative study of the teachings of Krsna and Christ in his 'Life of SriKrsna'[4].

(14) Balendranath Tagore (1870-1899). He has many writings on Vaisnavism. The most important of which was that he discussed the excellence of Joydeva's poetry in a brilliant essay entitled 'Jayadeva'[5].

(15) Akshayakumar Maitreya (1861). The noted historian, during his research and study of Vaisnava literature, was very much impressed with the architectural concept of 'Haribhaktivilasa'. He highly praised this book[6].

(16) Rev. Krsnamohan Bandopadhaya (1813-1885), edited and translated into English 'Naradapancaratra' in 1865.

(17) Rabindranath Tagore (1861-1941) and Sriscandra Majumdar (1860-1908), edited 'Padaratnavali' in 1885[7].

---

[1] Valsnavism in Bengal: by Dr. R. Chakravorty, p. 405.

[2] Ibid. p. 405.

[3] Pratahsmaraniyacaritamala: by Yogendranath Vidyabhusan, No

[4] 2nd ed. 1885.

[5] Hemchandra: by Manmathanath Ghose, Vol. 1, pp. 98-99.

[6] Balendranath's Chitra O Kavya (1894): BalendraGranthavali: Calcutta, 1952, pp. 34-42, pp. 196, 331-55.

[7] Sahityasadhaka Charitamala: Vol. 5, p. 50 (Aksayakumar Maitreya's letter to O.C. Ganguliguated here).

(18) Sisirkumar Ghosh (1840-1911), founder and the editor of the famous 'Amrita Bazar Patrika', was once a Brahma. His elder brother Hemantakumar Ghosh, converted him into Vaisnavism. Sisirkumar regarded himself as a 'marked servant of Caitanya'. He wrote biographies of Narottama Datta, ('Narrottamacharita', 1891), Caitanya ('Sri Amiyanimaicharita', 6 volumes, 1892-1011), Pravodhananda Sarasvati ('Pravodhananda Sarasvatir Jivanacharita', 1889) and Gopala Bhatta Gosvamin (1896). He published an edition of Vrndavana Dasa's CBH and Vaisnava Dasa's 'Padakalpataru' (3 volumes, 1897). 'Lord Gauranga or Salvation for All', his biography of Caitanya written in English, was published in 1897. He edited two Vaisnava journals, namely, 'Sri-Sri-Visnupriya Patrika' (first issue, dated Caitra, 1890) and 'Sri Sri Gauravisnupriya Patrika' (first issue dated, Phalguna, 1901)[1]

(19) Dinesh Chandra Sen (1866-1939), was the first historian of Bengali literature who discovered by long arduous research a great mass of materials for the study of Harekrsna movement and literature. His discussions and explanations are characterized by profound devotion for Caitanya and adoration of the Vaisnava poets. Some of his views are translated in the later parts of this text[2].

(20) Brahmavandhava Upadhyaya (1861-1907), celebrated editor of the anti-British newspaper 'Sandhya', a friend of the extremists, formerly a Christian and later an orthodox Hindu, may be said to have initiated the study of Vaisnava lore in a little known work named 'Palaparvana' in January, 1925[3].

(21) Brahmavandhava's example was followed by Dinendrakumar Ray (1869-1943). He wrote highly interesting sketches of Rathayatra, Jhulanyatra, Nandotsava in a remarkable work entitled Pallicitra

---

[1]   Vaisnavism in Bengal: by Dr. R. Chakravorty, p. 406.

[2]   Ibid. p. 406.

[3]   Ibid. p. 406-07.

(1904)[1]. The Snanayatra and the Dolyatra (holy) festvals are described in 'Pallivaicitra' in 1905[2].

Some characteristics of these memorable attempts should be noted.

The emphasis on the discovery of materials relating to the careers and activities of the leaders of the Harekrsna movement of Bengal was heavier than that of the Vrndavana phase of the movement.

---

[1] Pallichitra: 3rd ed. 1922, p. 85, 151-66, 209-34; Pallivaichitra: Anananda Publishers, Calcutta, 1982, p. 103.

[2] Pallivaichitra: Anananda Publishers, Calcutta, 1982, p. 103.

CHAPTER VIII

Influence of Harekrsna Movement on Intellectuals

Deshbandhu Chitta Ranjan Das (1870-1925)

Desbandhu (friend of the country) was contemporary of Mahatma Gandhi, had the same fame in India, was the president of the Indian National Congress, founder of the Svaraj Party and people lovingly gave him the title 'Friend of the Country'.

Sri-Caitanya occupied the mind and heart of Deshbandhu. Hemendra-nath Das Gupta has rightly written, "The devotion and love that became alive and burning in the heart of Caitanya, the flow of love that originated at Nadia, flooded Bengal, Bihar and Orissa and the happiness, the knowledge and the desire that led him to leave the loving family life, for the feeling of misery of the living soul, to extend his loving embracement to Brahmin and Candal (a class of lowest caste), Hindu and Muslims, became the essence of life of Chittaranjan."

The thought of Mahaprabhu (Caitanya) entered in every corner of his mind. The conviction of Mahaprabhu immensely occupied his thought and that inspiration made him a great Vaisnava. This love of Caitanya converted his emotion of youth to pure love to God. It was this love that used to make him absorbed in kirtana, raise his bhakti to God, inspired his unparallel sacrifice and dedication and prompted him to semi-renunciation. It was this love that raise his future hope of great union of human being, irrespective of their caste and religion"[1].

---

[1] Bangali Manishaye Sri-Caitanya: N.N. Gupta, p. 121-26.

The reference of Caitanya came time and time again, whenever he addressed the public "the imagination of the loving statue of Caitanya, has brought the change in my life". In 1917 at Bhavanipur, Calcutta at the presidential address of the provincial congress he said, "The National independence movement came as a cyclone, floated us in a very strong tide. We have survived this deep drowning flood and we have met the living soul of Bengal and possibly party understood, the stream of the history of Bengal."

It reminded us the songs of Chandidas and Vidyapati. The appearance of Caitanya was after them. The essence and the flavour of love that was appreciated in the songs of Vidyapati and in the love of Chandidas, became awakened, alive and glowing in the life of Caitanya. Chandidas was comparable like the dim rose at morning light, was to announce the appearance of the hot midday sun with its full luminous glow, Caitanya was about to come. The glory of the life of Caitanya has increased the glory of our mind.

It is difficult to limit our surprise, when we analyse how much inspiration could be generated, even by a glance of sight (tilek darshan) of this jyotirmoya, (the unbounded source of light) the immortal revolutionary[1].

In the presidential address of the Bengal convention of Literature at Dacca C.R. Das said "One day Mahaprabhu had put his two red lotus feet on this bank of River Padma, that's why (translation of Bengali rhyme) men and women sing Caitanya sankirtana all over this area and Bengal. Bengalis are fortunate because the appearance of Mahaprabhu was in Bengal"[2].

Saint Arabinda Ghosh (1872-1950)

The famous learned Indian Saint of the recent centuries. The great scholar, educated in England, gave up the top civil service job to participate in the Independence movement of India.

"The expression of Bengalis" religious mind has always been through emotion. It is said that Bengal is both the mind and heart of India. It is the

---

[1] The Lecture Notes of Deshbandhu C.R. Das, April, 1917.
[2] Ibid: 8 April, 1918, Dacca.

centre for Nayacharcha (Brahminical conservatism) and the birth place of Caitanya (the reformer).

Caitanya is like a spotless beautiful lotus at the highest peak of the Buddhist expression in Bengal.

To fulfill the requirement for the noble elevation of the thought of the self visualization of the soul of Bengal, one need to hold on the enthusiasm and the ideal objectives of the new movement, the way Caitanya surrendered his desire totally for Hari (God). It is this kind of love what is essential for the Bengalis for the Mother land. Svaraj (independence) will not come only by repeating the word svaraj. It will come if we all individually plan in our life the reflection of svaraj, by sacrificing our self-interest, raising the thought of national consciousness. As Caitanya did not stay as Nimai Pandit, but became Krsna, Radha, Balaram, similarly each individual of us, will have to forget our differences, irrespective of caste and creed. The perfect sense of self abandonment which Caitanya felt for Hari, must be felt by Bengal for the Mother .... Our passion to see the face of our free and glorified mother must be as devouring a madness, as the passion of Caitanya, to see the face of Sri-Krsna. We need the similar emotional love as Caitanya had. The way Jagai and Madhai gave up their administrative job, to join the namsankirtana of Caitanya, we need to sacrifice for the country, with similar enthusiasm[1].

The love of Caitanya is a heavenly spiritual feeling on the glorious destiny of expression of jiva-soul. I will not question whether Caitanya was an incarnation of Krsna or an incarnation of a mystic love (divya premer). The evident expression of that character, is perceived from the various description about him. From the available description of the intermittent, appearance of Krsna within him, the spiritual expression of the supreme personality in Caitanya incarnation, is noteworthy[2].

Rastraguru Surendranath Bandopadhyay (1848-1925)

The great scholar, famous Professor of Calcutta University, one of the top leaders of the country, ex-president of the All India National Congress, got

---

[1] "The Demand of the Mother" Bande Mataram, 11 April, 1908.
[2] The Purpose of Abatarhood: by A. Ghosh, Centenary Vol. 22, p. 418.

the title from the people 'Rastraguru', the teacher of the nation. He said in his writings:

"Such a day will come when our future generation will be surprised and think how was their respected fore-fathers who imposed cruel injustice on the woman. We do not know the future, but past is like an open book in front of us. The past has said to us, when Raghunandan introduced Nayasastra and Smriti book, at the heart land of 'Sanatan dharma' (Navadvipa), the contemporary reformer also was born at the same place.

There appeared the greatest reformer, the Bengal, or India, has ever produced, the prophet of love (bhakti), who would have no distinction between man and man, or between man and woman, who treated the Brahmin, the Chandal and the Muslim alike and enfranchised our woman from the bonds of enforced widowhood.

Who knows, in time there may be another personality like Caitanya, would emerge, at the famous centres of the Sanskrit teachings, to show the broad light of knowledge for the happy future, to rescue the Hindu widow. It is true that the social problems in India, are very hard and loaded with lots of complications[1].

There is not a single social problem within the Hindus, which has not got a religious link. If any social tradition, once can be projected as the intention of God, it then becomes firm belief of the people. It does not follow the rule of logic, but spread its root in the soil of emotion. Maintaining the practice over the generations, these have become very firm traditions. These are difficult to discard by the logic of common sense. The social reformer in India has to struggle against such a tradition and bindings, which are imagined as spiritual.

Time to time there has been example of success, as was shown by Caitanya which not only proved his very strong personality, but also gave the expression of the significance of the thoughts of the Indian people.

Caitanya came as an incarnation to the people and was the greatest social reformer of Bengal of all the time. Like Buddha he was also against the traditional unreasonable practices.

He declared war against the caste system and the unfair social restrictions for the widows. People found flood of heavenly light in his teachings,

---

[1] A Nation in Making: by S.N. Bandopadhyay, p. 101, 141, 396.

assurances in his love and so were inspired with noble enthusiasm and gave him unlimited support. They felt that Messiah (saviour), had come to replace the old and to preach the message of the new. There was no bindings of the practices, and there was no rules for conservatism. They found in him the immense source of inspiration, of the heavenly truth which he had projected in such a way that had touched the heart of the people and brought them closure"[1].

Bipin Chandra Pal (1858-1932)

The Vaisnav movement (Harekrsna movement) introduced by Caitanya, not only brought a spiritual message or a message of musical art or a novelty to the poetry-song (gitikabita), the best wealth of the Bengali literature, but brought a noble message to the society, for each to respect each and every individual. This movement was for the benefit of the individual and for the society as a whole. The Vaisnava movement was primarily a protest movement against the organisational structure of the traditional Hindu religion and its social and economical rules and restrictions. In Punjab from this protest movement a new religion Sikhdharma was born. As a result of this bhakti movement of late fifteenth and early sixteenth century, in various provinces of India, there was a period of extermination and reconstruction of the social structure, through which originated a new evolution.

As a result of this new development, there was a notable expansion of the provincial literature. Hindi in North, Marathi in South, and Bengali in East, were particularly encouraged with some new inspiration. The novel thought and perceptions were enunciated in literature. Consequently in the provincial languages, there was a build-up of religious and spiritual literature, which had so long been restricted within the boundary of Sanskrit language. This novel creation brought a message of freedom from the medieval Brahminical influence, to the intellectuals. In this way the uprising of the Vaisnavas revealed the path of mass movement all over the country.

In Bengal this movement was intense because the Bengalees already had passed the period of metamorphosis of the Buddhist cultural heritage.

---

[1]   Ibid p. 83.

In Punjub ancient Hindu religion was mostly replaced by the Sikh religion of Guru Nanak. New religious book Grantha Saheb occupied the position of Veda. In Bengal although it was not possible to be completely free from the Brahminical influence, the "Caitanya Caritamrita", became the principal religious book, amongst the followers of Caitanya. This brought great inspiration and enthusiasm among the Vaisnavas. Reading of this religious book everyday became the routine of many people. The eagerness of reading of the religious book in mother language, was very helpful, for the expansion of mass education. Even in the beginning of this century the number of people capable of signing were maximum within the Vaisnava community. In this society not only man, the woman also had some sort of education in their mother language. The education that was restricted within the limited top class Brahmins and some top class non-Brahmins, found its way to the vast majority of the Vaisnava society[1].

The Harekrsna movement of Caitanya brought the bulletin of freedom to the people of so-called lower class. In the society administered by the Brahmins, the restrictions of rules and law depriving the lower class, their legitimate right, were gradually weakening, which were completely broken with the advent of the movement.

Caitanya wanted to get rid of the untouchability of the caste system, introduced by the Hindu Brahmins. Those who were untouchable, or the water brought by whom was not drinkable, the cooked meal was not edible, by the look of the so-called higher class, such as Brahmin, Kayestha, Vaidya, were respected.

The intelligent and learned member of these community, were given high ranking position in his new Vaisnava soceity. In this new religious movement, these people were given equal rank of guru (teacher) by the side of their Brahmin colleagues[2].

The all initial gurus were called goswamins. All the non-Brahmin gurus were respected in the same ways, as the Brahmin gurus, who exclusively enjoyed this honour till that time. Moreover Muslims such as Haridasa, were respected so much as like a Brahmin. Again those Hindus who were downgraded, due to the involvement or the close contact with

---

[1] Bangali Manishay Sri-Caitanya: by N.N. Gupta, p. 83-84.
[2] Ibid: p. 85-86.

the administrative council of the Muslim rulers, were reinstated with the acceptance of the Vaisnava order. Some disciples of Caitanya such as Rupa, Sanatana and their nephew Jiva, became theorist and the most respected of the acharyas. Their hard endeavour gradually led to the build-up of the rich philosophy and metaphysics of the new Vaisnava movement (Harekrsna). All the changes along with the movement, deeply influenced the development of the rational thought of the Bengalees and the very conservative Hinduism. Its tradition of caste system and superstitious religious practices, all fled away.

This new movement, in fact, had built up a new society in place of the old one, where new systems were introduced in place of Smriti rule (Brahminical). Although this movement did not fulfill all the expectations of Caitanya, but it made tremendous changes in the outlook of the society. He wanted total change of the caste system according to the Brahminical rule. According to the rule of the new movement it was declared, the freedom of marriage ignoring the system of caste barrier, outside the Brahminical rule. Non-Brahmin bride and bridegroom could easily get married with the opposite number from the Brahmin community.

Beside these, the system of medieval child marriage was abolished and widow marriage was introduced.

The ceremony of marriage became much simpler. The foundation of this marriage was like some sort of gandharva marriage (a simple system of mutual declaration of marriage in an evening by the two partners), the mutual agreement between the two partners, irrespective of any caste, and to exchange either a garland of flower or Tulsi wood (a sacred plant to Vaisnava).

The new Vaisnavas also denied the old practices and traditions in sraddha (funeral ceremony). In place of old functions and ceremonies, they introduced namsankirtana (congregational singing of Harekrsna) with the fellow Vaisnava members and at the end to have a simple vegetarian meal together (mahotsava). In fact they denounced all the activities used to be performed by the Brahmin priests in the religious ceremonies, instead they had introduced namsankirtana and mahotsava.

The main notable feature of the Hare-krsna movement of Caitanya was its universal appeal. He totally denounced the prejudicial social and religious rights of the different caste of the Hindu religion.

He declared that singing of the name of God is the best worship. He also declared that Lord Krsna is the only one to worship. There is no need to worship, to any-body else of the three hundred thirty million of Hindu gods and goddesses. There is no need to organise a ceremonial puja by a Brahmin, with numerous material elements to sacrifice to God, which in fact are collected by the Grahmin priests for their own use. In this way the Vaisnavas of Bengal, without depending on the establishment of social aristocracies of the caste system, gave the highest right to each and every individual, in the field of religion. For this universal worship the only mantra is to utter the name of Hari.

"*Harer nama, Harer nama, Harer namaiva kebalam kalou nasteiva, nasteiva, nasteiva gatiranytha*". (explained in p. 58). Along with this Mahaprabhua also added, "*Trinadopi sunichena taroriba sahishnuna, amanina, manadena kirtaniya, sada Hari.*"

It means that—The utterance of the name of Hari should be associated with modesty, one should consider him as low level as grass who always stumped by people but never objects. Tolerance like a tree who never deprives any body from its shadow, even to the one who cuts its branches and one should not expect to be honoured but be ready to respect the others.

"*Disharsi param chetana*"—This verse explain almost the whole significance of the philosophy, the rule of conduct of the Harekrsna movement[1]. The root of endeavour of perception of God, is in every human being. Here the modesty (trinadapi sunicha) is not only simplicity or timidity, but self discipline or forgetfulness of the mundane attachment. This forgetfulness is the step to climb from the consciousness of jiva soul to over soul, the paramatma. The tolerance comes from the perception of world-wide sense of self-realization. The Vaisnavas pray for this self-realization through namsankirtana. In Vaisnava prayer the name of Hari is the path, destination and the destiny. This conduct of Vaisnavas made the Harekrsna movement of Caitanya, a great philanthropic movement.

In the past there were examples of non-Hindu became Hindu. But that conversion and assimilation was within the existing caste system. Caitanya denied the caste system, that was why he adapted this novel way through Hare Krsna movement. He sounded out the voice of freedom to

---

[1]   Bangali Manishay Sir-Caitanya: by N.N. Gupta, p. 87-88.

the people of very lower class. His idealism, was "Chandalopi dvijasreshtha haribhaktiparayana—" one from very lowest caste could be more respectable than a Brahmin if he possess the love of God in his heart (Hari bhakti). This idealism of Caitanya brought a silent revolution to the Brahmin dominated and caste—based society. By the teachings of Caitanya, almost all the non-Hindu tribes, became associated with the Harekrsna movement and with the simple Vaisnava way of life. Such example is very well evident in the North Eastern part of India, where all the Manipuri community became Vaisnava.

Dr. Ramesh Chandra Majumdar

In sixteenth century, there was an inauguration of a new Vaisnava community as a result of the advent of Sri-Caitanya. Previously Vaisnavism was in Bengal. The Gitgovinda of Joydeva and Padavali of Candidas (books of songs)[1], were the good evidence of that. Shortly before the birth of Caitanya, Madhavendra Puri preached this premadharma (the religion of love). Caitanya met Isvarpuri, Pramanandapuri, Srirangapuri, Keshabpuri and Advaita Acarya, out of main nineteen disciples of Madhavendra Puri and a close relationship was also built up. But Vaisnavism before Caitanya was not able to create any significant impression. Noneless there were few very serious Vaisnava devotee[2]. Advaita was the foremost of them and was very upset, as there were not many devotee of bhakti in the city. Caitanya was able to depose his sadness. According to Vaisnavas, love to God and total surrender to his lotus feet (prapatti), is the only way to attain mokshya. But this worldly non-attached love of God, is expressed itself through santa, dasya, sakshya, batsalya and madhura (explained in p. 63-64) phases. The attraction of Radha and Gopies toward Krsna, were the examples, of this madhura love. The insanity of this love became eminently evident in the life of Caitanya. But this love is spiritual and outside any physical attachment.

This is the core message of the new Vaisnava philosophy. Caitanya himself did not compose any informative book. But his principle disciples six goswamins, such as Rupa, Sanatana, Jiva, Raghunath Das, Raghunath

---

[1]   Bangali Manishay Sri-Caitanya: by N.N. Gupta,: p. 103.
[2]   Medieval History of Bengal.

Bhatta and Gopal Bhatta, inhabitants of Vrandavana, composed many religious books and put his new movement on a very strong philosophical foundation. Most of the instructions about their practices, code of conducts and religious functions are compiled in two books, named "Haribhaktibilasha and Satkriyasaradipika".

Before the composition of these books, the wave of insanity of premabhakti of Caitanya, in the ideals of the love of Radha and Krsna, sweft the whole country in an unprecedented way. Whole Bengal was flooded with the bhakti and love of God, inspired by namsankirtan and the songs on the Vrndavana activities of Radha and Krsna (Radha-Krsna lila). In this type of expression of devotion there was no room for any traditional practices of the Hindu religion, nor was there any discrimination of the castes of the participants. The aim of Caitanya was to initiate women, sudra, candal everybody, in the religion of premabhakti, to arouse the spiritual devotion and love of God, in every-body's mind. The archetype of the love affairs of Radha and Krsna was known in this country. But that was lack in spiritual love and gradually became the example of physical enjoyment. The forceful appeal of Catianya with pure spiritual love and unparallel personality, put the Vaisnava, the Radha-Krsna worshipper at a very higher level. The clear perception of premabhakti, the delirious melody of namsankirtana and the ideal love affairs of Radha-Krsna, what he harmonized in his own life, washed away all the obscenity. With this moral improvement and the example cited by Caitanya, the Hindu society of Bengal seemed, got a new life.

As a devotee of pure love, with intoxication, Caitanya used to roll on the ground. The example cited by Caitanya, intoxicated with namsankirtana, the devotee of pure love, is unparallel in the medieval history of India.

He was determined to improve the life of everybody irrespective of their caste and sex. With this purpose, he persuaded Nityananda, to come back to Bengal from Puri and not to become a monk, so that he could look after the needy, lower and outcasts. As a result of his movement, the strong binding of the caste restriction was broken and all the lower class of the Hindu society, who were deprived and ignored, joined the new movement of Catianya. It is mentioned before, the lower class Hindus in large number were accepting Muslim religion and this was stopped, due to the preaching force of Nityananda and his followers.

As a result of Caitanya's renouncing of the caste system, denouncing the social injustice and recognising equal right for the woman, led to a social revolution within the Hindu society. Caste barrier was abolished and some Muslims also accepted the Vaisnava religion. Person like Haridasa (Muslin) was respected[1].

Along with Brahmin, Vaidya, Kayestha and other caste, and Muslims (jaban) used to sing together Harinam sankirtan. Non-Brahmin started initiating Brahmins without any hesitation. Raghunath Das was a Kayestha, still he got a place among the six famous goswamins. Kalidas, uncle of Raghunath Das, ate the left over food of a Sudra and other lower castes Vaisnavs. Numerous Brahmins accepted initiation of Vaisnavism from Kayestha Narahari Sarkar. The tradition has still been continuing in the family of Narahari Sarkar of Srikhanda (a small town in East Bengal) that many Brahmins still take initiation from his descendants.

The situations has improved for the women also. It has been stated in the songs of Balaram Des "sankirtan majhe nache kuler bouhari". It means that young house wife openly used to take part in singing and dancing during namsankirtana. But all these changes did not accomplish, the intention of Caitanya fully. Along with these changes there were some undesired elements, came along with the movement, after the death of Caitanya. These elements might have diluted the gravity of the movement but were in no way obstruction for the abolition of caste system.

The Sahajiya Buddhists and the Tantric groups (ritualists) were already in this country. Their influence was very much reduced due to the spread of Vaisnavism. Soon these groups joined the Vaisnavas and increased their number. One aspect of the religious aspiration of these group was recognition of adultery. So when they became Vaisnava, they did not give up these practices. As a result some of the practices of the Kartabhaja sections of the Sahajiyagroup, such as kishoribhajan (love with adolescent girl), degraded the image of the Vaisnavas, to some extent[2]

The Harekrsna movement of Caitanya was a universal, noncommunal movement, irrespective of Hindus and Muslims, against the traditional religious belief and practices, based on bhakti and on belief in God, as was

---

[1] Medieval History of Benga; p. 106.
[2] Medieval History of Benga: p. 107.

preached by Ramanada, Kabir and Nanak outside Bengal, in the medieval period. But unlike Kabir and Nanak, he did not suspend all the link with the ancient religion and tradition. After Caitanya some of Sahajiya and Tantrics, become influential and founded some subgroups. Their influence and injection of some personal ideas, diluted the gravity and depth of the original philosophy of Caitanya in some areas.

Sahajiyas were divided and subdivided into many branches, such as Aul, Baul, Sai, Daravesh and Sahajiya. Besides these there were Karttabhaja, Spastadayak, Sakhibhavak, Kishoribhajani, Ramballavi, Jagonmohini, Gourabhadi, Sahebdhani, Pagalnathi and Gobarai etc. were considered as a class of Sahajiya. Although there were some differences about their belief and practices, they had common view about gurubad (to be initiated by somebody), free mixing of man and woman and adultery to some extent.

These Sahajiyas have many centres in places like, Ghoshpara, Ramkeli, Nadia, Santipur, Khardaha, Kenduli, Birbhum, Bankura and in Midnapore district.

Karttabhaja sampradaya (group) was founded by a religious person named Aulchand in eighteenth century. He preached in different areas of Nadia district. In 1769 when he died, Ramsharan Pal of Naihati, A Satgop (lower caste) became its head. He maintained not believing in caste system and his disciples included Hindus and Muslims.

People of this community used to regard their guru (kartta) as God or Krsna. Women of the lower caste were more in number within this community and they used pray for their guru in the same way as Gopies used pray for Krsna. In nineteenth century this community became quite influential under the leadership of Ramdulal Pal son of Ramsharan Pal. But according to the code of practices of the time, people were very critical of their attitude and behaviour towards this religion.

Ultimately they were disregarded and they lost their influence. Spastadayak sampradaya was just the opposite of Karttabhaja sampradaya. People of this community never used to consider their guru as an incarnation of God and the role of guru was also very limited. Rupram Kaviraj of Murshidabad district, disciple of Krishnachandra Chakravorty was the founder of this sect. Like Karttabhaja sampradaya they had many household followers. But the administrative power was mainly in the hand of a group of monks and nuns. They used to live together in a centre like brothers and sisters. They used to sing and dance praising the name of Krsna and Caitanya. Their biggest centre was in Calcutta.

The male member of Sakhibhavak sampradaya used to dress like ladies, name like ladies and used to dance like ladies, singing the name of Krsna and Caitanya. Their biggest centre was at Jangalitola of Maldah district. At Joypur and Benaras, they also had some influences[1].

In the outlook of the present days, some of their behaviour and attitude may be considered as unpleasant and objectionable, but some of their specialities, are noticeable. The Sahajiyas had the expressions of the liberal universal religious appeal, based on the pure love only between bhakta and Bhagavan (Jiva soul and Paramatma), as the view had Kabir and Nanak, who denied the traditional Hindu religious custom. But the source of this was in the book of Sahajiya Buddhist. These books were composed in the medieval period or a bit earlier. There is no doubt that the Vaisnava Sahajiyas were influenced by the Buddhist Sahajiyas.

The resentment against the traditional practices and the religious superstitions, remind as the renaissance of the nineteenth century (navajagaran), and this type of devotion had been continuing since the medieval period, as is proved by the like wise religious opinion of the Sahajiyas. As much as known about the life history of Caitanya, there is no reason to believe that he was influenced by Islam.

Caitanya and Sahajiya Vaisnavas all were more or less influenced by the devotional pattern of the Buddhist Sahajiyas. There is no evidence to prove that they were influenced by any other invocation.

Panchkari Bandopadhyay (1886-1923)[2]

The Gaudiya Vaisnava religion introduced by Caitanya is another element of the importance of the Bengalees. This Vaisnava religion (Harekrsna movement) is completely different from the Vaisnavisms in the other provinces of India preached by the Acharyas such as Ramanuja, Vallavacarya, Madhvacarya, Nimberka etc. I had the fortune to listen the Harikirtan and bhajan (devotional songs), at various places, such as Vrndavana, Mathura,

---

[1] Medieval History of Benga: p. 108.
[2] Bangalir Bashistata: Bangabani, Bhadra, 1329. (1935).

and at Nathadvara. In these bhajans and kirtans of Western India, swapchadi class (untouchables) of people were kept out. There is no such restriction in the Harikirtan in Bengal, introduced by Caitanya. All the castes higher or lower can enjoy equally the pleasure of listening namsankirtan. In these types of namsankirtan no—body, would lose caste, just by the touch of the swapchadi class. Not only this, on the ground where kirtan is held, a higher class Brahmin with sacred thread may not have any hesitation to roll under the influence of emotion with kirtan, in the dust shredded by the feet belonging to all castes, the singers and the participants. In the crowd of all the kirtan singers, if some lumps of sugars are thrown as prasadam (small quantity of good graced with the blessing of the God), during kirtan, would be picked up and put in the mouth by every-body from the lowest class candals to the highest caste Brahmins. So much not had been possible by the Vaisnavas of any the provinces apart from the Bengali Vaisnavas. These sorts of incidences regularly occur at the kirtans of the Gaudiya Vaisnava at Vrndavana[1]

There was a revolution of the Hindu society and its literature, when it came in confrontation with early Islamic religion and Muslim civilization. As a result of this revolution, there appeared Goraknath, Ramananda, Nanak and Caitanya as social reformer, staying in one side[2].

The fear of spreading the Muslim religion in India, axed the root of the caste system. Those who were at the lower level and at the bottom of the Hindu society all along in their life, became the most honourable members by the grace of the Islam.

The candals (lower castes) who as a Hindu could never dream of sitting in a same place with a higher caste, could sit in a same place with Muslims and Kshatriya, if he became a Muslim. Consequently, the Sudras the financial backbone of the society and the expertise of the industries, started changing their religion to be Muslim, in large number. There appeared an uneven revolution in the society. On the other hand, the poetry and the composition of the poet such as Sadi, Hafez, Ferdousi and Omar-Kshaium, brought new ideas and new message in-front of the Hindus. There were innovations of the Hindu ideas also (bhava-biplab). For the self-defence

---

[1] Medieval History of Benga: p. 109.
[2] Bangali Manisay Sri-Caitanya by N. Gupta, p. 78.

from this insurgence, the Hindu intellectuals, were about to make an understanding with the Islamic force. Goraknath began the propaganda, about the spread of the Saiva dharma, irrespective of caste. On this account Ramananda wanted to make the Vaisnava religion for the service of all the castes. Immersing the practice of religion or morality in bhakti, mixing up with renunciation and by a compromising formula of Hindu and Muslim, Guru Nanak created the Sikh religion. At last by flowing the flood of pure and perfect Haribhakti (devotion to God) and by conquering all the obstacles, Sri Caitanya of Bengal, created a noble religion, by adopting a policy of true love to God. Depending on the spirit of the highest stage of love God, and considering him as a beloved, he distributed Hari namsankirtan to welcome everybody irrespective of their castes. In this way there were some compromise between the Hinduism with the Islam. There was some adjustibility in the Hindu society which became evident.

Subsequently there was some uprising in the Hindu literature also[1]. When Pathan invaded Bengal in the first time, the influence of Buddhist religion was very high in Bengal. When they came and occupied some parts of West Bengal, the Sahajiyas and Buddhist welcome them with a place of very high affection. Consequently the castes of the lowest level of the half of East Bengal accepted the Islamic religion and established a relation with the Pathans, through marriage. The period during the down-fall of the Pathan and the uprise of the Mughals, has been considered as the great critical moment in the fate of the Bengali nation. During this period Caitanya appeared, also appeared Krshnananda Agambagish, Smartha Bhattacharya Raghunandan. In this time also occurred the melbandhan of Devibar and attempt was made to rebuild the social structure of the Bengalis. These one and a half or two centuries were the Augustan period of Bengal and the Bengalis. On one side there was social injustice and unrest, and on the other side at Navadvipa the light of knowledge was lit with hundreds of flames. During these period, the foundation of the importance of the Bengalis, was laid. The work on nation building started. It is difficult to keep the count of so many foreigners who came and lived in Bengal, during the three centuries, when the Pathans were in. Many of the Pathan leaders married Bengali ladies and lived together as husband and wife. Sona bibi

---

[1] Nabin Chandra O Jatiya Abhyuthan: Sahitya, Magh 1315 (1921).

was a big example of these. Gulam Habishi of Abisinia, Juju, Ujbeck etc. many ferocious Muslims came to live in Bengal and due to the relaxation of the Buddhist system, created many half caste class of people. Sri-Caitanya, Nityananda, Krishnananda, Debibar, Agambagish, Raghunandanan, etc. the intellectuals, tried to build up the society, which was very relaxed under Sahajiyas and Buddhists, some sort of classified, disciplined and implied some importance on it. They were in fact the creator of the Bengali Hindu society (modern) and possibly it will not be an exaggeration, if it said that they were the ancient gods of Bengal[1].

After Sir-Caitanya there was no such an exceptional sannyasin (monk), in Bengal. He was not only a monastic. He showed in himself, all the stages of devotion (consciousness) and all the manifestations of bhakti and the order of their expression, one by one, by adopting, practising and incorporating into his own body and mind. His followers used to imagine him as the actual Godhead himself, as they used to visualise, all the manifestation of bhakti full bloom in him. It is doubtful, if anybody else in India, was able to show such a living example of bhakti[2].

Keshab Chandra died before Vaisnavism became full blossom in him. That work was done by Ramakrshna paramhansha. His disciple Swami Vivekananda managed to expand that work. Vaisnava religion has not been fully galvanised yet in Bengal. By the grace of almighty, in future, if any really altruistic monk of great personality, adopt the same principle after renunciation, then he will be able to renovate the Vaisnava religion.

Mahatma Sisir Kumar Ghosh (1804-1911)

Sisir kumar Ghosh, a very well known journalist, has many writings about Caitanya. His comments and observations have been referred previously. Here is one quotation from his writings[3].

"In Sourastra people still show that Banyan tree under which once Sri-Caitanya sat and took rest for a while he was touring on feet. I am quoting from the article I wrote in the magazine called Vishnupriya.

[1] Banglar Upasak Sampradaya: Bangabani, Kartick, 1329, (1935).
[2] Prabahini: Sisirkamar Ghosh, 20 Poush, B.S. 1321 (1927).
[3] Bangali Manisay Sri-Caitanya: by N. Gupta, p. 54.

(Ramjadav Bagchi, a follower of Gauranga, once went to a South Indian tour, to visit the cave of Ilora. Within this cave there are various types of half-broken temples. This place is very remote a few days journey from Bombay. After taking lots of trouble to reach there, when appeared Ramjadav babu found a Radha-Krsna temple there.)

He found there was arrangement for regular evening prayer and was very surprised by watching an incidence there, when the prayer started. He saw a few Vaisnavas of that country started singing our sankirtan (Hare Krsna . . . .), with drums and kartal of our country in front of the images. The reasons for saying our sankirtan, as it was exact like our sankirtan, although the accent was different. Ramjadav babu was surprised to hear the name of Gauranga, while they were singing. His body was shaken with the astonishment. Ramjadav babu was amazed, on thinking how our sankirtan and the name, the son of Brahmin of Navadvipa, reached such a remote dense forest. At the end of the singing he asked the Vaisnavas about this information. But they could not say much. Ramjadav babu was very determined to gather this information. For this purpose he stopped there for two days and after the intense search he met an old Vaisnava. Being asked he answered, "this drum, kartal and kirtan have come the same Bengal where you are from. When asked how did it come from he answered again "the one who was Caitanya deva in your country once sang and danced in front of this temple". On his tour on feet, Gauranga once danced in front of the temple of Ilora. That was four hundreds years ago. That word and waves are still existing there. Please try to appreciate this fact then you will understand what sort of powerful material Gauranga was"[1].

Rangalal Bandopadhyay (1827-1887)

A quotation "I had to stay for the Government work in the country of Utkal (Orrissa) for many years. It had been changed hundred times than what I saw when I came first. The education has spread enormously. The light of knowledge has reached the remote areas, like the sunshine in a very deep dark cave of a mountain. By watching the past work and the activities of the

---

[1] Bangali Manisay Sri-Caitanya: by N. Gupta: p. 54.

people here, any kind hearted person, would realize that there were many hidden seeds of glorious power, in the mind of the people of Utkal.

Once they were armed with bravery and knowledge. Being the neighbouring country, they were well acquainted with the Bengal, since many years. To save himself from the tyranny of the Muslins the last Hindu ruler of Bengal, took shelter in this very country. Biswambar Misra the best descendant of the Vaidic Brahmin, who later became famous as Bhagavan Sri-Krsna Caitanya, during his tour in western India, once in this very country, managed to preach his view (Hare Krsna movement) very successfully and drive out the Buddhist religion from this country. To speak truly at least one-third of the whole population of this country, are of his followers and they respect him as an incarnation of God.

Nearly 370 years has passesd, since Caitanya deva preached his view at Srikshetra (a place in Orissa). At that time he himself saw the downfall of the Buddhist religion. King Prataprudra deva also originally belonged to Buddhist religion. Possibly these were the reasons, why Sankaracharya, Ramanuja, and Caitanya, had to plan a special skilful strategy, to bring back the people of Utkal, who were loyal to the very deep rooted Buddhist religion. They instead uprooting the tree of Bodidruma (tree of Buddha religion) of Buddhist view, might have trimmed some of its additional branches like practices and converted that into a shape of a tree of Sanatana dharma (Hindu Religion).

In the Vaisnava religion mentioned in the Vedas, the prescription of violence such as sacrifice, by killing animal, were in practice. The non-violence or the prohibition of killing animal, were the views of Ramamanda, Ramanuja and Caitanya, but were in fact the non-violence, the main objectives or the advice of the Buddhist[1].

Raj Nararayan Basu (1826-1899)

Caitanya deva appeared shortly after Vidyapati and Candidasa. The disciples of Caitanya contributed enormously in the development of the Bengali literature. When Caitanya had been organising the work of social reform in Bengal, Nanak had been doing the same work at Punjab and Luther in

---

[1]   Kanchi Kaveri (Itroduction and Footnote): Kartic (November) 1877.

Europe. At that time there was some weather of a religious reform in the world. The inspiration of religion is contagious. Caitanya used to be able to stimulate others because he himself was insane with religion. 'At the last stage of his profession in general teaching, hardly any other word would come out from his mouth apart from the name of Hari. He was equipped with an extraordinary charming appearance and no doubt this had helped him enormously to accomplish his work. In those days there were no easy transport and communications, (or louhabarta), still Caitanya managed to tour from Rameswar Setubandha to Vrndavana, and preached his own religion with immense enthusiasm. I have seen myself at places such as Kanpur etc. Hindusthani (inhabitant of Hindu dominated India) followers of Caitanya. To perform the sort of work, related to the religious reform, the learned person of the nineteenth century became scared. Caitanya was able to achieve part of it, under the influence of the contagious, religious insanity.

He was able to make the start of the remarriage of the widows, inter-caste marriage and conversion of some Muslims within the fold of the Vaisnava religion[1].

The preaching of the Vaisnava religion of Caitanya, at this time gave a new life to the mind of the Bengalis. This was the time when Bengali language received new enthusiasm and pleasure and many religious books were composed.

At this time Rupa Goswami composed "Ragamaya Kosh" related to control the passions, Sanatana Goswami composed "Rasakalika", Jiva Goswami "Karchai", Vrndavana Das "Caitanya Bhagavata," Lochan Das "Caitanya Mangal", and Krishnadas Kaviraj composed "Caitanya Caritamrita".

In this period other people such as Rai Sekhar, Basudeva Ghosh, Narahari Das, Jadu Nandan, Jnana Das, Govinda Das, etc. poet singers also composed of many songs known as padavali kirtan.

---

[1]   Ibid: p. 119, Lecture on Bengali Language and Literature, 1878.

Rabindranath Tagore (1861-1941)

The Tagore family in general was very much admirer of the Vaisnavas. They appointed Vaisnava nuns as teachers for the ladies of the family[1]. Professional Kirtana singers were very often employed to sing padavali kirtan in Tagore house[2]. Rabindranath was deeply impressed by the language, rhythm and the spiritual touch of the Vaisnava poetry and songs. He witnessed the beginning of the nationalist movement, during his adolescence and early youth. Many national leaders were inspired by the nonviolent movement of Caitanya. He himself developed great interest for Vaisnava literature as it was very much a part of Bengali culture. This was evident from his edition of 'Padaratnavali' anthology in 1985[3]. His liking of padavali kirtana particularly of Vidyapati and Candidasa is evident in many of his songs and poem. His view was that "Vidyapati sings of the happiness of love and Candidasa's theme is the soul stiring agony of love".

In a letter to Brajendranath Sil Tagore wrote that he had imbibed the spiritual ideas from the Upanishads and Vaisnava poetry[4]

The poet admired Caitanya mainly for three reasons:

(i) He thought that it was Caitanya who by his Harekrsna movement, put an end to the Bengal's insularity.

(ii) It was Caitanya who had the supreme courage to preach the gospel of universal love at a time when Brahminical orthodoxy was trying to make the artificial caste divisions extremely rigid.

(iii) The advent of Caitanya brought about a brilliant literary efflorescence[5].

---

[1] Vaisnavism in Bengal: by R. Chakravarty, p. 445.

[2] Gharer Katha O Yugasahitya: by Dineshchandra Sen, pp. 182-83.

[3] Rabindra Sahitye Padavalir Sthan: by Bimanbihari Majumdar, pp. 12, 103-01.

[4] 'Chithipatra' Rabindra Rachanavali, Visvabharati ed. Vol. 2, 1939, p. 528; Vaisnavism in Bengal: by R. Chakravarty, p. 447.

[5] Bangali Manishaye Sri-Caitanya: by N.N. Gupta, pp. 127-28.

The poet attributed the sixteenth century renaissance in Bengal to the Vaisnava concept of universal liberation and the cult of divine love. Tagore wrote:

> *"Liberation was not the monopoly of the few fortunate.*
> *God cannot be confined within the scriptural corpus.*
> *As soon as this sublime idea was postulated, all the*
> *sleeping birds of our country woke up and began to sing.*
> *Bengal discovered herself only during the Vaisnava age.*
> *During the Sakta age Bengal remained spiritually poor.*
> *But Vaisnava brought her fulfillment."*

The beauty of the nature reminded him of the rhythm of Vaisnava poetry. He believed that the 'eternal' Vrndavana lay in the every fresh beauty of the nature.

In describing the influence of Harekrsna movement in poetry and songs the poet's view was like this[1]:

The uproar produced by the Vaisnava religion in Bengal due to the advent of Caitanya, was extraordinary in relation to a religion. By these the released soul of the human being was eager to express itself with the emotion of the thought of bhakti. In these circumstances, people not only enjoy as an inmate object, but create as an ambulatory one. For these reasons on that day, Bengalis started to reveal itself in poetry and songs. At that time it was not possible to continue the usual tradition of composition, with the repetition of prayer, and Tripodi style and to recite it repeatedly. It broke the limitations which was not in fact a disastrous flood but a tremendous flow of creation.

In the sky, there is a divine beauty of the vastness. But the expression of the creation is not of this vastness. The end of the creation is in the identification of each and every star which stand out as an individual and makes several, the great unity of the universe. This great emanate of individual identity in Bengali literature is known as Romantic movement in English (literature).

---

[1]   Ibid: p. 127.

This individual endeavor was not only visible in poetry but in songs also. The fallacious songs could not stand in-front of such a great flow. At that time, music was looking for such a tune which would not express the general beauty of the Ragas and Raginis, but express the significance of the individual emotions of the heart. Before the Caitanya era, as Vaisnava religion was ignored by the Pandita (teacher) of Sastra, similarly kirtan songs were not favoured by the teachers of music[1].

There is another importance of the kirtana which is for the historical reasons. There came once in Bengal, the era of democracy in the practice of religion or in the enjoyment of the thought of the religion and these were due to the strength of the thought of the Vaisnavas. On that day, the emotions of the aggregated soul, wanted to be expressed through the aggregated voice. These expressions were not at the conference hall, but in the roads and streets. The kirtans of Bengal provided, a very broad voice, for blending with the sound of the expressions of the emotional thought of the people.

When a natural devotee is born in a society, habituated with the image worship, due to his extraordinary power, sometimes can see the inner objects in it, beyond the image. His inner vision cannot be restricted by some visible boundary, from the infinity. His mind supersede that what is in his sight, with the speed of a thunder.

The external pretexts are his habit only and it is not necessary to get rid of them.

The very material world is like a story to him, and the image even less important. As a person acquainted with the alphabets, does not see TREE as letters when written on a piece of paper, but sees immediately with his inner vision, a real tree (plant) with branches and leaves; similarly he does not take notice of the object situated in front of him, but enjoy the real pleasure of the inner meaning of it (*jato bacho nivatante aprapya manasa saha*). But this enchantment is possible only by supernatural genius. Caitanya had that type of talent[2].

---

[1]   Bangali Manishaye Sri-Caitanya: by N.N. Gupta,: p. 127.
[2]   Ibid: p. 128: Sakar O Nirakar: Rabindra Rachanabali, Centenary.

Bankim Chandra Chattopadhyaya (1838-1894)

He was a Deputy Magistrate and very famous Bengali novelist.

Bankim Chandra interpreted ancient Indian History and suggested that the future religious prospects of India would depend in terms of Vaisnava idealism (HKM).

Bankim Chandra's deep acquaintances with Vaisnavism and Vaisnava lyrics is evident in many of his novels. In 'Durgesnandini" (1865), a fool named Gajapatividyadiggaja takes himself as Krsna, and regards a Muslim lady named Asmani as Radha[1]. A mendicant Vasnavi named Girijaya sings many Vaisnava songs in 'Mrinalini' (1869). Girijaya is depicted as a mysterious figure. Hardasi Vaisnavi is a key figure in the celebrated novel 'Visavrksa' (1873). She is an expert singer[2]. In the novel 'Visavrksa', there is a reference to murial paintings of Krsna and his queens[3].

In 'Indira' (1873) a young and sprightly girl sings a Vaisnava song to entertain her sister and brother-in-law[4]. Popular Vaisnava songs are recorded in 'Chandrasekhara' (1875)[5]. Vaisnava song which was composed in Hindi, is quoted in 'rajasimha' (1882)[6].

Bankim Chandras 'Anandamath' may be regarded as a "Vaisnava" political novel, since its principal characters are Vaisnava Goswamins, however, did not belong to the Gaudiya Vaisnava order, though they sang the songs of 'Gitagovinda'. Satyananda Goswamin, their leader, said that Vaisnavism (HKM) in the real sense of the term meant the suppression of roguery and the redemption of the world. Real Vaisnavism was a combination of love and spiritual strength[7] The Goswamis of 'Anandamath' are described great patriot who had renounced the world with the sacred purpose of liberating their motherland from the Yaban, as he decribes.

---

[1] Bankim Racanavali: Ed. Jogesh Chandra Bagal, Sahityasmsad ed. 1956, Vol. p. 70.

[2] Ibid: pp. 273, 285.

[3] Ibid: p. 333.

[4] Ibid: p. 382.

[5] Ibid: pp. 404, 466.

[6] Ibid: p. 647.

[7] Ibid: p. 750.

He appreciated GaudyaVaisnava indifference to caste system. He thought that the Vaisnava worship of Radha-Krsna was but the worship of a symbol[1]. His interpretation of 'Priti' or Friendship was influenced by the Gaudiya Vaisnava ideologoy[2].

Miachael Madhusudan Datta (1824-1873)

A famous Bengali poet was well known for his 'Virangana', 'Vrajangana Kavya' and 'Meghanathabada Kavya'.

It is already mentioned before that 'Vrndavana' particularly the activities of Radha was hardly known before the appearance of Caitanya. Since then hardly there was any well known Bengali writer who did not use the activities of Vrndavana in his composition.

Though himself was a Christian and well versed in English and continental literature, he became famous for his Bengali composition on the material of 'Ramayana and Vrndavana'. He was deeply impressed by the Radha-Krsna legend. On the theme of separation of Radha from Krsna, he composed 'Vrajangana Kavya' (1861). He could not forget Sita and Radha. Some of his Christian friends disliked his high regards for the Hindu heroines. In a letter to Rajnarayan Basu he wrote: "I think you are cold towards the poor lady of Vraja. Poor man! When you sit down to read poetry, leave aside all religious bias. Besides Mrs. Radha is not such a bad woman after all"[3]. The language, the mood and the metrical form of the Vrajangana Kavya are quite different from those of kavi, padavali and the panchali songs. The central theme of viraha or the pang of separation, was described in the book in a tasteful language as something intensely human and distinctly individual. The influence of Vrajangana Kavya is seen in some of the contemporary Kavyas (poetry). Michael used the Vrndavana imagery even in his celebrated 'Meghanadavadha Kavya' (1860).

The life and experience of the famous poet were not happy. He suffered from dire poverty in the later part of his life. It was perhaps quite natural for him to seek escape in the soothing Vrndavana legend. Krsna and the

---

[1] Bankim Racanavali: Vol. 2, p. 269.
[2] Ibid: pp. 339, 905-06.
[3] Michael Madhusudan Datter Jivancharit: by J.N. Basu, 1983, p. 341.

enchanting music of his flute are very often referred to by the sensitive poet in 'Meghanadavada Kavya' and other poems[1]

Navinchandra Sen (1847-1909)

He was also a Deputy Magistrate and a well known writer and poet.

According to him both Buddha and Krsna rejected caste and thus laid the foundation of the Indian brand of socialism. Buddhism was what later transformed into Vaisnavism[2].

The story of Krsna, the founder and the organiser of the socialistic Mahabharata, or Great India was the subject of Navinchandra's trilogy, Raivataka (1889), Kuruksetra (1893), and Prabhasa (1896). The poet also wrote a kavya (a book of poetry), on Caitanya in twelve cantos entitled Amrtabha.

Navinchandra described the non-violent and vegetarian Vaisnavism as branch of Mahayana Buddhism[3] He rejected caste system and his writings were against conservative Brahminical authority. He stated the following reasons for describing Krsna in his trilogy as a leader of the down trodden Sudras[4].

(1) According to the legend of the Bhagavata Purana, Krsna even in his boyhood had repudiated the ceremonial Yajna, and preached the philosophy of Karma.

(2) The Brahmin priests were so angry with Krsna that they refused to give him any food even when he was once terribly hungry.

(3) Krsna and his Kshatriya friends, the Pandavas, once humiliated Durvasa, an ever angry Brahmin sage.

(4) Brahmin sage named Bhrgu once gave Krsna a terrific kick on his breast.

---

[1] Vaisanvaism in Bengal: by R. Chakravarty, pp. 442-43.

[2] Amar Jivan: by Navinchandra Sen, Ed. Sajanikanta Das, Part I, Vol 2, 3, and 4, p. 460.

[3] Ibid: p. 15.

[4] Ibid: p. 464 465; Vaisnavism in Bengal: by Dr. R. Chakravarty, p. 428.

(5) The logical conclusion is that a powerful sections of the Brahmins somehow became the unrelenting enemies of Krsna. These Brahmins formed a league with uncivilized non-Aryans, and ultimately affected the total destruction of Krsna and his family.

Vijoykrsna Goswami (1841-1899)

He was a prominent Brahma preacher and social reformer. Gradually he had detached himself from the Brahma movement and became a Vaisnava guru. Vijoy Krsna Goswami was an 'eclectic' Vaisnava. He was a friend of the Vrndavana Goswami, the Naga ascetics of the mountains, the Muhammadan Fakirs, the Tantrika mystics, the Gaudiya Vaisnava Babajis of the Akhdas (the full time Vaisnavas of the centres), the Christian Salvation Army, the Brahmins and the Brahminical priests. With so many and such varied links, Vijoykrsna was certainly an uncommon Vaisnava. His guru was an Brahmananda Svamin who was almost as old as Methuselah, and who lived in the unexplorable regions of the mystic 'ManasaSaravara' in the Himalayas[1]. It is interesting to note that his views on caste were similar to those of Kedarnath Datta. According to him there were only three castes, in accordance with three qualities of Sattva, Raja, and Tamas[2]. Most of his disciples were house holders such as Asvini kumar Datta (1858-1932), Manoranjan Guhathakurta, Bipinchandra Pal and Svarna kumari (1867-1932). All of them were very prominent people and helped for the propagation of HKM. Some of them were ascetic also like Satish Chandra Mukhapadhaya, Kiran Chand Darbesh (d. 1878), and Kuladananda Brahmacari (1867-1930).

---

[1] Ibid: p. 437 438; Sadguru Sri Vijoykrsna: by Tarinicharan Choudhuri, 1973, pp. 563-75.

[2] Sri Sri Sadgurusanga: by Kuladananda Brahmachri, Vol. 2, pp. 115-16; Vol. 3, p. 118.

5.Travels of a Hindu: by Bholanath Chandra, Vol, p29.

Bholanath Chandra (1822-1910)

A pupil of D.L. Richardson, published, his 'Travels of a Hindu' in two volumes in 1869. In volume one of this work, he gave a very lucid account of the HKM of Caitanya and its effects. He wrote, "Caitanya is now truly appreciated by the discerning generations of the nineteenth century as a reformer[1]. He had special emphasis on Caitanya's struggle against the Tantrikas, his strong opposition to the caste system and his propagation of the cause of the remarriage of Hindu widows[2]. He wrote "an innovation of Caitanya have produced an important era in Bengal which deserve a prominent recognition that history has not yet taken"[3].

Jyotirindranath Tagore (1849-1925)

Jyotiridranath Tagore did not share, his father's respect for caste differences. He wrote that it was not an essential duty for the genuine Hindu to observe caste rules. According to him Caitanya, who was decidedly a Hindu, violated no social law when he converted Haridasa, a Muhmmadan.

He wished the rebirth of a great man like Caitanya with the mission of flashing out caste distinctions[4].

Shoshee Chunder Dutt

An uncle of Ramesh Chunder Dutt (1848-1909), ICS, and an eminent Bengali intellectual.

Shoshee Chunder described as "new idea for Hinduism, ... With the glorification of the faith of Caitanya, also repudiated the caste. This changed the character of Vaisnavism completely and greatly raised it in importance . . . . the success of his religion was at the outset was almost as great as that of Buddhism under Sakya. One great concession it made to humanity was that it did not demand the renunciation of home and family

---

[1] Travels of a Hindu: by Bholanath Candra, Vol. 1, p. 29.
[2] Ibid: p. 30-31.
[3] Ibid: p. 36.
[4] Sahitya Sadhaka Caritamals: by J.N. Tagore, Vol. 6, pp. 66-67.

ties". Dutta however noted that some of the Vaisnavas from the upper caste followed the caste restrictions[1].

Aksayakumar Datta (1820-1886)

A journalist and a great researcher of Hindu religion, published in the 'Tattvavodhini Patrika' which he edited between 1832 and 1845. He collected materials for a detailed study of the Indian sects. The result of his research was in the form of a book 'Bharatiya Upasaka Sampradaya' (two volumes, 1870-1883).

A detailed, unprejudiced and objective account of 99 Vaisnava, 59 Saiva and 24 Sakta sects was given in these two volumes. The total number of sects mentioned in the volumes was 182.

Two decades earlier, Wilson did similar study and published in his 'Sketch of the Religious Sects of the Hindus' (1846) and gave the account of 45 sects[2].

Rashikchandra Ray (1820-1893)

Rashikchandra Ray composed some Vaisnava poem complete different from Padavali. Some other poets who also wrote new types of Vaisnava poems, were Banoarilal Ray (1863), Jadavananda Ray (1870), and Ganeshchandra Bandopadhyaya (1864). In fact hardly there were any well known poet existed at that time who did not write about Caitanya or Vaisnavism. In between 1858 and 1900, there were records of seventy-five poets who wrote nearly five hundred lyric poems which had the touch of Vaisnava influence.

The well known literate Dr. Harekrishna Mukhopadhyay, the master of the Vaisnava literature, gave an account in his publication of 'Vaisnava Padavali' of two hundred twenty six poets, writing about four thousands Vaisnava lyrics[3]. This undoubtably proves the enormous amount of material,

---

[1]   India: Past and Present, by Shoshee Chunder Dutt, pp. 159-62.
[2]   Vaisnavism in Bengal: by Dr. R. Chakravorty, p. 421.
[3]   Vaisnava Padavali: by Dr. Harekrishna Mukhopadhyay, Calcutta, Sahitya Sansad, 1980.

the Vaisnavism has provided to the poets and writers, over the years to make the Bengali literature so rich.

Jogindranath Bhattacharya

He explained the sociological significance of the HKM movement in his book 'Hindu Caste and Sects' (1896). His assessment of the movement was mixed. While he was a supporter of the Brahminical Tantrika tradition and was not prepared to recognise Caitanya as a 'great reformer' but accepted him as a genius like a statesman[1]. He was generous enough to admit that "of all the great teachers of the world no one has done more to popularize religion than Caitanya". He concluded that the inevitable result of the movement was to cause relaxation of religion from the grip of thought of the old Hindu Rishis (monks who usually pray in lonely forest). Max Weber describes Jogindranath as "An upper pandit, loyal adherent to English dominion and the caste order, and hater of the plebeian gurus"[2].

Suniti Kumar Chattopadhyay

The professor describes here his view about Caitanya. How his philosophy, his movement influenced the Bengali and Sanskrit literature and their effect on the Bengalis and on the Indian Hindus as a whole.

"The expansion of Bengalis, similar to which we understand as greater Bengal to-day, occurred only once and as a noble one too, due to the influence of Caitanya deva, prior to Mughal period. But there was no Gaudiyaism or Bengalism in knowledge, at all like in our time. The advent of Caitanya would not let Bengali stay as house bound or introverted. The invitation he gave for preaching the name of Hari, would not let him to be restricted in his own house or village. He had to come out. He had to be prominent once more for spiritual reasons, if it was not for the political one and had to be an Indian, rather than a Bengali. Caitanya was an ideal man among the Bengalis and was the best among the prominent Bengalis. But he does not belong to Bengal only, he was placed on a very much higher level than

---

[1] Vaisnavism in Bengal: by Dr. R. Chakravorty, p. 421.

[2]

that of Bengalism. It would be unfair and unscrupulous, if his name was used to increase the status of Bengalism and it would be an indignity for his departed soul if it was done.

I heard from a Oriya pandit at Puri saying with deep devotion with bhakti "Mahaprabhu (Catianya's another name) was a super natural person; He does not belong to any particular community (caste) in India. He was amongst the Bengalis during the childhood and at adolescent, within the people of central and south India some part of his adult life and the last phase of his carrier he had spent amongst the Oriya."

As the result of the teaching of Caitanya, there was the establishment of the Gaudiya Vaisnava sampradaya (community), Bengalis went to Puri, the temples of the remote Vrndavana were rescued and the development of Vrndavana was made, as one of the main centres of Vaisnava thought and philosophy.

After the Hindu period again the pandit (teacher), devotees and workers of Gaudiya Bengal started moving and residing outside Bengal.

Since the sixteenth century, due to the residence of the Vaisnava Gosamins, such as Sri-Rupa, Sanatana, Jiva etc., Vrndavana became one of the foremost centre for the Sanskrit pandita of Bengal and Gaudiya Vaisnava religion.

During the Muslim period apart from the Vaisnava religion introduced by Sri-Caitanya and his disciples no other movement evolved from Bengal that had spread all over India. Because it was a religious movement, there was nothing particularly of Bengalism in it. The major portion of the Bengali culture was nourished due to the advent of the great personality of Caitanya.

The teachings and the life history of Caitanya had created or introduced many new systems in Bengali culture. The prestige of the sanskrit knowledge was not eroded in his hand. The philosophical justification in the sanskrit language and the composition of thought in this region, were introduced. The original books, criticism, and poems were composed by the Vaisnava gurus (teacher), regarding Caitanya and the Goswamins and that of Vrndavana, were unprecedented creation in the Bengali culture, from the point of view of knowledge and intellects. The expression of the heart and the sense of appreciation that is noticeable in Vaisnava padavali (mamoth composition on the activities of Radha and Krsna at Vrndavana), is the result of the inspiration from Caitanya. Besides these the image adopted in the popular folk songs, and the very tastes developed in kirtanas, the life of the Bengali music, are the prasadam (the sacrificed food for the god after worship) of Caitanya. Leaving the family and home, the introverted Bengali, went to Puri, Gaya, Kashi, Vrndavana, Joypur and further west with new enthusiasm, and in sixteenth and seventeenth century really established a glorious greater Bengal.

The influence of Caitanya was noticeable here also"[1].

Gopal Chandra Halder

The author described his view about the influence of Caitanya and Harekrsna movement in the Bengali literature, which in turn, influenced the heart of the numerous people across the general mass of population over the centuries[2].

"The love (prem) appeared only once in this world, and that was in Bengal." this was the version of the very famous historian of the Bengali literature, the late Dinesh Chandra Sen. This statement may be felt as an exaggeration to some people. But it is the view, not of his own. It is the view of the majority of the general Bengalees, male and female. Caitanya was an incarnation of love to many of them and as a living image of the supernatural great thought to even more of them. If it is analysed from the historical point of view, of the Bengali literature, the unprecedented inspiration that was provided by this love insane sannyasin (monk), to the life and history of the Bengalees, then the appearance of Caitanya must have to be accepted as the greatest incidence of the Bengali literature. Possibly apart from Rabindranath (the World Poet), no one else was able to make the Bengali literature so blithe some, with the inspiration of creation. So although he himself did not write a lot, Caitanya was the prime person in the history of the Bengali literature, in the preBritish period.

In the medieval period in India, Europe and in many other countries, the appearance of many of these types of religious persons with spiritual thought and their preachers, were visible.

---

[1] Bangali Manishaye Sri-Caitanya: by N.N. Gupta, p. 139.
[2] Ibid: p. 141.

Nothing is strange in it; because the society was restricted with strict rule of the boundary period. The effect of these restrictions were sometimes unbearable to the kind hearted people. They were the great men of those days, and the unconscious dissidents. Their revolt in those days, naturally used to take place, under some religious cover.

By these way the strict administration of the practical political power and from the power of the society, could be avoided. Many times the tyranny of the administrative force could be avoided also.

Of course, it is not that this revolt would not have any effect on practical field. At the time of the boundary period when the whole society was hesitant and organized on the policy of division, this spiritual and profound prem bhaktibad would not differentiate man from man. This spiritual policy of indifferentiation wanted to wipe out the line of differentiation between man and man. their followers came from the common people. For these reasons, almost in every country, these religious preachers and followers, had been tortured, by the ruling force. This was particularly very true in case of Sufi devotee of Persia and the Sikhs, the disciples of Nanak. In the medieval period what was true for other religious leaders, was true for Caitanya also. His view about the religion of love, in fact was a protest, against the traditional system of the society, but was not completely free from it. His policy did not agree with the system of the society, at the same time, he was not prepared to deny it completely. Caitanya as a representative of the cultural dissident group, against the Hindu society under the Muslim rulers, was in favour of a very fair and open minded Hindu society. He did not revolt directly against the caste system only. But denying the system of the society, he preached the ideals of showing kindness to all the living creatures, the devotion of bhakti to God, particularly the religion of the name of Hari, the namsankirtan. In this country of the different rights, for the different class, he preached for the religion of equal right from the top class Brahmin to the lowest class Candal, through namsankirtan. The namasankirtan in an aggregated mass in the roads and streets of Navadvipa, in the Rathayatra festival at Puri, was in fact the great get-together of the love of the people of all the castes. There even Yavan Haridas (Muslim) was regarded as his closest associate; all these prove the endeavor of Caitanya for the great reform of the society[1].

In this country, in this society, comparing with this period, surely we may call this idealism and endeavour of reform a democratic one, in terms of the modern language, although it remained neutral about the political force and not eager to deny the force of the society also. In this regard Caitanya deva is comparable with Buddha deva. Both of them were great reformer of the society, but none of them were terrorist or political dissident totally.

The role of Caitanya also was as a principal social reformer and dissident as a thinker, unlike other ordinary religious teacher in the medieval period. We can see him exercising his own role also, in the Bengali society. One side by stopping the (sechchhachar) misbehaviour amongst the aristocrat and on the other side, by preaching the name of Hari through namasankirtan and giving equal right to everybody irrespective of their caste, he gave a real shape to the cultural reform movement of the oppressed class. Thirdly, Caitanya helped to build up a Hindu society of closer link of all by brining the top and lower class together to each other, with the same principle and same idealism of simple religious practice. He managed to remove from the mind of the society, the luxuries of the ceremonial religious functions of the early days to some extent and instead in that mind arouse in general, some sort of love for the period (that's why devotee of Caitanya like to think *"pranamaha kaliyuga sarvayuga sar"*) and the value of humanity. The most negligible person could be pure in heart if he pray for Krsna (*"muchi hoye suchi hoy jadi krsna bhaje"*)[2]

As a result of this cultural reformation of the society, an unprecedented luxury of thought was evident in the literature, music and philosophy of the Bengalees.

But this elevation of the Bengalees were not complete because it did not reach to all the areas of the practical life and political field. Still that development was a great celebration, and in literature, primarily it was a gift from Caitanya and his followers.

Caitanya himself did not organise any particular community. But even during his lifetime, there were more than one sect developed around

---

[1]   Bangali Manishaye Sri-Caitanya: by N.N. Gupta, pp. 7, 142.
[2]   Bangali Manishaye Sri-Caitanya: by N.N. Gupta, p. 142

him who believed in the Harekrsna movement. Instead of vaidhibhakti, the one prescribed in the scriptures, the followers of Caitanya accepted, raganuragabhakti as the means of best devotion.

His followers at Navadvipa regarded Caitanya as the Godhead himself. At Sri-Khanda the conception was different. Caitanya and his devotees were regarded in the similar way, as were Krsna and Gopies at Vrndavana, as nagar (male lover) and nagari (as female lover) respectively.

After the death of Caitanya few of these subgroups became prominent, such as one around Advaitaya Acharya, one around Gadadhar (Gauranga paramyabad or Gauranga pujari sampradaya), and another group around Nityananda. The group which was under Nityananda, also included sixteen hundred Nada Nedi, who originally belonged to the nearly obsolete Sahajiya tantric sects of the Buddhist religion. It is understandable that the Harekrsna movement of Caitanya was like an open gate for the Sahajiya tantric from the very beginning. The influence of Sahajiyas are also noticeable amongst the Vaisnavas of Srikhanda and in the name of Nityananda it was the Sahajiyas who became the largest sections of the Vaisnavas. That was the reasons why the prakriti sadhana and parakiya tatta (devotion to women and extra-marital love) became easily incorporated among the Vaisnavism[1].

The singing of Harekrsna is common in all these various groups of Vaisnavas. All these branches are still alive to some extent; although some branches have become more prominent. But actually the Gaudiya Vaisnava religion was established, by the six Goswamins staying at Vrndavana. The great renunciated devotees, very well versed in bhakti sastra (knowledge about religion), all these Goswamis were at Vrndavana, far away from the feud of all these branches in Bengal.

By staying at Vrndavana in the atmosphere of other devotees such as the followers of Ramanuja and Madhva, composed and edited their own views, information, and system of devotion based on smriti sastra and purana, particularly founded on Bhagavata purana and bhakti sastra. According to that view also Caitanya was the incarnation of God. But Krsna and his Vrndavana activities were the main theme of their philosophy. The raganuraga bhakti is the main path of devotion according to them also. But in practice the pure and simple attitude prescribed in the scriptures, were

---

[1] Bangali Manishaye Sri-Caitanya: by N.N. Gupta, p. 143.

the main advice given by the Goswamins. The Vaisnava society of Bengal was organised gradually to adopt the rule prescribed and preached by these Goswamins. Of course, raganuraga bhakti is the one what is suppose to wrap up all their endeavour of creation, with the beauty of the poetry and establish the name of Caitanya above all the yugas[1].

Bipin Chandra Pal

In *Bengal Vaisnavism*, p.103. mentioned "Outside the Hindu communion, Mahaprabhu's message proselytised entire non-Hindu clans by initiating them in the name of the Lord. We thus find the whole clan of Manipuria in northeastern India becoming Vaisnavas of the school of Sir—Caitanya Mahaprabhu".

E.P. Rice

In, *A Hisory of Kanarese Literature*, p. 21. has pointed "And finally, in the sixteenth century, a wave of Vaisnava enthusiasm, inspired by Caitanya preaching the doctrine of Krishnabhakti, swept over the peninsula (South India), and completed the alienation of the people from the austere teaching of the Jainas"

Dinesh Chandra Sen

A song from a great poet singer Chandidas, is like this:

> *"Aju kego murali bajay, eta kabhu nahe syamaray.*
> *Ihar gaur barane kare alo, chudati badhiya keva dila . . .*
> *Chandidas mane mane hashe, arup haive kon deshe."*

—It means, who is the one still playing flute ? It never could be syam (Krsna). His golden colour emits light. Who has styled his hair as a crown? Candidas wondered himself, where would this be possible? Repeating the question, where could this be possible? The author answered like this The

---

[1] Bangalli Manishaye Sri-Caitanya: by N.N. Gupta, p. 143.

love of God appeared only once in this world and that was in Bangladesh. Candidas was not alive at that time to watch it. There was opportunity of meeting between Candidas and another great singer poet Vidyapati and also meeting took place between Caitanya and Roy Ramananda, which was very nice. But it would have been much nicer and wonderful if Candidas stayed till the appearance of Caitanya to meet him. The blending of the love insanity to the music and the love insanity of life, would have taken place in the similar way as the blending of the perfume of the roses with the perfume of the lotus. In the description of Candidas the preface, the anxiety of Radha, the pure love and the spiritual love insanity of Radha, all were very evidently shown in the life of Gaur Hari (Caitanya).

If the appearance of Caitanya did not occur, then the important moments in the life of Radha, such as "Jalad nehari nayane jharu lor"—means on watching the dark coloured cloud. Radha used to have tears in the eyes with the thought of Krsna, cuddle with the dark plant (kadamba) by mistake as the body of dark coloured Krsna, to stare at the neck of the peacock and pea hen (mayur mayuri), and the sweetest dream of thought of the new acquaintances (purbarag), would have remained as the imagination of a poet. This loss of self memory as a result of the expression of emotional thought would have been neglected today, as a dry imagination of a poet.

But Gaur Hari has proved the reality and the truth of the Bhagavata and the Vaisnava songs. He had shown that this enormous sastra (religion) is standing on the base of bhakti, in the loving tears of bhaktas (premasru), and in the devotion of the heart (soul). The stream of the tastes of the activities such as preface, separation, meeting and union etc. are not imagination, are appreciable and have been appreciated.

The wonderful expression of love made the body of Gaur Hari nearly a Kadamba tree, the sound of the wave of ocean became the musical sound of river Yamuna, the Chatack hill became Giri-Gobardhana and the people of this period, became conscious of Krsna.

The characters of the Vrndavana activities would be better understood with the help of the padavali kirtana, with the help of the characters of the Vrndavana activities and both would be better understood with the thought of appreciation of Gaur Hari. I would try to explain these—Candidas described the state of Radha's loss of consciousness with the thought of Krsna like this, *Tulakhani dila nasika majhe tabe bujhila sous ache.* Similar description is given of Caitanya when he became unconscious at the house of Sarbavouma, *Suksha tula ani nasha agrete dhariala, ishat chalay tula dekhidhairja haila.* The meaning of both the quotation is same, as they were tested with some cotton fibres, held in front of the nostril to see if they were breathing at all.

Description of Radha when she watched Tamal tree (*Bijane alingani tarun tamal*) she cuddled the dark colour tamal tree with the mistaken identity as Krsna. Similarly her state of mind when watched the dark coloured cloud (*Chahe megh pane na chale nayaner tara*) when she saw dark cloud stopped blinking and hardly could take her eyes away. In the life of Caitanya also similar incidences were described, *Chatak parvat dekhi Gobardham bhrame, dhaiya chale artanad karia krandane. Jaha nadi dekhe taha manaye kalindi, maha prema bashe nache prabhu pade kandi. Tamaler briksha ek sammukhe dekhiyia, Krsna bali dheye giye dhare jadaiya. Ban dekhi bhrama kare ai Vrndavana.* He had emotional outburst in cry with joy for mistaken identity such as Chatack hill, as Giri-Gobardhana, any river as Kalindi or Yamuna, dark coloured tamal tree as Krsna and any forest as Vrndavana.

In innumerable places Radhika had to be aroused from the state of unconsciousness with the thought of Krsna by uttering his name (*Krsna Keshaba Krsna Keshaba Krsna Keshaba raksha Rai*), similarly, Caitanya had to be aroused in innumerable time by uttering the name of Hari (*Kakhana hai prabhu anande murchhita, karnamule sabe Hari bale ati vita*).

In emotional imbalance, Radhika used to fall on the feet of the person who used to utter the name of Krsna to arouse her from emotional unconsciousness (*paye dhari dande se chikur gari jaye, sonar putali jena bhutale lutaye*). Similarly Caitanya in innumerous time did the similar things.

Krsna anurage sada akul hriday, sunile Krsner nam asru dhara boye. Jadi keha Radha bali uchcha sabda kare, amni asru dharajhar jhar jhare. Prana Krsna bali jadi daibe keha dake, dheye giye alingan karen tahake.

Radhika used to be impatient and would ask her friends with tearful eyes where she could meet Krsna (*Puchhaye Kanu r katha chhala chhala akhi, kothaye dekhila shyam kaha dekhi sakhi*).

Caitanya also used to be emotional and ask his friends where he could find Krsna (*Gadadhare dekhi prabhu karaye jiggas, kotha Hari achhen shymal pitabas. Sambhrame balila Gadadhar maha saye, nirabadhi achhen Hari tomar hridaye. Hridaye achhen Hari bachan suniyia, apan hridaye prabhu chere nakh diya*). Once Caitanya in his emotional state asked Gadadhar where he could find Krsna. Gadadhar answered that Krsna was in the heart of everybody. Immediately Caitanya started to scratch his chest in the semiconscious state.

Being immersed with the thoughts of Krsna, Radhika sometimes used to be happy, by writing with her nail, the name of Krsna on the ground (*bharame tomar nam kshiti tale likhi*). Chaitanya deva also used to write the name of Krsna or draw his portrait on the ground.

The renunciation of Caitanya has created the taste of a drama in the history not only of Navadvipa, but of Bengal as a whole.

Describing the heartbreaking loss of his mother Sachidevi and young wife Vishnupriya, and their shedding of tears, the composers, have poured the stream of melody in the same way as was described in the unbearable condolence of Yasoda and Radha when Krsna left Vrndavana and went to Mathur).

The physical appearance of Caitanyadeva was like a full blossom kadamba flower impregnated with love and his eyes were like the petals of a lotus with full of dew on its surface. A very minimum of the everlasting joy of his love, could be tested to some extent in the description of Candidas. Other poets give the impression of watching him from quite far and composed the songs like a scared audience. The books like "Padakalpataru", tried to give a touch of the account of the super human love of Caitanya. Those who are not acquainted with the activities of his life, may mistake to compare the features of Radhika drawn by the Vaisnava poet, with Audrom, Juliet or Didor. For these reasons I have searched for so many examples. The padavali of the Vaisnava may be thought like a noble or illusion of a magic; but this is a real truth. In the eye of a bhakta (devotee), dark cloud has been mistaken as Krsna (*kena meghe dekhe Rai amon haili*) etc. I have tried to determine the relationship of the Padavalli literature with the numerous books which contributed for the enrichment of the Bengali literature.

1. BangalivManishaye Sri-Caitanya: by N.N.Gupta: pp. 135-38.

P.K. Parameswaran Nair

From, *History of Malayalam Literature*, Chapter VI, p. 64. "This was the period when Vaisnava poets were encircling most literatures of India with their mystic outpourings; . . . there were in the north Kabir, Surdas and Tulsidas writing in the various earlier forms of Hindi. The tide of devotional literature was steadily rising in the south as well. The sojourn of Sri-Krishna Caitanya, he came to Kerala also and heralded a renaissance in the cult of Krishna worship."

Kazi Nazrul Islam (1899-1976)

In Duti Gaur Giti (Two songs on Gaur) the famous, revolutionary poet, wrote like this:

> *"Barnachora thakur ela rasher Nadiay tora dekbi jadi ay,*
> *tare keu bale Srimati radha, keu bale tay Shyamaray . . . ."*

The God with hidden colour (disguise) has come at Nadia full of thoughts (raser Nadia). You may come and watch if you wish.

Some people think of him as the image of Radha, some people think he is Sri-Krsna himself, some people consider him as the combined image of Radha and Krsna, some people call him Gaur Hari and some people conceive him as the incarnation of God head.

Some devotee watched him as Vishnu with six arms at the house of Srivash and some devotee at Nilachal (Jagannath temple at Puri).

Some people watched him as Sri-Ram with bow and arrow in his hands and some people as Krsna with flute in his hand.

Many people saw him as a sannyasi (monk) with a stick and a sac (bag) in his hand.

> *"Pathe ki dekle jete amar Gaur devatare . . . ."*

Have you seen my God Gauranga in the street, the one who invites everybody and distributes his love, before one approaches him.

The noble monk with his handsome, charming appearance makes people crazy and always with his tearful eyes with the thought of God, travels door to door to beg them to render their love to God Krsna. Those who are immersed in the mud of sin such as Jagai and Madhai are easily forgiven and accepted by him, if they utter the name of Hari. With his generous and magnanimous heart he gives shelter to the people of all the caste and ceed and takes them to the next life, once utter the name of Hari. Have you seen such a God of love like Jagannath[1].

Translation of some songs about Gauranga written by various poets including some Muslim ones.

Lal Mamud

In his *Gaur Lila*, the golden man has come to Nadia. He floats with his disciples, on the wave of love of God at the house of Srivash. The tears of love automatically shed, on watching the shine of beauty of his golden appearance. He brought the flood of the name of Hari (Harekrsna movement) and made the world grateful. There is no interruption of singing Harekrsna by his troupe by the process of continuous singing Harekrsna day and night with his troupe, created an atmosphere of flood and has been trying to float the lives of Kali yuga to the ocean of love.

He is running forward as a golden man with golden appearance, golden nupur in golden feet and is emitting shine of gold everywhere. By his influence many ordinary people of all sects adopted his principle of salvation, in Gaur incarnation. Those who pray for golden man, also ultimately become golden man. But Lal is not aware of these, he has spent his whole life in wrong doings, now he does not know whom he is suppose to blame.

(The poet is repenting and blaming himself).

Shah Akbar

In his *Gaur Lila*, long live Oh Gora (Gauranga), the captivator of my mind. You dance being absorbed with your own thought. Along with your song the drum (khol) and Kartal are played and your followers dance with pleasure.

---

[1] Bangali Manishay Sri-Caitanya: by N. Gupta, p. 130.

You keep on moving forward and cannot be still with joy. It is strange magic and I extend my congratulation to you. Shah Akbar is begging to you for your love[1].

Rauf

Gaur Viraha (Feel for Gaur in Separation) It is thought that the poet is trying to say his friend when Gauranga left Navadvipa after renunciation.

Friend I would go to see, Gora at Nadia. I will ask him on touching his feet, "Listen my master, listen carefully. Why did you live me alone? What fault did you find in me? I know that I am guilty of hundreds of errors. But I beg you earnestly, on touching your feet, please forgive me, please be kind to me, knowing that I am very sad. Otherwise I would sacrifice my life on traveling to look for you. "Raul begs him on touching his feet to see him at the time of his death[2]

Abul Hassan

Describing the appearance of Gauranga the poet is saying, in his *Gauranger Rup* (appearance of gauranga) "I am unable to explain the beauty of Gauranga with my only one mouth. The beauty of Gauranga is super natural accomplished with the colour of purity. The only comparable objects with this beauty is the electric spark (decoration). With his golden complexion, accompanied with sweet voice and handsome appearance has involuntarily attracted the mind of the young ladies. Abul Hussan says after knowing the importance of Gauranga that he wishes to have the two feet of Gauranga at the time of his death"[3]

Kabir Gossain

Poet is giving his thought about Doyal Gaur (the kind Gaur)

---

[1] Bangali Manishay Sri-Caitanya: by N. Gupta, p. 130.
[2] Bangali Manishay Sri-Caitanya: by N. Gupta, p. 131.
[3] Ibid: p. 131.

"Kind Guar, there is nobody for me except you. All the time I think and sing of your qualities during eating, sleeping and the walking on the road. You are the helpmate, you are the assets, you are the thoughtful (prudent) destination and you are holding with you, the inaccessible and prohibited place for the jiva soul. You are the heaven, you are the earth, your name, the place of your original residence, all are blended in you, the kind master. Please give shelter at your lotus feet. You are the Brahmana, you are the Vishnu, you are the Jesus and you are Krsna, please give me the blessing of your feet at the time of my death. I do not want any thing else. Kubir says by touching your feet," I watch you in every pilgrimage, please remove my all the desire of the material world"[1].

Chhaifa Banu

The poet is expressing here, on Gauranga Sannyas (Renunciation of Gauranga), her feeling pretending as mother of Nimai, when he left home.

"Where have you gone my Nimai, on uttering the name of Hari? Why you did not wake me up, at the time of your departure? What have you learnt from your guru (teacher)? You have virtually killed your mother this morning, when you left home with the only possession, your sacred thread and a tiny piece of cloth, for your wearing. You are using coconut shell for your drinking pot, begging door to door for your living and all the times you are chanting the name of Hari. In the sorrow of loosing Gauranga, Chhaifa says she would achieve Gauranga if she meditate for him"[2].

Jadubindu Gossain

The poet here is blaming himself for his inability by saying, in his *Gaur Prem* (love of Gaur):

"I feel that I am not in love with Gaur. In the name of Gaur, or in the love of Gaur, I did not become charmed. Never I have spoken with an open mind, with a pious man about Gaur.

---

[1] Ibid: p. 131.
[2] Bangali Manishay Sri-Caitanya: by N. Gupta, p. 133.

In no way I could be immersed myself in the thought of Gaur, so I wonder along road to road. The impurities in my mind is too dense and I have not cleaned it with the soap of knowledge. Possibly I like to enjoy the amusement of the material world fully, I am too greedy to taste all sorts of delicious food, I like to have all sorts of comfort and never suffered from any misery. Those who have the urge of devotion in mind, have got rid of the feeling of the caste and pedigree, accepted Gaur as their master and the aim of destination, will have the pleasure of achieving Gaur and fulfill their desire because they have not taken any pleasure of this material world. Jadubindu was not organized in this thought, never took seriously, the name of his Guru (teacher) Kubir, wasted his time on frequent smoking and never thought the feet of Kabir in his-heart[1].

Lalan Fakir (1775-1891)

The very famous Muslim poet singer addressing 'Gauranga' imagining him as an insane with the thought of God.

"Do not anybody go close to this insane (Gauranga). Three of them have met together at Nadia. One reveal his insanity by giving love to everybody, irrespective of castes. He seems he has not got any sense of caste system; Such a person is hardly noticeable. The main utensil he uses for daily use is a coconut shell for drinking etc., utter always the name of Hari and roll in the dust on the ground. If you go to watch him, you may be an insane also and may end up in leaving the house and family as a monk, and then you will realize. The name of these insanes are such that, dependent Lalan is too eager to utter them. They are Caitanya. Nityananda and Advaita.

It does not matter if I leave family and house, so long I achieve Gaurchand. It is true that birth and death is inevitable and family and house-hold, would not accompany anybody at the end. Then why one is to be proud for them only for a short while? No point on paying too much attention on family when these are unreal for us. Only reality is Gauranga the destination within the unknown and the real boat to cross the giant wave of the stormy ocean, for the next life. Lalan says "when I have left the

---

[1]   Ibid: p. 132.

desire for the material world and adopted the principles of Gauranga, I do not need to be scared of anybody"[1].

Dinabandhu Mitra (1830-1873)

Here the poet is giving a short description of Gauranga's rejection of superstitions and caste system and also of his renunciation, in *Bharat Tapan Gauranga* (Rising Sun of India):

"Gauranga with golden complexion, sweet nature and very pure in heart, the rising sun of India, is the Lord. The one who would perform the miraculous activities in future was notable in the childhood. During early student life he gave up ceremonial religious workshop. In response to the angry reaction of the family guru (religious teacher), he answered that he did not need to show the external worship. It has something to do in the mind. He was like a god with supernatural thought. He was so knowledgeable, as was like the goddess Swaraswati (goddess of knowledge), was sitting in his tongue. He was very modest, calm and religious in heart. Still he was very spirited, determined and authentic in devotion. He rejected the caste system based on birth, the worship of images and the superiority of the Brahmins by birth. He the light of knowledge, was really the religious adviser. By judging his strength, people adored him with bhakti and called him Vishnu himself. To preach his favourite religion, Sanatana dharma, he abandoned his family. He, left his elderly mother and young loving wife. The Lord was in deep love with his wife. Vishnupriya like an ordinary person. But for the benefit of the mankind to teach and preach them he decided to sever the material contact with his wife"[2].

Dwijendra Nath Thakur (1840-1926)

The poet here describes how Gauranga conquered the heart of many people.

"Gauranga the Aulia in attitude and in behaviour as a Vaisnava, flooded the country with his movement (Hare Krsna) and broken all the barriers

---

[1] Bangali Manishay Sri-Caitanya: by N. Gupta, p. 134.
[2] Bangali Manishay Sri-Caitanya: by N. Gupta, p. 15.

of restriction. How to describe the glorious activities that the two brothers (Gaur and Nitai) are doing".

The two together have conquered the heart of many unkind people.

Hundreds and thousands of people hardly could turn their eyes away on watching the appearance of the two. Nobody has seen any where else, such a strong wave of love which is capable of breaking the barrier of caste and pedigree. Some-times they dance and sing with rising two hands and in other time they roll in the dust on the ground with the joyful tears in their eyes with the emotion of love for God"[1].

Kumud Ranjan Mallik (1882-1970)

The poet here describes the movement of Gauranga as a flood.

"I love the invasion of flood that extends up to the horizon".

I receive invitation from the infinity through the sound it creates by the flow. The water of pale colour (gairik gala), capable of creating resonance is everywhere. What a celebration of emotion! It is very exciting. It is the flood of thought and the flood of love, the incredible shake up. It is like the feeling, at the irresistible youth, in the full bloom spring. The tremendous flow that sweeps away everything in the bank, has come.

It seems each drop of water has an intention of a new creation. This type of flood (of civilization), once came at Kapilabastu, Takshasila and Nalanda, Saranath. Sankaracharya also once brought such a flood and at that time, there were building up and establishment of many temples and missions. The new flood that has come this time drowned Nadia and Santipur. After affecting the mind and society, the flow has gone too far and wide. I love this flood water made of the followers of Gauranga and my heart dance with joy when I see these singers robbed with pale colour, dance in front of the Ratha of Jagannath"[2].

---

[1] Bangali Manishay Sri-Caitanya: by N. Gupta, p. 17.
[2] Swarna Sandhya, 1961.

Mahatma Gandhi

The last comments in this chapter is from the most prominent figure in the history of India in this century, the Father of the Nation, Mahatma Gandhi. Non-violence was Gandhi's ways and means in politics and he was well known all over the world, for his movement of 'nonviolence'. But what Gandhi did in this century was demonstrated by Caitanya four and half centuries earlier when he disregarded the order of Chand Kazi not to stop 'namsankirtana'. Rather he went with thousands of people to see Chand Kazi, on singing 'namsankirtana' and ultimately Kazi was convinced and became a follower of HKM[1]. What Caitanya could foresee and the action he initiated, became alive, obvious and the weapon of success of Mahatma Gandhi. Caitanya's weapon was as mentioned in CCM[2], "*Ebe astra na dharila prane kare na marila chitta suddhi karila sabhar*".

It means that—neither he picked up any weapons, nor he killed anybody, but won everybody, by conquering their heart. This was true in case of Gandhi also. Like Caitanya, he was against caste system, and nonviolence was his motto. An analysis would have shown that Ghandi's mind was full of the thought of Caitanya. There are many important quotations what Gandhi made about Caitanya, could be cited. Only a couple of them are mentioned here. In 1927, during his speech at the Chittaranjan Seva Sadan, he said that the Bengal that had given birth to many great men, such as Rammohan, Keshab Chandra, Rabindranath, Ramkrishna and Vivekananda, was fortunate, gratified and virtuous at the appearance of Caitanya.[3].

Gandhi was not particularly against the English education, he himself being a Barrister of English education. But to stress on the fact of national feeling and thought of national interest, in response to a question, in a meeting, the answer he gave, expresses clearly the very high regard, he had about Caitanya. Rammohan Ray was a great social reformer, and was well known for his attempt to make a law through British Parliament to stop,

---

[1]   CCM: Adilila Vol. 17 p. 321-22.
[2]   Interview with B.S. Swami Maharaj, the in Charge Caugiya Vaisnava Mission, London, 1991.
[3]   Gandhi's Work: Vol. 32, p. 65.

the 'sati' (the widow burning) and Bal Gangadhar Tilak was one of the great national leader for the independence movement of India. Gandhi's remark was like this "I have deep regards for Rammohan and Tilak. But I believe that if they did not receive English education but the national education, they could have done much 'greater revolution' like Caitanya[1]. This single sentence is strong enough to understand the distinctive importance, he gave on the HKM of Caitanya.

---

[1] 1 The Speech of Gandhi in Orissa: Publishsed in 'Young India', 13th April, 1921.

CHAPTER IX

Popularity of Harekrsna Movement

Assessment of the popularity

It is a daunting task to assess the popularity exactly, of any particular belief in a country, full of people of all the religion unless a survey is conducted covering all the population. During the earlier census, there might be mention of the religion such as Hindu, Muslim, Christian etc. but not as the sects such as Vaisnava, Sakta, Saiva etc. So one will have to depend on the published views of the important persons and other circumstancial evidences. HKM was very popular among the Bengalis from the very beginning of its start. After a quieter phase for about three centuries, there was a resurrection of enthusiasm in nineteenth and early twentieth century. This was the time, when Bengali intelligentsia, in large number, were in search of thought to bring the Hindu community together, to raise the community spirit and the national feeling.

In 1851 Rev. Lal Bihari De, a distinguished Christian noted that not less than eight million worshipped Caitanya. The great popularity of the sect, he attributed to its simplicity. Lal Bihari De parised the simplicity and the emotional appeal of the Gaudiya Vaisnava doctrine, and expressed his appreciation of the Vaisnava's obliviousness of cast. He also praised the Viasnava mass medium of Kirtana. He wrote: "We regard the system of Caitanya as an interesting development of the religious consciousness of India. It is a sign of the time, and an index of the march of liberal ideas in the religion". He favourably compared Caitanya with Martin Luther[1].

---

[1] Calcutta Review: Vol. XV, 1851, pp. 169 201.

The highly knowledgeable missionary, James Long, never belittled the strength of the HKM. He noted that one-fifth of the population of Bengal, were followers of Caitanya, and that the strength of HKM was increasing. Long gave many interesting data about the places, situated on the banks of the Bhagirathi river[1]. In this study an attempt was made to assess the popularity of HKM in Bengal through circumstantial evidences. For the purpose three regions were chosen, such as Bankura the heart of Bengal, Midnapore, Utkal, the western part of Bengal, and Sylhet and Dacca, the Eastern now in Bangladesh

Harekrsna Movement in Bankura

There were some influence of Vaisnism in Bankura before the era of Citannya. At least there were two temples in Bankura, namely Jagannath temple at Vishnupur (built 1449) and Gopala temple in the same place (1545)[2]. But real change started since Srinivasa Acarya converted Vira Hamvira, the Malla king into the fold of HKM. After Vira Hamvira's conversion the Malla kings vigorously pursued the policy of spreading the Krsna cult far and wide.

Their policy produced some interesting results. The introduction or rather revival of Vaisnavism by Srinivas Acarya turned the tide for ever in favour of civilization and humanity. HKM deeply influenced the prevalent tribal culture of Bankura district. The whole of the local Kora tribes were Vaisnavised. The Koras began to worship Radha-Krsna. The Kora tribe has more than 2054081 members according to the census of 1961[3]. A very popular tribal reform movement, known as 'Sridharma' movement, was initiated by the Santals, koras, Khairas, Lohars, Mogadhiya Doms, Baghdis and Bauris. It derived its inspiration from Vaisnava liberalism. The movement emphasized the necessity of cultivating the ethics. The weavers of Bankura, renowned for their silk pieces, were converted into Vaisnavism

---

[1]   Selected Papers: by James Long, Ed, M. P. Saha, pp. 57-101.
[2]   Late Medieval Temple of Bengal: by McCutchion, p. 2; Bankura Jelar Pura Kirti: by A.K. Bandopadhyaya, p. 53.
[3]   The Census of 1961: by Das, Rraichaudhuri and Raha, Book of W.B, PP127-129.

by lesser Mahantos (preacher) and ascetics. The weavers of Sonamukhi, for instance, were converted by Aul Manohara Das, a disciple of Janhava Devi[1].

The spread of HKM in Bankura-Visnupur formed the background of a brilliant architectural and sculptural afflorescence which formed an essential part of the glorious Vaisnava culture of Bengal.

The leaders of this efflorescence were the Malla kings and Queens of Visnupur[2]. The king of Visnupur was Bagdis (lower caste) by caste. It is also believed that real civilization of Visnupur began with the introduction of HKM. Many Vaisnava temples were built before seventeenth century. Sixty four of them were studied by A. K. Bandopadhyay and D. McCutchion, of these twenty-three were around the Visnupur town and the adjoining areas. Raghunath Simha, Vira Hamvira's successor, built numerous Vaisnava temples in many distant villages in order to make HKM popular with the tribal population of the villages.

The temple-building was one of the methods of spreading the HKM in Bankura, which was earlier a centre of Jainism. There is no doubt that the Vaisnava king of Visnupur made a special effort by building temples in which Vaisnava deities were installed.

The Vaisnava king patronized the evolution of Visnupuri style characterised by Ekaratna or the uninspired temples. Apart from the Vaisnava temples other types of temples are rare in Bankura, these days. A check list of the named temples are given here with the year, they were built but there are many other unnamed Vaisnava temples also[3].

The name of the temples are: Syamaraya (1643), Krsnaraya (1655), Kalachand (1656), Lalji (1658), Radhagovinda (1659), Madangopala (1665) founded by Queen Siraomani, Magangopala (1665) founded by Queen Cudambini, Radharamana (1687), Madanamohana (1694), Joramandir (1726), Radhagovinda (1729), Mahaprabhu (1734), Radhamadhava (1737), Radhasyama (1758), Radhakrsna (1800), Krsna-Balarama, Kisoraraya, Nikunjabihari, Nandalala, Sridhara, Rasamanca founded by Basu family, Rasamanca founded by Vira Hamvira, Jadava Raya

---

1   Gaudiya Vaisnava Jivan: Vol. 1, p. 5.
2   History of Bishnupur Raj: by A. Mallick, pp. 18, 27.
3   Bankura Jelar Purakirti: A.K. Bandopadhyay, pp. 28, 50-51, 52, 56-58, 61-62.

(1650), Radhakrsna Temple (1672), Radhakanta (1678), Syamacandra (1694-1704), Rasamanca (1800), Vrndavanacandra (1638), Gokulacandra (1643), Laksminarayana (1652), Gopala Temple (1653-54), Syamacand (1600), Ramakrsna, Syamasundara (1600), Madanamohana (1670), Radhakrsna, Laksminarayana, Balarama, Syamasundara, Radharamana and there are many other unnamed ones.

The depth of the influence of HKM in Bankura is reflected by the number of Vaisnava fairs and festivals are held in town and villages of Bankura, where thousands of people come and join in singing Hare Krsna and devotional songs. Many Vaisnava fairs are held during Holy festivals at places such as Brajapur, Rudra, Simlipal, Bhalaidaha, Nandarbani, Chandrakona. Similarly there quite few fairs are held during Rasa festivals, of which the most crowded one are, at Visnupur Town, Tiljhatka and at Sabrakon. The fair for Rathajatra festival is held at Visnupur which is a very crowded one.

Another important result of the spread of HKM in Bankura, was the evolution of district school of classical music, which is known as Visnupur Gharana. The school was first developed during the reign of Raghunatha Simha (1626-1655), the builder of the numerous temples. The Visnupur Gharana was patronized by leading Rajas and Zaminders of West Bengal. The main classical type of songs were Dhrupada, influenced by the four styles of Kirtana, which developed during the sixteenth century[1].

HKM also inspired the local artists, who developed a particular type of Radha-Krsna paintings towards the beginning of the eighteenth century. These old paintings were collected for the Vangiya Sahitya Parisat, who exhibited for the first time in Calcutta in 1906[2].

In Visnupur even card playing was influenced by HKM. The so-called Dasavatara cards were invented. These cards, one hundred twenty in number, were divided into ten bunches according to ten incarnations of Visnu[3].

---

[1] West Bengal District Gazetteers, Bankura, pp. 205, 206.
[2] Daksin Pascim Bager Silpa: by R. Bandopadhyaya (1929), pp. 563, 573.
[3] A. Mallick: op, cit, pp. 125, 126.

Harekrsna Movement in Midnapore and Utkala

Syamananda, a Sadgopa by caste, and his chief disciple Rasikamurari spread Vaisnavism in Midnapore and Utkala country.

In this area HKM, for this reason, is known as Syamananda Movement. According to one authority, Syamananda was born in 1556 and died in 1630. He accepted Vaisnavism at very early age, initiated by Hrdayacaitanya. Syamananda visited Vrndavana and there he became pupil of Jiva Gosvamin. They were patronized by the local chiefs. But they carefully maintained the contact with the masses. In early nineteenth century, Midnapore district belonged to Orissa. Two-thirds of the district consisted of jungles. The district had, in 1814 or thereabout, a population of 1.5 million. The district was dominated by Bhuiyans or landlords[1].

After returning from Vrndavana, Syamananda set up his permanent head quarter for preaching the Vaisnavism at Nrsimhapur village near Dharenda. His first important disciple was rasikamurai, son of Acyuta, king of Rohini. The other notable disciples wee Damodara Yogin and Sher Khan, a pathan Governor. The most important of them all was Rasikamurari who managed to transform the Syamananda movement in Midnapore and Utkala almost into a mass movement.

It was probably after Sher Khan's conversion that Syamananda andRasikamuari could hold some Vaisnava festivals through which the movement was spread among the people. The important festivals Rasayatra and Holy, were at Badakola, Alamganja, Naihati, Nrsimhapur, Gopivallabpur, Syamsundrapur, Govindapur and at Dhareda. Each of these festivals, gave a golden opportunity to Syamananda and Rasikamurari to convert hundreds of people into the fold of Harekrsna movement. Money for these festivals came possibly from the local king or Zaminder.

A noticeable feature of the HKM of Syamananda and Rasikamuari was its very close association with the local Hindu and Mahammadan landlords. Syamananda converted Acyuta, the King of Rayani, the landlord of (Ghatsila, Bhimadhan Bhuiyan, the landlord of Govindapur, Rajyadhara)

Raya, the landlord of bush-covered Bagdi, Uddanda Raya, the Bhuiyan of Nrsimhapur, and Sher Khan, the Pathan Governor. Rasikmurari coverted

---

[1] Description of Hindusthan: by W. Hamilton, Vol. 1, pp. 136-42.

Vaidyanatha Bhanja, rular of Mayurbhanja, Gajapati, king of Patashpur, Harinarayana of Pancet, Chandrabhanu, king of Mayna, Bhima and Srikara, tyrannical Bhuiyans of Dharenda and Ahmed, nephew of Ibrahim Beg, Subahdar of Orissa. The conversion of so many leading men of Midnapore made it possible for the two leaders to convert large segments of the local population without any serious opposition[1]. The villages of Midnapore which became the powerful centres for the Syamananda movement, are named here such as:

1. Alamganja, 2. Balarampur, 3. Bagdi, 4. Badakola, 5. Badagrama, 6. Basantapur, 7. Banpur, 8. Bhanjabhum Rajgarh, 9. Bhograi, 10. Cakuliya, 11. Dharenda Bahadurpur, 12. Patepur, 13. Ghatsila, 14. Gopivallabpur, 15. Hariharpur, 16. Hijli, 17. Jhatiada, 18. Kasipur, 19. Kesiadi, 20. Keonjhar, 21. Mayana, 22. Mayurbhanja, 23. Muktapur, 24. Nrsimhapur, 25. Rayani, 26. Raghunathbati, 27. Ranihati, 28. Remuna in Balasore, 29. Syamsundarpur, 30. Garbeta, 31. Jadagrama.

Syamanada and Rasikamuarari had many disciples who also spread the HKM in many villages. Thirty one notable disciples of Syamananda and two hundred three disciples of Rasikamurari are recorded in the the local newspapers named 'Rasikamangala' and 'Premavilasa'[2]. The important point is that many Brahmins, accepted, Syamananda and Rasika as their preceptors. Rasika's disciple Govinda Bhattacharya went to 'Vanga' and there he is said to have converted hundreds of Brahmins. The Vaisnava festivals helped the liberaisation of the caste system. The Brahminical opposition to the Syamananda movement was perhaps rendered negligible by the patronage extended to it by the local kings and Bhuiyans.

The Syamananda movement in Midnapore and Utkal produced some important results. So many people embraced Vaisnavism that they were regarded as Vaisnava caste. Towards the end of the nineteenth century and the beginning of the twentieth century, Midnapore had at least 1,000,000, counted Vaisnavas. The caste Vaisnavas numbered 96,178, according to the census of 1879[3].

---

[1]   Valsnavism in Bengal: by Dr. R. Chakravorty, p. 247-49; Variouis publications of the local news papers named 'Premavilasa' and 'Rasikamangala'.

[2]   Vaisnavism in Bengal: by Dr. R. Chakravorty, p. 250.

[3]   A Statistical Account of Bengal: by Hunter, 4, p. 51.

The Kayesthas of Midnapore and Balasore raised their caste status by joining the HKM[1].

It is interesting to note that Vaisnavism in Midnapore was linked with the prevailing system of land tenure. Hunters noted that Midnapore had as many as 272 Vaisnavottar holdings.

Vaisnavottara land was tax free and rent free donated to the Gurus and Mohantas by their disciples or the sympathetic landlords. It also led to the spread of the Brahminical culture among the tribal people.

As elsewhere in Bengal, the Vaisnava mystic and the Muhammadan Fakir formed a syncretic brotherhood in Midnapore[2]. But the emphasis of Syamananda and Rasikamurari was rather quantity than on quality. No distinguished poet or Padavali composer of very high calibre emerged out of the Syamananda movement. Since both Syamananda and Rasikamurari were married, it is conceivable that they did not preach any lofty ideal of asceticism, which could not be followed by the house holders.

There strong link with the 'feudal' element might have a secular motivation. As elsewhere in Bengal, the HKM in Midnapore and Utkala country probably strengthened the position of the landlords. The kinds and the landlords might have supported the two leaders for two reasons.

Firstly Vaisnavism helped them to elevate their position in the caste hierarchy[3]. Since an initiated Vaisnava had no recognizable caste, he was above caste. Secondly it may perhaps be argued that Vaisnavism, with its emphasis on nonviolence and faith in the world redeemer Krsna, made the down trodden peasantry mild tempered. So far as the Rajas and the Bhuiyans were concerned, this was a most desirable development.

An important result of the Syammananda movement was the evolution of the 'Reneti' style of Kirtana in the Ranihati Pargana in Midnapore. This type of Kirtana is comparable in style and design to Hindusthani classical Thumri songs which is quite popular in India.

---

[1]   Bengal District Gazeteers, Midnapore, pp. 64-65.

[2]   *Rameswara Rachanavali:* by Panchanan Chakravorty, p. 43. *"Fakir balen tera jati nahi jabe, Rama Rahima aye samsare ekai janibe".* Fakir said, you will not loose your caste, try to feel, Ram (a Hindu) and Rahim (a Muslim), are the same.

[3]   Social Change in Modern India: by M.N. Srinivas, (1982) ed, p. 1-45.

The spread of Vaisnavism in Midnapore formed the background of the construction of a very large number of Vaisnava temples in the district. There was however no remarkable deviation from the Pirha, Sikhara, Cala and Ratna styles (architectural) of temple building during seventeen and eighteen centuries.

Many of these temples were endowed with Vaisnavottara lands. The Midnapore temples, however, had not the brilliant terracota ornamentation of the temples of Bankura and Visnupur. The approximate number of Vaisnava temples within the jurisdiction of the present police station is given here[1].

Police stations, number of temples are:

Bhagavanpur	5	Chandrakona	15	Contai	1
Garbheta	7	Daspur	26	Gopivallavapur	1
Danton	3	Keshpur	6	Debra	8
Mahisadal	2	Dihivallabpur	1	Midnapore town	14
Egda	11	Mayana	1	Ghatal	10
Patashpur	2	Sabang	3	Pingla	3
Salbani	1	Binpur	1		

These 121 notable temples are mentioned here. There are many other small temples which are not mentioned. The proportion of Vaisnava temples to any other kind of temples are, 3 to 1.

Among other mentionable cult, Dharma had a considerable following in Ghatal and Tamluk subdividions[2] and Saktaism was strong in Karnagarh, Midnapore town and Chandrakona. The Proportion of Vaisnava followers and other type of cult in the present day is approximately 3 to 2[3]. Vaisnava

---

[1] Vaisanvism in Bengal: by Dr. R. Chakravorty, p. 255-56; Field work by touring in the different part of the district and personally visiting the temples.

[2] Dharma and Serpent Worship in Bankura District: by Ashutosh Bhattacharya, p. 207.

[3] Field work by the Author by interviewing the people in public places, shopping centres, market places and village fairs.

fairs and festivals that are held in a year at different villages and towns, are more than 116 notable ones.

Harekrsna Movement in Sylhet and Dacca District

The assessment of the extent of the influence of HKM in Hindu society of Sylhet and Dacca was based on local traditions which in many instances due to the presence of temples and performances of religious activities. Many Saiva and Sakta Zaminders built numerous Vaisnava temples. Like West Bengal, Eastern and Northern parts of Bengal too had many sects which adored Caitanya, yet remained unrelated to the orthodox Gaudiya Vaisnava order. Caitanya himself went after his first marriage with a view to paying a visit to his ancestral village in Sylhet, and making money[1]. His biographers aver that he paid a visit to Ramkeli village of Malda on his way to Vrndavana[2]. At this village which was a centrre for learning Sanskrit, he met Sanatana and his brother Rupa.

It is certain that Caitanya was able to make an impact to common people of the villages through which he made his long journey to Northern India.

A sizeable number of people, with whom Caitanya was intimately associated, in Navadvipa hailed either from Sylhet or from Chittagong. Advaitya Acarya, Srivasa Pandita, Chandrasekhara Acarya, Jagadisa Pandita, Murari Gupta, Stalwarts of the Caitanya movement in Navadvipa, hailed from Sylhet. Gadadhara Pandita, Gopala Dhananjoya Pandita, Mukunda Datta, and Vasudeva Datta hailed from Chittagong. Khagendranath Mitra has suggested that Vaisnavsm was imported into Navadvipa from Sylhet[3].

The fact that the Caitanya milieu in Navadvipa was fundamentally a Sylhet Chittagong mileu, in which Advaita had a central position remains indubitable. But not much is known about the pre-Caitanya Vaisnavism, in Sylhet. The Srihatta Vaisnavas certainly confronted to caste rituals and Brahminical norms.

---

[1]   CBH: Adikhanda, Ch. 12, pp. 83-89.
[2]   CCM: Kalna ed. Madhyalila, Ch. 16, pp. 409-11.
[3]   Srihatter Loka Samgit: by N. Bhowmik and G. Datta, p. 67, (Mitra's opinion quoted).

In all probability Advaitya Acarya brought the men from Sylhet and Chittagong close to Vaisnavism. They were converted into Vaisnavism by the disciples of Madhavendra Puri among whom Advaita and Isvara Puri had a prominent position.

In the seventeenth and the eighteenth centuries four influential Vaisnava families, namely the Thakurvani, the Thakurjivana, Vaisnava Raya and Vancita Ghose held the torch of the HKM aloft in Sylhet[1]. According to local tradition two Vaisnavas named Madhava Dasa and Rama Dasa, spread HKM among the Hajongs of Susang Durgapur[2]. A Hajong leader named Pathura Hajong even went to Puri on pilgrimage. The economic effects of the spread of Vaisnavism in the Hajong tribal area are not known; but it is not difficult to surmise that the agriculture in the area grew extensive and that much Jungle was cleared by the Vaisnava tribals.

According to one authority Chitom Thomba, king of Manipur in Assam and his subjects were converted into Vaisnavism by the Adhikari Vaisnava of Sylhet who were Brahmins. The conversion took place sooner after 1715[3]. King Bhagycandra of Manipur was converted by Ramnarayana Misra, a descendant of Caitanya's uncle who lived in a village Dhaka Daksina of Sylhet[4].

The Vaisnava of Manipur have a high regard for Caitanya. Hundreds of them visit Navadvipa every year, and attend the festival held every year in commemoration of Caitanya's birth. A distinct 'Gharana' or school of Rasa dance with a remarkably high degree of sophistication evolved in Manipur.

The HKM came to Tripura towards the beginning of the seventeenth century. Rajadhar Manikya, king of Tripura (1611-1623), was converted into Vaisnavism. King Govinda Manikya (1658-1660) even visited Mathura and Vrndavana[5]. The spread of HKM in Tripura, a hilly and tribal area, paved the way for the spread of Bengali culture among the local tribes.

Dinesh Chandra Sen saw among them a tremendous enthusiasm for reading or to listening to the recitation of classics like CCM.

---

[1] Achyutacharana Tattvanidh, op. cit. Vol. 3, p. 303.
[2] Ibid. CH. 1, pp. 142 143.
[3] Brihat Banga: by Dinesh (Ch. Sen, Vol. 2. p. 1096.
[4] Daudiya Vaisnava Abhidan: Vol. 2. p. 1919.
[5] Brihat Banga: Vol. 2, pp. 1035-1036.

Towards the end of the nineteenth century, Raja Viracandra Manikya of Tripura donated a tremendous some of money for the publication of Vaisnava works. Radharamana press was set up at Baharampur (Murshidabad) for printing Vaisnava works, as mentioned earlier[1]. The HKM was popular at Tripura. The evidence of its strength lies in the numerous Vaisnava manuscripts discovered in the Chittagong district[2]. Many of these manuscripts are on Radhaviraha or varamasya.

The manuscripts are written by the local poets early in the eighteenth century. An anthology of seventy 'Padavalis', composed by the Hindu Vaisnava poets of Chittagong have been recently published[3].

Radha-Krsna concept on a popular level, literary expressions of which are found in Sylhet. Mymensingh, Comilla and Chittagong districts had nothing to do with the sophisticated Gaudiya Vaisnava theology. In Chittagong Krsnarama Datta composed 'Radhikamangala', a Mangalakavya on Radha[4]. The ideas and the language of this work conform to the 'Mangalakavya' style.

It is interesting to note that not a single companion of Caitanya belonged to the Dacca, Faridpur, or Barisal districts. Caitanya's visit to East Bengal was before his renunciation. So He did not have any direct influence in spreading the HKM in East Bengal.

Much later a disciple Isana Nagara, a disciple of Advaita and Caitanya's personal *carrier*, was probably commissioned by Advaita to proselytise the people who lived at the villages of the western part of the Manikganj subdivision of Dacca and adjacent region of Faridpur. He converted the local landlords and there after the HKM movement gradually became popular there. Some followers of Gadadhara Pandita built up powerful bases in the Manikganj subdivision of Dacca district. One of them was Vallabhacaitanya Goswamin[5].

---

[1] Sajjanatosani: 1895, Vol. 7, pp. 289-91; 1896, Vol. 8, p. 289.

[2] Bangla Prachin Puthir Vivaran: by Abdul Karim Sahityavisarada, Parts (I II).

[3] B Akadami Patrika: ed. No. 4, B.S., 1971, 'Chattagramer Hindu Kabir Padasahitya' by Ahmed Sharif.

[4] Radhikamangala: Published by the Vangiya Sahitya Parishat, in B.S. 1905.

[5] Vaisnavism in Bengal: by Dr. R. Chakravorty, p. 283.

Vallabhacaitanya set up a Sripata (a centre) in the populous place Vikrampur. Soon the centre became popular. His descendants had gradually spread the HKM among the local Hindu peasantry.

Kasthakata Jagannatha, another disciple of Gadadhara Pandita, set up a powerful centrre at the Kathadiya village of Vikrampur Pargana, and converted a good number of people of the neighbouring villages. The Kathadiya Goswamins had powerful influence in nineteenth century.

One of them was Harimohan Siromani, who had followers in Vrndavana, Navadvipa and Puri[1].

The HKM assumed the shape of a bigger movement in Dacca proper when Virabhadra visited there. From a catalogue of temples of Dacca district, Wise found that 75% of the population worshipped Krsna in one or other of his numerous forms, and only 21% worshipped Kali, Durga or Siva. B.C. Allen noted that a large proportion of the Hindus of Dacca city were Vaisnavas[2]. There is clear evidence of Nityananda's and Virabhadra's influence among the non-Brahminical castes of Dacca city. The weavers of Dacca, the creators of the world famous 'Muslin' embraced the HKM. The conchshell ornaments makers of Dacca, who belonged to the caste of Samkha Vaniks, are mostly Vaisnavas. Lalmohan Saha a very affluent leader of the community, claimed that 'Vangavasi Caitanyadasa', a medieval composer of the Vaisnava devotionals, was his ancestor. From Dacca the HKM spread to the neighbouring villages and towns, such as 'Savar' and 'Dhamrai', where the Rathayatra festival soon became very highly popular.

According to local tradition, a Vaisnava Goswamin named Bhikhan Lal Thakur installed in Narayanganj five Narayancakras and converted many people. Gradually the riverport of Narayanganj became quite a sizable centre for HKM. Bipin Pal, the eminent Brahma and nationalist leader, visited numerous Vaisnava monasterires or Akhdas at Naranganj city towards the end of nineteenth century[3].

---

[1]   GVA: Vol. 2, p. 1903; Vaisnava Vivrti by Harilal Chattopadhyaya; Vikrampur by H. Chattopadhyay, Vol. 2. pp, 287-88.

[2]   Vaisnavism in Bengal: by Dr. R. Chakravorty, P. 284; Wise: Notes on the Races, Castes, and Trades of Eastern Bengal, p. 147.

[3]   Bangla Bramhan: by Bipin Chandra Pal, Vol. 2, p. 44.

The survey given above may not be adequate, but makes it plain that the spread of the HKM in Bengal, was the result of the advent of Caitanya.

Slowly but surely Vaisnavism became an essential element of the Bengali way of life. One of the methods of spreading the faith in peace was in collaboration with the landlords and the Brahmins. Such a collaboration was unavoidable.

Even Nityananda could not gain any foothold in Kangalpukuriya and Benapole in Jessore and Khulna because of the opposition of the local landlord, Ramacandra Khan, who was a Tantrika. But one may say that the Gaudiya Vaisnava Mahantas found it easy to make a compromise with the Brahminical culture because they were protected by their own Smriti and religious sophistication. Those Vaisnavas whose commitments were more extensive, were compelled to mix with heterogeneous elements, gradually grew deviant.

The Vaisnava ladies like Hemlata Thakurani and Haripriya Goswami symbolized the advent of a new age when the upper caste Bengalis might no longer be Asuryampasya, invisible to the sun. Their contribution to the spread of the HKM in areas, where elements hostile to the Vaisnava ideal were active, can never be estimated[1]. Most possibly the preparation of the anthologies in the seventeenth and eighteenth centuries, had some connection with the spread of the faith. The 'Kirtana' became highly popular throughout Bengal. The common listener did not care for their style. They were moved by the human appeal innate in them. Still another cultural result of the spread of the HKM was the construction of a large number of Vaisnava temples. The temples were built both the rich and common people. Sanyal shows that a quite large number of Nabasak' and other castes built temples between 1700 and 1900. During the period the upper caste built 678 and the lower caste also built 568 temples. The Radha-Krsna cult was undoubtedly the main inspiration behind the revival of the Hindu art and architecture[2].

In general assessment, there are some other circumstancial evidences to suggest the popularity of the HKM. In thirteen districts of West Bengal,

---

[1] Vaisnavism in Bengal: by Dr. R. Chakravorty, p. 303-304.
[2] Temple Promotion and Social Mobility in Bengal: by Hitesh Ranjan Sanyal, pp. 341-71; Dr. McCutchion, op. cit, p. 1f.

Vaisnava fairs and festivals are held through out the year. The common festivals are the 'Rathayatra' (observed in the Bengali month of Asada, about July), and the 'Rasayatra' (observed in the month of Kartika, about November), 'Dolyatra' and 'Jhulana' etc. The following figures have been roughly computed from the list given in the four volumes of book named 'Paschim Banger Puja Parvan O Mela' edited by Asoke Mitra[1].

Districts	Number of festivals	Districts	Number of festivals
Bankura	72	Jalpaiguri	10
Birbhum	33	Malda	10
Coochbihar	24	Midnapore	116
Darjeeling	1	Murshidabad	62
Hooghly	65	West Dinajur	13
Howrah	41	24 Pargonas	128

An account of total 575 well known fairs and festivals are given here. There may be even more in number which are less popular.

No other cult hold so many fairs and festivals. None of the other comparable cults such as Sakta, Saiva, or Dharma, can claim to hold, even 20% of the above number. It is worthwhile to mention about the celebration of Durga Puja, Kali Puja and Swaraswati Puja. All these events are quite popular among the Bengalis for the purpose of celebration in the towns and villages, but very minimum number of people usually take part in religious activities and prayers. Moreover the celebrants of these events do not have any cult comparable with the Vaisnavas. It is also notable, during the celebration of Durga Puja, at many places it is arranged or there is a tradition for acts of play such as Yatra (Opera), Krsna Yatra (play about the activities of Krsna) or Kirtana songs.

---

[1] Vaisnavism in Bengal: Dr. R. Chakravorty, p. 277.

Vaisnava names for the places may be an indication of the popularity of the religion in Bengal. The following datas are collected for the name of places in West Bengal[1].

Villages of West Bengal[2] named after Krsna or his various appellations:

Jagannathapura	72	Gopinathapura	65
Purusottampaura	36	Krsnapura	86
Gopalapura	142	Balaramapura	76
Govindapura	125		

The other names which are frequently heard of Madhavapura, Syampura, Krsnanagara, Syamasundarapura, Radhavallabhapura, Mathurapura, etc. A few villages are named after Caitanya, Gauranga, Vasudeva, Nityananda, Lakshmi and Radha. Thirty two per cent of the Vaisnava names are heard in Midnapore.

There are eight hundred villages named after Rama, three hundred nineteen villages named after Visnu, and fifty three villages named after Radha[3].

The name of the children usually used to be selected in Bengal by grand parents and sometimes parents till a generation ago. These names sometimes signify the families outlook towards their religious devotion. The religious families sometimes select the name which is synonymous with the name of the favourite God or Goddess. The thought behind this was involuntarily or subconsciencly, one would utter the name of the God whenever the child is to be called.

Certain very common Bengali Hindu names are mentioned here which are the names of Vishnu, his incarnation or the associates of his incarnations, such as Vishnu, Krsna, Rama, Lakshmana, Bharat, Satrugana, Shyam, Shyamchand, Shyamnath, Shyamaroya, Shyamasundara, Hari, Haripada, Gaur, Gauranga, Giridhara, *Giridhari, Govinda, Gopal, Gopes,*

---

[1]   Vaisnavism in Bengal: Dr. R. Chakravorty, p. 277.
[2]   Paschim Banglar Gramer Nam: by A.K. Bandopadhyay, (1980), Ch. 3.
[3]   Vaisnavism in Bengal: by Dr. R. Chakravorty, p. 277.

Gopinath, Gobardhan, Gaurhari, Gadadhar, Ghanashyam, Basudeva, Balarama, Bhajahari, Benudhara, Banamali, Brajesvara, Bangshidhar, Bisvesvar, Bisvambar, Advaita, Abhiram, Aniruddha, Kanai, Kala, Kalachand, Kalashashi, Kishore, Krsnapada, Krsnanath, Krsnachandra, Kripasindhu, Vishnupada, Sridama, Sudama, Keshav, Madhav, Madhusudan, Madanmohan, Mukunda, Murari, Pranesvara, Prangovinda, Prananath, Raghupati, Rakhal, Raghava, Radhehyam, Rajaram, Nitai, Nilamani, Natabara, Narasingha, Narayana, Dinabandhu, Dinanath, Dayal, Dinadayal, Jagannath, Jadava, Jadubar, Jadunath, Jadupati, Jagatpati, Janardhan12.

These common Vaisnvaite names were enlisted fromfrom the common Hindu crowd, after interviewing ten thousands people. There are many more Vainavite names which are less common, so not been enlisted here.

In other comparative sects had only a few names such as Mahadeva, Mahesvara, Shiva, Sankara, Bholanath, Nataraj, Nilkantha and Panchanan in the Saivaites and Uma, Parvati, Gauri, Sankari, Sati and Tara in the Sakta sects. The names about the other less important or local cult are only very few to mention.

These people were all above forty years of age. These names were selected by the grand parents in about forty per cent of the cases and was not known in the rest of the cases.

This shows the Vaisnavism was voluntarily or involuntarily was associated with most of the Bengali families, till at least up to one generation back.

Diviant Vaisnavas and Proliferation of Guruism

Bengal witnessed the development of numerous deviant Vaisnava or semi-Vaisnava sects in the wake of the HKM. Most of them were emerged as an indentifiable sects during the seventeenth and eighteenth centuries.

The Auls and Bauls were prominent even in the sixteenth centuries[2]. The Sahajiya order stemmed from as mentioned earlier from the Buddhist Sahajiya tradition[3].

---

[1] Field work by the Author. Interview with ten thousands Hindus at random.
[2] CCM: Antya Vol. 19 p. 37-40.
[3] Obscure Religious Cult: by S.>B. Dasgupta, p. 113.

The reasons for the sprouting of the numerous deviant orders in the seventeenth and eighteenth centuries were various. First of all was due to the lack of the very strong leadership within the Vaisnavas to keep them very closely adherent. There were other additive factors also. The slow consolidation of the British power in Bengal before 1757, and the quick down fall of the Mughuls after 1709, made life and society in Bengal very highly hazardous. The internal and external markets for the indigenous were dying out. The Nawabs of Bengal, lacked the administrative organisation, for coping with the various problems of the 'period of transitiono'[1]. The Bengalis of West Bengal were harassed by the Maratha raids which first began in 1742. The penetration of British mercantile capital into the traditional Bengali industries, upset the old economic order. Both the Bengali peasants and the Bengali weavers were very badly affected by the work of the foreign monopolists.

On the other hand caste was not yet abolished and the superstitions were growing stronger. The Brahminical exclusiveness led to the development of the diverse sects among the lower orders.

The professor of the guru (who initiate into the religious sects deeply), grew very lucrative. The intellectuals suffered heavily. Even highly talented poet like Kavikankana Mukundarama Chakravorty once failed to bring food for his starving children[2]. Another poet Jivan Maitra had starved sometimes[3].

Many Vaisnava poets described themselves as 'Dukhi' or affected. There was a sharp division in the society between rich and poor.

This division was nicely described by the Sakta poet Ramprasad Sen "Mother you have given some people servants, wealth, elephants, horses and chariots. Are they your grand fathers? Mother! you remain unmoved even though you see my miserable condition[4].

---

[1] The Passing of the Empire: 'The Maghul Case'; Modern Asian Studies (1975), pp. 385-96.

[2] Chandimangala: Sahitya Akademi Edition, Section 6, p. 3.

[3] Ramesvara Racanavali: by Pancanan Chakravorty, pp. 252-54.

[4] Bangalir Gan: One of the traditional song of Ramprasad, "*Kore dile dhanajna ma, hasti asvs ratha chaya; Tara ki tor baper thankur, ami ki tor keho noi?*"

The Brahmins or the upper caste intellectuals might yet survive the turbulence of the 'transition' by using their writs and caste status. But the low castes had no such chance. Some men and women of the lower castes became gurus. The HKM had at least theoretically obliterated the caste. A low caste man could be a Vaisnava guru or even a Tantrika guru and live comfortably from the income through the guruism without doing any professional work. The common people were constantly encouraged to believe the life in this world was absolutely worthless, and that their joys and sorrows were preordained by 'Karma'. If they did 'pious' deeds in this world, they were sure to be reborn in rich and happy families. Guru worship was a pious deed. The gurus had to preach this theory with a view to ensuring their survival in the cruel world[1].

The gurus also used to take advantage of the natural calamities or epidemic of diseases such as cholera, small pox etc and these were considered as the kindness of Mother 'Sitala'. The only way to be saved from this disaster, was to get the blessing from the guru who would organize a puja of 'Mother Sitala' or other local god or Goddess concerned to save every-body and guru would have some earning, through these proceedings.

The Gaudiya-Vaisnava-Brahmina equation made some of the Gaudiya-Vaisnavas reactionary in the social sense of the term. They did not emulate the noble example set by Caitanya, Nityananda and Advaita. Most of them forgot the miseries of life in the contemplation, remembrance and analysis of the Radha-Krsna sports. Talented Vaisnava poets did not turn their attention to the various problems of the common people.

They invariably wrote the sophisticated songs on the Vrindavana sports. Ultimately their songs grew extremely artificial and stereotyped.

Some of the gurus were not only the spiritual teacher but also became a medicine man who was expected to cure incurable diseases. The amulets, protective 'mantra' (Raksasmantra), 'thought reading', 'rice reading', 'palm reading' and 'plate reading' grew extremely popular mainly because there was no viable system of law and order. There was no social hygiene. The amulets, the mantras, the kabachas were prepared both by the Vaisnava and

---

[1] Vaisnavism in Bengal: by Dr. R. Chakravorty, p. 347.

Sakta gurus[1]. The gurus who used to pretend to feed hundreds of people with rice cooked only for few persons, or the gurus who could pretend to cure tuberculosis, cancer, or leprosy simply by his special mantra or kabacha, grew wealthy.

If the legend of the miracles performed by a guru was accepted by the people, none dared to question the guru's antecedents or qualifications. The problems of poverty, hunger and disease compelled the helpless masses to flock to the gurus, and accept their creeds.

Due to the proliferation of these various guruisms, there were also introduction of many new sects around some comparatively stronger gurus over the years. There are many sects and subsects. Sometimes it is difficult to decide whether it is worth while to recognize a group of people around a comparatively strong guru, who introduces some of his own thoughts into the practice, he adopted originally and continue to preach these to his disciples.

A check list of the Vaisnavas and semi-Vaisnavas are given here. Not necessarily all of them has got very strong support in the society; some of them merely got some identification around a guru. All of them has one thing common. Besides their various activities which may differ in various groups to some extent, all sing and chant Hare-Krsna as their main means of prayer.

A checklist of the Vaisnava and semiVaisnava Sects21.

1. Aul.	22. Hazrati.	42. Sahaja.
2. Asimatyaja.	23. Haridasi.	43. Akhibhavaka.
3. Asramorodhi.	24. Jaganmohani.	44. Sambhucandi.
4. Advayavadi.	25. Kartabhaja.	45. Spastadayaka.
5. Baul.	26. Kalikumari.	46. Sain.
6. Balarami.	27. Ksepavama.	47. Sahebdhani.

---

[1] Puthiparichaya: by Panchanan Mandal (many manuscript Black Magic written in Bengali).

[2] Caitanyottara Yuge Gaudiya Vaisnava: by N.G. Goswami, pp. 163-201; Vaisnava Vratadinirnaya: by N.C. Goswami, pp. 51-52. Kartabhaja Dharmamantra O Itihasa: Field Works particularly for the lat three in the list.

7. Curadhari.	28. Kanupriya.	48. Sisyavilasi.
8. Caranpankhi.	29. Kisoribhajana.	49. Sitarama.
9. Darbesh.	30. Khusivisvasi.	50. Smaranapanthi.
10. Darpanarayani.	31. Maddhavirodhi.	51. Sect of the 'Mother in Law'.
11. Darisannyasi.	32. Naresapanthi.	52. Sect of the Elder
12. Gauravadi.	33. Nathabhaya.	53. Saddhvianthi.
13. Gaurasyama.	34. Nitairadha. Brother and Mother	
14. Gharpagla.	35. Nyada.	54. Varnaviragi.
15. Guruprasadi.	36. Paramahamsa.	55. Vamakaupina.
16. Grhi-Baul.	37. Pratapacandi.	56. Vamsidhara.
17. Gairikavirodhi.	38. Ramavalllabhi.	57. Yugalbhjana.
18. Gauresvara.	39. Ramadasa	58. Shyamanandi.
19. Gadai-Gauranga.	40. Radhesyama.	59. Gaudiya-vaisnava
20. Gobrai.	41. Ratbhikari.	60. Ramthakura Sampradaya.
21. Haribola.		

61. Matua Sampradaya.

62. International Society for Krishna Consciousness (ISKCON).

All these sects except the last three claimed to be the branches or have some links with the original Gaudiya Vaisnavas, at Navadvipa. But the Gaudiya Vaisnavas do not agree with this. They feel that they were the original Vaisnavas and the mainstream Vaisnavas.

The Vaisnava ideals, principles and the main organization, is still with them; the various other groups may follow some Vaisnava principles, but they are the deviated group from the original body and they should not be considered as the Vaisnavas[1]. Each group has some point of speciality which they stress more, as the name suggests in many of them. There are some differences in the practices also, but they all have common way of sending their prayer through Harekrsna namsankirtan and devotional songs, except the Matua Sampradaya.

The members of this group chants the word 'Haribol' along with devotional songs, as the main way of sending their prayer. As controversies exist about who should be levelled as proper Vaisnava, although all of

---

[1] Personal interview of the author with 'B.S. Swami Maharaj' in charge of The Gaudiya Vaisnava Mission in London, 1991.

them accept Vishnu as their god, and all of them sings Harekrsna, for the purpose of this study, it has been called Harekrsna movement. Individual membership of any of these above groups are not very significant for the country as a whole except the last four. But the aggregated membership of all these groups is significant and makes a big mass. Moreover except the ISKCON, and possibly the Gaudiya Vaisnava Mission, none of the sects has got any membership register to enlist all the members. Some of them may have some address book of the prominent members, for the communication purpose only[1]. It is the understanding of the members only who belonged to which sects. It can be assessed only by observing, the attendance, at 'Namayajna' (continuous singing of Harekrsna for a certain period by an aggregated mass), fair and festival, organised by a particular sect.

Again there is no restriction of attendants in all these events. So members of one sect may freely join the events, organized by the others.

This also does not help to estimate the actual members[2]. Besides these there is a general mass of population who does not belong to any particular sect but accept Vishnu, as their Godhead. They are the main bulk of Vaisnavites. For the purpose of this study from now on this population will be described as 'General Mass Vaisnava' (GMV). In true sense the popularity of any belief whether Vaisnava, Saiva, or Sakta depends on this general mass rather than on the registered members of any sect. Possibly their number may be even bigger than the aggregated mass of the recognized sects. They do not take initiation from any particular guru of any sect; nor do they follow the strict principles prescribed by any of the Vaisnava sects. But they follow some simple principles of Vaisnavism preached by Caitanya and Nityananda, such as the acceptance of Vishnu as Godhead with his various incarnations, the devotion based on bhakti only and not dependent on knowledge, the simple way of praying through 'Nama sankirtana or devotional songs, rejection of caste system. The leaving of family (renunciation) is not essential to practice religion[3].

---

[1] The author's observation by visiting many of the Vaisnava fair, festivals, namayajnas and interview with many Gurus.

[2] The authors 'Field Works' by visiting many Vaisnava fairs and festivals.

[3] The author's observation from the personal interview with numerous people extending over forty years mainly in Bengal and United Kingdom.

The GMV in general are the more open minded people than many strong supports of some particular sects. Although the allegiance of these people remain towards Vishnu, they do not mind to participate in the celebration of Kali puja or Durga puja (Sakti); rather they enjoy the celebration, unlike some very arrogant sectorians who may not even like to take part in the discussion about the other goddesses. This view is best expressed by the song written by a very famous Bengali Muslim poet, Kazi Nazrul Islam, "*Ami Shyama mayer kole chade japi ami Shyamer nam, ma halen more mantra guru thakur halen Radheshyam.*"

This means, while I ride and enjoy in the arm of Shyama (Sakti), I pray for Shyam (Krsna). Mother (Sakti) is my religious teacher (guru), but Krsna is my God[1].

For the purpose of this study, a survey of ten thousand people belonging to Hindu community, over the age of forty years, male and female almost equal number, selected at random from the common place of aggregation such as market place, sports ground, rail stations meeting in the Independence day etc., avoiding the place of religious aggregation. They were asked, whom they consider or pray as their God, "either Vishnu or His incarnations, Siva or His incarnations, Sakti or Her incarnations or any other belief they feel strongly about."

The answer was fifty five percent for Vishnu, Twelve percent for Sakti, and less than one per cent for Siva. It was interesting to note the view of the rest about thirty two percent of the people.

These group strongly feel it does make any difference if one calls them in one name or the other. Many of them even feel if one prays with the names of goddesses, outside these three, would achieve the grace of Almighty, provided one maintain good conduct and has the devotion of worthy of it. In other words, these were the teachings of bhakti, preached by Ramkrishna. He believed in that the Omnipotent God is the same person, but people call Him different names.

The Matua Sampradaya particulary do not stress on the name as Harekrsna, instead they stress on 'Haribol'. They have got strong followings

---

[1] Nazrul Giti: by Nazrul Islam. The song was sang by many famous Bengali singers. The author heard from the famous Sital Mukherjee, currently at Coventry.

in Jessore, Khulna, Faridpur and 24 Parganas. Due to the developments of sects and semisects, within the Vaisnavas, it makes difficult for one to assess the way of practicing Vaisnavism.

The Brahminical Influence in Vaisnavism

The Gaudiya Vaisnavas had to make out a case which might be acceptable to the regional upper castes. They had to tone down the egalitarian implication of bhakti. This was done by Gopal Bhatta Goswamin in Haribhaktivilasa. The most remarkable feature of this work is its emphasis on Vaidhibhakti or 'ritualistic' devotion. The caste ridden Hindu society of upper India was not prepared to accept bhakti without clearly articulated rituals, because nonritualistic bhakti might be a menace to the social and religious predominance of the Brahmins.

Although in general 'Haribhaktivilasa' is accepted as the most comprehensive compendium of the Vaisnava rituals, many have doubt whether Gopal Bhatta faithfully represented the social ideal of Caitanya, particularly for the certain rituals to keep the superiority of the Brahmins[1]. For these reasons certain advise in the rituals of Bhaktvilasa, subsequently have been ignored by many Vaisnavas, instead new rituals and systems were introduced, leading to the development of many sects and subsects. However it was possible that 'Haribhaktivilasa' was made to let the Brahmins and local aristocrat know that HKM was also based on coservative and Brahminical norms.

To the Vaisnavas of Bengal however Gopal Bhatta's work was of not of much use, mainly because it had no provision for the worship of Caitanya. The rituals of Caitanya worship gradually evolved in Bengal with sectarian variations. The idea of 'Pancatattva', first enunciated by Svarupa Damodara, turned out to be the basic ideology of the Vaisnavas in Bengal[2]. Karnapura explained the concepts of Swarupa Damodara aboaut 'Pancatattva' in the following manner[3]:

---

[1] Vaisnavism in Bengal by Dr. R. Chakrovorty, p. 306. Brahmonical Influence in Vaisnavism 202.

[2] CCM: Adilila / 7 / 19 30; GGD: Verses 6 12, pp. 9-11.

[3] Ibid: p. 147.

Caitanya : represents Krsna.

Nityananda : represents Balarama.

Advaita : represents Siva.

Srivasa and others : represent real devotion.

Gadadhara Pandita : represent the Sakti
(power of the female principle) of devotion.

Shorn of the elemental or universal symbolism, the pancatattva doctrine established the primacy of the Bengali leaders over the Vrndavana group. The Vrndavana leaders did not try to debunk the 'Pancatattva" doctrine. Any attempt to debunk it might have rendered the gulf between Navadvipa and Vrndavana unbridgeable.

'Pancatattva' did not create any difficulty for the Krsna worshippers. To them it was merely a local interpretation of the Vaisnava hagiology. But even in the Radha-Krsna temples certain rituals, such as before singing Kirtana, during Mahotsava, their stress on 'Gauracandrika' and the intermixing of castes became fashionable. The Goswamins of Vrndavana tried to lend sophistication to the HKM. But the unprecedented social mobility generated by the HKM in Bengal to a great extent inhibited the 'Sanskritisation' of the rituals[1].

Every genuine Vaisnavas of Bengal, including the different varieties of Sahajiyas and Bauls used to worship Caitanya. But the worship of Caitanya had no generalised strict rituals. It mainly depended on the various composition of the talented poets associated with the movements. But due to the variations in the outlook, interpretation, compositions of songs and the strength of influence of the leaders of different sects, explanations provided by certain sectarian leaders in the past are difficult to accept by the intellectuals, today. Some of them are mentioned here. The Srikhanda Vaisnavas and the followers of Gadadhara Pandita infused into the Caitanya worship, the spirit of 'libidinous' mysticism. Siddha Caitanyadasa, a famous Vaisnava mendicant of the nineteenth century, regarded himself as Krsna's or Caitanya's wife. He considered Bhagavana Dasa of Kalna as a cowife, and quarreled bitterly with him on the ground that he was trying to entice Krsna / Caitanya away to Kalna. Bhagavana Dasa had the sense of humour

---

[1] Social Mobility of Bengal: by H.R. Sanyal, 1981, pp. 58-64.

to advise Siddha Caitanya Dasa to keep a close watch on Krsna / Caitanya who have reported to have visited, many other wives, in a surreptitious manner[1].

The followers of Nityananda might have adhered to the friendly point of view. The followers of Advaita, on the other hand, began to attach a primary significance to his role. This was evident in the biographies like Advaitaprakasa, Advaitamangala, Valyalilasutram, and Sitagunakadamva[2].

The Pancatattva doctrine signified an attempt to unify the different views by establishing the equalities of the cardinals. Those who did not support the doctrine became deviant Vaisnavas.

Even among the Gaudiya Vaisnavas there were men who were not prepared to accept the theory of the equality of Caitanya's cardinals. The followers of Gadadhara Pandita, for instance, believed that he was the incarnation of Radha. Sometimes in seventeenth century, Radha-Krsna Gosvamin, a leader of the 'Gaudia Gauranga' sect, wrote a ritualistic work called 'Sadhanadipika'[3]. This work was regarded even by the influential Vaisnavas of Vrndavana, as a genuine compendium of the specific rituals of the sects[4]. In all probability the Vrndavana Vaisnavas, had to form an alliance with followers of Gadadhara Pandita who had considerable influence among the people of the districts, Burdwan, Birbhum, Midnapore and Dacca. But many Vaisnavas found it either impossible or impractical to worship, Caitanya and Gadadhara Pandita as the incarnations of Krsna and Radha. The CCM had already depicted Caitanya as the singular incarnation of Radha-Krsna conjugality[5]. Those who believed in this theory might have found difficult to accept Gadadhara Pandita as the incarnation of Radha.

---

[1] Gaudiya Vaisnava Jivana: by Siddha Caitanya Dasa, Vol. 2, p. 91.

[2] Vaisnavism in Bengal: by Dr. R. Chakravorty, p. 307.

[3] Ibid: p. 307.

[4] Sadhanadipika: by Radhakrsna Gosvamin, edited and published by Haridasa Dasa; Ibid: Introduction, p. 1 2.

[5] CCM: Adikhanda, 4 / 165 166; "*Radha purna sakti Krsna purna saktiman, Dui bastute ved nai sastrer praman. Radha Krsna aichhe aki svarup, Lila rase asvadite dhare dui rup*", it means Radha and Krsna in fact is the same character, but adopted two personality in the incarnation, for teaching the jiva souls.

At Navadvipa the relatives of Vishnupriya Devi and their descendants popularized Vishnupriya worship. A thousands names (Sahasranama), were coined for her and rituals of her worship were composed. Vishnupriya worship was considered by some as important as that of Radha[1].

There was also unending controversy on the nature of Krsna's loves. The majority of the Vaisnavas believed that Krsna was the paramour of the milkmaids (gopies). The rituals of Krsna worship generally conformed with this idea. But some Vaisnavas including Jiva Goswamin regarded Krsna as the husband of the milkmaids. The rituals of the Svakiya—ideology (Krsna as husband) were different from those of the Parakiya-concept (Krsna as lover). The Sakiya rituals were not accepted by the majority of the Gaudiya Vaisnavas.

The minority viewpoints might have been reflected in the conservative spirit of Haribhaktivilasa. It was stated in Sadhanadipika that Jiva Goswamin had enunciated the Sakiya doctrine in Srikrsnasamdharva in accordance with the request of Vaisya disciple named Gopala Dasa[2].

The Ritualistic and Ceremonial Synthesis

What was therefore necessary a synthesis of the rituals, which should simple to work out within the ambit of the Parakiya theory which was supported by the majority of the Vaisnavas. But the problem really the Vaisnavas had to solve, was the one of affecting a viable juxtaposition between Krsna and Caitanya on the one hand, and Vrndavana and Navadvipa on the other. The problem was partly solved by the stress laid on the remembrance, contemplation, and analysis (Smarana, Manana and Nididhyasana).

Both Krsna and Caitanya did many types of religious sports.

Since Caitanya was the incarnation of Krsna, his sports might very well be brought within the ambit of the Smaranamangala formula of Rupa Goswamin. A Vaisnava saint named Krsna Dasa Babaji, who lived in Vrndavana, ultimately effected the synthesis. His aim was to enable the Vaisnavas to follow the Raganuga bhakti rituals without any hitch.

---

[1]   Sri Sri Vishnupriyasahsranama Stotra: by Haridasa Goswami, 1322.

[2]   Sandhanadipika: by radhakrsna Goswamin, p. 260.

Krsna Dasa Babaji was born in Orissa in the third decade of eighteenth century. He went to Vrndavana and became pupil of Vaisnava Dasa, the compiler of 'Padakalpataru' anthology. Krsna Dasa belonged to the branch of Narrottama. He lived in Jaipur, for nearly a decade, returned to Vrndavana and became a disciple of a hermit named Jayakrsna Dasa. He mastered the Vaisnava scriptures and became very prominent for his knowledge. Following Krsnadasa Babaji's instructions his disciple, Krsna Dasa II, compiled the following works[1]:-

(1) Bhavanasarasamgraha.
(2) Gutika.
(3) Gauragovindarachanasmaranapaddhati (GGCMP).
(4) Sadhanamrtachandrika.

The first part of the GGCMP deals with the rituals for the worship of Krsna. Sadhanamrtachandrika established the synthesis between Krsna and Caitanya in a ritualistic background. This synthesis grew popular even among the Vrndavana milieu towards the end of the eighteenth and the beginning of nineteenth century. The anthology attached considerable weight to the purely contemplative aspects of Gaudiya Vaisnavism. The emphasis on Smarana, the remembrance, naturally led to the simplification of the rituals.

As an incarnation of Vishnu, Krsna was accepted not only to the Brahmins but also to the Saktas. But the Gaudiya Vaisnava emphasis on the paramourhood of Radha was misunderstood by the conservative elements. The Radha concept was grossly misused by the Sahajiya Gurus, who invented the theory of 'Aropa' or Attribution, which was used for the attribution of Radha, qualities to their female disciples, and the qualities of Krsna to themselves.

The Goswamins of Vrndavana and their followers in Bengal had popularised the worship of Manjaris. A time came when the Manjari, maid servant of Radha seemed more prominent than Radha herself. The Gaudiya Vaisnava ascetic was expected to practice penance as a manjari or sakhi (female companion) of Radha. A very respectable and scholarly Vaidika

---

[1] Valsnavism in Bengal; by Dr. R. Chakravorty, p. 309.

Brahmin of Barisal, named Gopal Bhattacharyia, used to dress up like Lalita Radha's principal companion and achieved great renown, not only for his patience, scholarship and Brahmacarya, but also for the interesting and immaculate behaviour pattern attributed to Sakhi Lalita[1]. A rival concept was that of 'brotherly' or 'friendly' adoration. An ascetic named Siddha Gauracharana Dasa Babaji Maharaja, who lived in Vrndavana during the first half of nineteenth century, regarded himself as Radha's 'elder brother'[2]. Radha was worshipped mainly by the followers of Gadadhara Pandita. In 'Sadhanadipika' an attempt has been made to present the worship of the Gadadhara Pandita school as the best of all other forms of Vaisnava worship[3]. It has also been claimed that Gadadhara Pandita was the greatest cardinal of Caitanya[4].

Siddha Krsnadasa and his disciples simplified the rituals of the worship of Radha and gave them a Brahminical colour, so that they might be acceptable to Brahminical elements. These rituals are mentioned in Sadhanamrtachandrika, where in Radha is given the highest position in the hierarchical order. Her female friends and manjaris are recognised as lesser divinities[5].

The synthesis to finalise to clear the concept of Krsna-Caitanya and Vrndavana-Navadvipa was prepared by Siddha Krsnadasa and his disciples. This was accepted by the majority of the Vaisnavas and still this is the basis for the most of the sects. According to this view, the duties of an ideal devotee as prescribed in 'Sadhanamrtachandrika' are listed below[6].

Duties at the early hours of the Morning:

Singing of Kirtana.
Salutation to Guru.

---

[1]   Gaudiya Vaisnava Jivana by Caitanyadasa Babaji, Vol. 3, p. 374-386; Lalita Dasir Punar Janma by Ramadassa Babaji, Vol. 4 p. 219-231.
[2]   Ibid: Vol. 2, pp. 78-81.
[3]   Ibid: pp. 166-204.
[4]   Ibid: pp. 188.
[5]   Sadhanamratnachandrika: Krsnadasa V 11, pp. 28, 59-63.
[6]   Ibid: pp. 1-37.

Salutation to Pancatattva, Navadvipa and the river Ganges.

Salutation to Krsna, Radha, and their companions.

Salutation to Balarama, Yasoda, Nanda, Rohini, Vrshabhanu and Kirtida (Radhas parents).

Salutation to Rupamanjari and other manjaris.

Salutation to Paurnamasi, Vrndadevi, Tulasi, Vrndavana, the Yamuna river, the Gobardhana mountain, the Syamkunda, the people of Vrndavana, and the Vaisnavas of Vrndavana.

Beginning of the Kirtana on the early morning sports of Caitanya and Krsna.

Contemplation of the state of Krsna at sunrise.

Utterance to the name of Hari according to the required number of times.

Once again the salutation to the Vaisnava Guru.

Performance of the Vaisnava Achamana.

Bath.

Prayer to the Guru before and after bath.

Contemplation of Krsna.

Smearing of the Tilaka markings.

Visit to the temple of Hari.

Worship of the Idol.

The temple utensils are washed.

Flowers and leaves are picked up.

The Morning Duties[1]:

> Tulsi leaves are plucked.
>
> The procedure of worship is settled.
>
> The conchshell and the Bell are placed.
>
> The water is springkled on the Idol.
>
> The morning sports of Caitanya and Krsna are remembered.
>
> The Guru is worshipped.
>
> The Dhyana of Caitanya and Krsna.
>
> Worship of Caitanya.
>
> The Dhyana of Nityananda.
>
> Worship of Nityananda.

---

[1]   Sadhanamratnachandrika: Krsnadasa 11, pp. 38-77.

The Dhyana of Advaita Acarya.

Worship of Advaita Acarya.

The Dhyana of Gadadhara Pandita.

Worship of Dadadhara Pandita.

The Dhyana of Srivasa.

Worship of Srivasa.

Obeisance to the Vaisnava Gurus.

Dhyana of and obeisance to, the female Guru.

Contemplation of the soul.

Contemplation of Krsna.

Contemplation of the eight female companions Radha.

Contemplation of Vrnda Devi, the presiding deity of the Vrndavana woods.

Contemplation of the manjaris.

Worship of Krsna.

Worship of Radha.

Recitation of devotional poems.

Worship of a Vaisnava.

Worship of the Tulsi leaf.

Duties of the Forenoon:

Remembrance of the forenoon sports of Caitanya and Krsna.

Duties of the Noon:

Bath.

Offering of food to the Idol.

Worship of the Tulsi leaf.

Salutation to the Guru.

Listening to the Kirtana composed in Brajabuli language.

Eating of the leftover of the Idol.

Afternoon Duties:

Chanting of names according to a fixed number of times.

Listening to the recitation of hte bhagavatapurana and Bhakkktisastra.

Remembrance of the afternoon sports of Caitanya and Krsna.

Evening Duties:

Bath.

Wearing of Tilaka.

Rousing of the Idol from slumber.

Offering of Vayabhoga to the Idol.

Remembrance of the evening sports of Caitanya and Krsna.

Duties at the early hours of Night:

Offering of food to the Idol.

The Idol is laid to rest.

Nocturnal Duties:

Remembrance of the nocturnal sports of Caitanya and Krsna.

Recitation of relevant poems, as given in Bhavanasarasamgraha.

and other Samranamangala works, dealing with prayer to the Manjaris.

Some elaboration of the salient features of the duties of an ideal Vaisnava, may be worth while. Remembrance of Caitanya and Krsna is not simultaneous. At first the sports of Caitanya and later that of Krsna are to be contemplated. The cardinals of the Caitanya movement in Bengal have been partially deified. Considerable Importance have been attached to Navadvipa and the river Ganges. The singing of Padavali songs composed in the Vrajabuli language, is regarded as a religious duty. The rituals of Radha worship has been simplified. While stress is laid on the worship of Guru, the worship of manjaris is regarded as item of less importance.

The followers of HKM who worked hard for the unity of Gaudiya Vaisnavas in nineteenth century, were in fact mostly the disciples of Krsna Dasa II, such as Nityananda Dasa, Balarama Dasa, Madhusudana Dasa,

Bhagavan Dasa of Kalna and the millionaire Bengali Zaminder Lala Babu of Calcutta[1].

Remembrance solved many problems. There were provisions for the house holders who could perform their worldly duties while contemplating the sports of Krsna and Caitanya. They were not always required to count the beads of the Yaparosary. It was not easy for the landlords, traders, and persons of the middle rank in the society, to pose as Tilakdhari (decorated with twelve yellow markings on the body each as a symbol of a Vaisnava deity) and contemplative Vaisnavas. The simplification of the rituals made HKM, extremely popular. Remembrance made the Vaisnava rituals, quite different from the Brahminical rituals, which could hardly be observed without the assistance of a professional priest. In the rituals of Sadhanamrtachandrika, neither the priest nor the caste system has got any place. The primacy of the Guru was not challenged.

Certain specific rituals were laid down for male and female Vaisnavas, regardless of caste, who wanted to become mendicants.

Later these rituals were selected and laid down in a systemic manner in a work entitled 'Vesasrayavidhih'[2]. Certain sects of Vaisnavas, kept observing the caste rituals (by Brahmonical influence in some areas). But according to the Vaisnavas who have accepted Vesa or Bheka are not required to observe the caste rituals. Bheka may be taken up on any day at any time. The Vaisnavas who wish to take the Bheka, have to seek the blessing of their Guru first. They are to observe the following sacraments or sacramental duties as a part of the procedure[3].

1. Fasting.
2. Shaving of the head.
3. Bath in holy water (the water from the river Ganges).
4. One has to wear a garland of Tulsi beads.
5. Smearing of Tilaka marks.

---

[1] Vaisnavism in Bengal: by Dr. R. Chakrovorty, p. 315.

[2] Vesasrayavidhih: Bengali Translationby Ramanarayana Vidyaratna and Published by Vrajanatha Misra, in Murshidabad.

[3] Vesasrayavidhih: Bengali Translation by Ramanarayana Vidyaratna and Published by Vrajanatha Misra, in Murshidabad, pp. 12-24.

6. One has to wear Mudramarkings.
7. Rechristening.
8. Constant conformity with the 'mantra' given by the initiating Guru.
9. He has to wear 'kaupina' (the loincloth). This is not obligatory to the female Vaisnavas. The kaupina is the symbol of male continuance.
10. Absolute dedication of self to Krsna.

After the performance of the procedure of the sacraments, the mendicant Vaisnava has to practise the ritual worship of Krsna, living in seclusion and continence. He is forbidden to use any ritual object touched by a non-Vaisnava. He has to fast on 'Janmastastami' (the birthday of Krsna) and 'Ekadasi' (eleventh day of the fortnight cycle of position of moon)[1].

The Bhekahari mendicant has to practise austerity and penance.

The ceremony of 'Sraddha' (service after bereavement) of this type of Vaisnavas, consisted singing of kirtana and a vegetarian feast of Vaisnava. The observance of the rules of Sadac-hara or good conduct is obligatory after Bheka.

Even if a Bhekadhari was a Brahmin previously, he is not required the sacred thread. But his scalp has adorned with an unknotted tuft of hair, called 'Sikkha' (which may be translated as flame). A Vaisnava mendicant has to eschew the cultivation of scriptures of Knowledge and action and has to dedicate himself wholly to the cultivation of bhakti[2].

The dead body of a mendicant usually has to be buried[3]. The Syamanandi Vaisnavas of Midnapore, wear the sacred thread after initiation like the Brahmins, regardless of caste[4].

The Vaisnava initiation is said to bestow on all castes the high status of the twice born. Some Vaisnavas of Vrndavana used to regard the bestowal of the sacred threat, as a part of the ritual of initiation. Some Vaisnavas

---

[1] Ibid: p. 25-56.
[2] Vesasrayavidhih: Bengali Translation by Ramanarayana Vidyaratna and Published by Vrajanatha Misra, in Murshidabad, pp. 28-32.
[3] Ibid: pp. 33.
[4] Gaudiya Vaisnava Itihas by Madhusudan Tattvavachaspati, p. 253.

discern no distinction between the Brahminical sacred thread and the Vaisnava garlandof Tulsi beads[1].

All these facts lead to the conclusion that ever since the time of the starting of HKM, the Vaisnava society in Bengal had been moving towards what may be described as Vaisnava Brahmin equation.

Some of the Vaisnava ceremonies in Bengal are personal and some are social. HKM in Bengal has created far more social festivals than any other faith. The festivals Rathayatra, Janmastami, Jhulana, Rasayatra, and Dolayatra are held throughout Bengal. They are organized by many sects and rich individuals and the purpose is to disseminate the HKM among the peasantry.

These festivals are the source of income to the Vaisnava gurus, goswamins, mohantos of the sects, sometimes for themselves and sometimes to run the organisation.

Vaisnava ceremonies and festivals are organised in a particular localities by the active goswamins, mohantos and their followers.

Most of these festivals owe their inception to the descendants of the Vaisnava guru goswamins of the sixteenth and seventeenth centuries.

Most of these descendants live in the district of West Bengal. In Nadia, Murshidabad, Rajshahi, Midnapore, and Hooghly, certain places has become the centres for Vaisnava festivity. From these sort of centres the influence of HKM radiate and keep the Vaisnava spirit alive and flourishing in Bengal. A study of the location of the Vaisnava festivals makes it plain that the HKM is strongly entrenched into the villages.

It must also be noted that in some laces, such as Birbhum, Bankura, Midnapore and Hooghly, the HKM has become well-adjusted with Saiva and Dharma cults. Vaisnava Sankirtana is held in certain Siva temples of Midnapore during Sivaratri festival.

The Gajan, which is connected with the Dharma and Siva cults, is held for the Vaisnava God Syamaraya, in Bandipur village of Hooghly, and many other villages of Burdwan, Birbhum and Bankura.

Vaisnava festivals such as Rathayatra, Janmastami, and Rasayatra and Namayajna and kirtana, have in the course of the centuries, become an inali enable ingredient of social life in the villages of Bengal. Vaisnava fairs such

---

[1]   Ibid: p. 254-255.

as the Kenduli fair of Birbhum, the Ratha fair of Mahesh, and Dhamrai (Dacca), the Janmastami procession of Dacca and the Rasa of Santipur, are famous throughout Bengal. The commemorative Dandamahotsava at Panihati near Calcutta is also very popular.

It is indeed significant that all along from the beginning of the movement, Navadvipa, had been providing the leadership of the HKM until the foundation of ISKCON, about twenty years ago and establishment of its headquarter at Mayapur. Since then the adjacent town Mayapur has become the centre of activity and attraction. Mayapur is the place where Caitanya was actually born. There was a temple of the Gaudiya Vaisnava at Mayapur for a long time. But it did not draw much significant attraction. Since the establishment of a very attractive temple, convenient residence for the pilgrims and nice musium etc. by the ISKCON, Mayapur has become a pilgrimage and tourist centre at the same time. Old Gaudiya temple has also been renovated.

So Mayapur has superseded the superiority of Navadvipa. People attend all these attractive religious places, take part in the various activities, singing, praying, eating together regardless of their caste. The feeling of caste system has not disappeared, completely from the life of Indians. But if one visits, the religious places like these, would feel for a moment that caste system does not exist in the fair, festival and get-together of the Vaisnavas[1].

Practices of Religion by General Mass Vaisnavas (GMV)

Before the advent of Caitanya, it became difficult for common people to practise Hindu religion due to the hardship of the rituals, the strictness of the rules and the restriction of the caste system. The HKM of Caitanya brought the revolution in the Hindu society. The caste barrier was rejected, philosophy and practice became very simple, as one had to live a good life and to sing or chant the name of Hari with premabhakti in heart. After the death of Caitanya situation within the Vaisnava community changed to some extent. There appeared various sects with some rivalry amongst them. To bring them together, due to the necessity of the adjustment

---

[1] Field Work by the author by paying visit to many of these places and gathered information through the other pilgrims.

for the acceptance of the religion to the local population and due to the Brahminical influence in some areas, over the years through many process of synthesis and resynthesis of rituals, though some standard practices have been prescribed in Sadhanamrtnacandrika[1], it is not easy for many people to join the movement as a full time devotee, as a mendicant and follow the rituals. Instead the Caitanya philosophy being very close to their heart, many people prefer, the simple way of practising religion, without giving up their worldly commitment as family person.

General Mass Vaisnavas

For this study purpose this group has been named as General Mass Vaisnavas (GMV). They like to remember the stress, bestowed on the remembrance, contemplation and analysis (Smarana, Manana, Nididhyasana)[2]. Many of them very strongly believe that the good way of practising religion is, the observance of the rules of Sadachara or good conduct, voluntarily not to do any harm to anybody, practising of nonviolence as much as possible, and to think, talk, or sing the name of God, when time permit after fulfilling their primary worldly responsibilities.

Some of them give importance on diet and take strictly vegetarian food and other do not give much importance on diet. It is worthwhile to mention that the mendicants of the Gaudiyia Vaisnava Mission and ISKCON, are strictly vegetarian. Among the members of the various other sects, some are vegetarian and some are not. Their way of praying varies enormously according to their wish, interests, and suitability. It may be simple thinking of God in mind, or some formal or informal prayer. The prayer again may vary enormously, some of them are mentioned here.

Everyday Prayer

Many people of this group have a habit of sitting for prayer in the evening everyday for a moment, after finishing the days work, either alone, or with

---

[1] Sadhanamrtnacandrika by Krsna Dasa 11, edited and published by Vrndavna Dasa.

[2] Vaisnavism in Bengal by Dr. R. Chakravorty, p. 309.

some, or all the member of the family together, either formal or informal way. The prayer may include just simple salutation to God, chanting Harekrsna or other names of God, devotional songs, reading religious scripts such as Gita, Bhagavata etc. or simply religious talks. Many people have a designated house for the purpose named 'Thakurghar' (house for the God). Those who have not got any spare room, usually designate a small corner of a suitable room for the purpose. It has been noticed during survey, people with strong religious feeling in this group, particularly single persons or students, sometimes put a picture of his or her favourite deity on a corner of the dressing table or on the reading desk, for the purpose of prayer. In many families usually the ladies do not take their food in the morning before praying and offering food to Gopal (Krsna).

Once a Week Prayer

People who do their prayer everyday or people who cannot manage to do the prayer everyday sometimes, attend prayer once a week, usually in the temple nearby or organise in the house who has not got any temple around, usually in the Sundays. Some people do arrange for devotional songs, regularly or the prayer could be variable as mentioned in the previous page.

Monthly or Once in while Prayer

Apart from the method of prayer mentioned, sometimes people arrange regularly a bit bigger prayer group, on monthly basis or once in a while following a 'Manat' (promise in mind to God). Sometimes people at the time of crisis or distress during some court cases, illness of the nearest one etc., wishes to arrange a prayer with the belief that by this way one would achieve, the blessing of God.

Yearly Events of Prayer

Some people of the above group, or those who cannot arrange regularly frequent meetings, try to arrange a bigger one, on some special day of the year such as 'Janmastami' (birthday of Krsna), 'Gaurpurnima' (birthday of Gauranga), Bengali New Year day, or to fulfill the manat (promise) or may arrange these bigger meetings without any occasion but for the religious feeling only.

These meetings may be organised by individuals, religious sects, or just social club with religious interests. These bigger meetings are usually designated as 'Mahotsava' or 'Namayajna'.

These sorts of yearly events are very popular in rural Bengal. In certain districts such as in Khulna and Jessore, one or two of these events are arranged in most of the villages, in every year, in the Bengali months, Phalgun, Chaitra and Vaishakh, corresponding to the spring months in England.

Mahotsava[1]

The meaning of the word Mahotsava like this Maha means great and Utsava means celebration. So the meaning of the word 'Mahotsava' means great celebration. This celebration, in fact, is the enjoyment of the devotional songs by an aggregated mass. These are usually arranged by individuals, groups of people, leaders of sects of Vaisnavas or by the social clubs with religious interest. The duration of celebration varies according to the desire of the organisers, from few hours to few days. The priest is not essential to conduct the events here. Usually one of the leading singers conduct the ceremony, by organizing the informal sequence of the singers. The events always starts of, with songs about Gauranga called 'Gaurachandrika'. There may be one song or many songs of this kind, may be sung by one individual or a group. This is followed by varieties of other kinds of devotional songs, including Baul, Padavali Kirtan, Lila Kirtan, Pala Kirtan etc. There are usually few principal singers, who perform the main singing and are helped by a group of supportive singers. But most of the other attendants usually listen quietly. It is believed in general that the effect is the same in achieving, the blessing of the God either as a singer or as a listener.

---

[1] Valsnavism in Bengal: by Dr. R. Chakravorty, p. 309.

Namayajna[1]

Nama means here the name of 'Hari' or 'God', Yajna means 'sacrifice' or 'worship'. So the the name 'Namayajna' means singing the name of Hari in the form of a yajna. The purpose of this yajna is to ensure the well being of the individual, his family and domestic and ultimately the whole community.

Namayajna again a special event usually arranged once in a year, regularly by some people and as a special occasion or if this is a 'manat'. The organisers are of the same type as in case of Mahotsava. In Namayajna singing pattern is completely different from Mahotsava.

The singing here in fact is the constant repetition of the name of God like this *"Hare-Krsna Hare Krsna Krsna Krsna Hare Hare Hare Rama Hare Rama Rama Rama Hare Hare"*. In Bengali or in Sanskrit these count in each cycle exactly sixteen word (name of God) and thirty two letters. The believer in this yajna and the organisers like to maintain very strict discipline not to break the cycle, and to maintain the continuity for a definite period of time, they declare before the starting of the 'Yajna'. If there is any break either in the cycle or in the continuity, then the 'Yajna' would be imperfect and the desired effect of the blessing of Krsna may not be achieved. The time for arranging this 'Namayajna' has to be for a fixed period set before hand and in term of Indian timing called 'prahar' (each prahar equivalent to three hours), such as one prahar, four prahar, eight prahar, sixteen prahar, twenty-four prahar (three day and night) etc. Sometimes it could be for seven days. It is claimed in one temple in Navadvipa that there is a continuous namkirtana which had started many years ago. The continuous namasankirtana is maintained by the participation of many different groups of singers known as 'Kirtaniyas'.

1. The Author's Interview with B.S. Swamimaharaj, in charge of Gaudiya Vaisnava Mission, London, a few famous poet singers (kabi gayak, they are known as Sarkar) of Bengal, with vast knowledge in Hindu religion, Rajen Sarkar, Bijoy Sarkar, Nishi Sarkar and Rasik Sarkar: The meaning of Hare, Krsna and Ram Ram and Krsna are the incarnation

---

[1]   Field Work by the Author by attending many Mahotsava and Namayajna.

of Vishnu, so are the same. Hare is the vocative of the word 'Hara', a name of Radha. Radha is a part of Krsna. So all the three word has the same meaning;

2. The Science of Self Realisation: by A.C. Bhaktivedantaswami Prabhupada, p. 147-48, "the word Hara is the form of addressing the energy of the Lord, and the words Krsna and Rama are forms of addressing the Lord Himself. Both Krsna and Rama means supreme pleasure and Hara is the supreme pleasure energy of the Lord, changed to Hare in vocative."

Each group comes in turn to sing for a variable period of time, depending on the number of group of participants and the availability of the time, usually from half an hour to two hours. During the later part of the singing of a group, another group gets ready in a place arranged for them, nearby could be some yards away, where they start their tune, rhythm and the melody of 'Raga' and enter the stage before the other group finishes. In this way there is always expected to be an overlapping for a short period to maintain the continuity. Moreover to make sure about maintaining the continuity, always there is a Vaisnava present, there one side with his Tulsi bead to continue the chanting constantly, so that there would not be any chance for interruption. The constant repetition of the name of the God, by which an ecstatic state may be attained. The magical potency of the name is so great that even a 'blasphemous' repetition of the name of Krsna may secure beatitude. Not only the singing, the success of the Yajna, the blessing of the God depends on the good conduct and the modesty of the host also. All the attendants are really treated like an honoured guest. It has been observed particularly in the Namyajna in the rural area, even sometimes the feet of the attendants are washed either by the host of their representatives, before they are asked to sit for Yajna. They like to create the atmosphere of a holy place, such as Vrndavana and Navadvipa etc. Many people really believe in the traditional Vaisnava rhyme "*Adyavadi sei lila karen Gora Roy, kona kona bhagyavana dekhibare paye*", it means still Gauranga plays the same sports, only some fortunate ones can visualise that. On the other hand if one concentrates in the events, can have the pleasure of seeing the deity in a holy place.

The serious thinkers really believe that God physically presents there, which again could be illustrated with the traditional Vaisnava rhyme[1], *"Je nam sei Krsna bhaja nistha kari, namera sahite achhen apani Sri Hari"*, it means that there is no difference between the name of God and the God himelf, one need to concentrate seriously on devotion to find him adherent with the name.

In CCM it has been mentioned like this, *"Krsna nama Krsna guna Krsna lilavrnda, Krsner svarupasama save chidananda".* It means the name of Krsna, the qualities of Krsna and the sports (lila) of Krsna like his physical presence bring ever delight in the heart. Besides all these the singing itself with the right tune, accompanied with the melody of the 'Raga' of the Indian classical music, appropriate for the hour of the day, performed by an experienced Kirtaniya, with bhakti in his heart, can create an atmosphere, the depth of which cannot be expressed or described by any language, only a devotee can fee, what could be called 'premabhakti'. It has been observed many times, to roll down the tears of emotion, from the eyes of many spectators during the flow of this kind of kirtanas.

The smoking or any sort of habit that may cause addiction, even drinking tea, are strictly prohibited in this sort of occasion. The food is usually served in this sort of occasion and it is always, strictly vegetarian. A religious person of any belief may have some feeling of the spiritual atmosphere, if visited.

There is no chaste bar in this sort of occasion. People of any caste could be freely involved in Mahotsava and Namayajna, either as an organiser or as a participant.

Each sect has few special features of their practices, but all sects utter Harekrsna as their main word of prayer, except 'Matua Sampradaya', (Harichand sect) who stresses on the word 'Haribol' more.

---

[1]   Field Work by the Author by visiting many Namayajnas.

Matua Sampradaya or Harichand Sect[1]

The sect was founded by the person called Harichand Thakur (1711-1777). His followers believe that Mahaprabhu Caitanya came back as an another incarnation as 'Harichand thakur', at the village 'Odakandhi' in the district of Faridpur of East Bengal. They have strong followings in the district of Faridpur, Jessosre, Khulna of Bangladesh and Northern part of 24 Parganas, and Bagula area of Nadia of West Bengal. The most of the 'Namasudra' caste of these districts belonged to Mutua sect. Their followers do not arrange any 'Namayajna' instead they arrange 'Mahotsava'. Their biggest Mahotsava is usually, once in a year and is called 'Barani'.

Ramthakur Sect[2]

The founder of this sect, Sri Sri Ramthakur (1859-1949), was born in the village 'Dingamanik' in the district of Faridpur of Bangladesh. His activities were mainly at the district of 'Nowakhali' and the adjoining district of Bangladesh. After Independence of India many of his followers have migrated to India, and set up their main centre at Jadavpur, in greater Calcutta. The centre is called 'Kaivalyadham'. They also have set up an important centre at Delhi. They sing Hare Krsna. They arrange 'Mahotsava' instead of 'Namayajna'. One of the features of the Mahotsava is that they arrange 'Satyanarayan Puja' which is an essential element of their Mahotsava. They believe Ramthakur was an incarnation of God. Some of their activities, suggest that this sect has got the effect of Brahminical influence, such as 'Satyanarayan puja'.

---

[1] Sri Sri Harililamrta by Tarak Chandra Sarkas; The Author's Interview with P.R. Thakur and his son Kapil Thakur, the great grand son and the great great grand son, respectively of 'Sri Harichand Thakur' and with numerous other leading members.

[2] Sri Ramthakur Prasange by Jatindra Chandra Debroy; The Author's interview with many of their leading Mahantas, Particularly Mr. B.S. Chatterjee, Head of the Delhi temple.

CHAPTER X

Harekrsna Movement Outside India

First western Vaisnavas

In the last century and early part of this century many Indian religious leaders had visited the West for lecturing and touring and for the purpose of preaching. There is a record that a Gaudiya Vaisnava named Premananda Bharati (1857-1914), preached in Europe and U.S.A.[1]. A Caitanyasamaja was established in U.S.A. in about 1897 by an American convert named Professor Osman. Real thought about this originated at the time when Bhakti Vinode Thakur became the in-charge of hte Gaudiya Vaisnavas. He founded a formal central organization named Gaudiya Math and Mission. After him, his son Bhakti Siddhanta Swaraswati Thakur took a further step to organize the Vaisnavas. In his time there were at least sixty-four Maths (centre) were established in various places of India. He had a vision to preach the Harekrsna mantra to the West. He himself was not able to come for the purpose, but sent a mission of a few members to England in 1933. Among them Tridandi Swami Bhakti Pradip Tirtha Maharaj was prominent[2]. With his easy and simple approach towards the religion, and discussion with reasoning attracted many people. The first formal meeting they organized was at Kensington Hall. Among the many attenders was Miss Daily Cicilia Bowtell, a British lady with her mother. The subject of discussion on that day was 'Life after death'. She was very much impressed

---

[1] Caritasudha: by Ramadasa Babaji, Vol. 1, pp. 270-298; Sajjanatosami: 1897, Vol. 2 p. 3.

[2] Author's Interview with B.S. Swami Maharaj in charge of the Gaudiya mission, London 1991; News Letter by the Gaudiya Mission, London, 1991.

with the discussion. That was really a remarkable day in her life also. Since then she was deeply involved with the thought of the question, life after death. Within a few days, she came to encounter the Swamiji, involved with more deeper and detailed discussion. She was very much convinced and became his disciple promptly and was known as Srimati 'Vinodevani Dasi'[1].

Since then Vinodevani became a keen learner of the Vaisnava literature. She had another friend named Steela Horrish, who was impressed by the change and progress of Vinodevani and also became a Vaisnava disciple. Vinodevani realized the necessity for a Vaisnava centre at London. She did not have many helpers or supporters. Steel with her own ability, she bought a house at 27, Cranhurst Road, London, N.W.2. and soon after she made a will to donate the house to the Gaudiya Mission, Calcutta.

Since then the house was not much in use or active. After her death in 1981, other members of the Gaudiya Mission had come to make the house, an active centre for the Gaudiya Mission, since 1985[2]. So Vinodevani was the first recorded Vaisnava disciple in the West, after Professor Osman.

For preaching the HKM in the west, apart from the mission just mentioned, Bhakti Siddhanta Thakur requested many of his other disciples. One of them was A.C. Bhaktivedanta Swami Prabhupada. He was requested to spread the teachings of Lord Krsna, including the Harekrsna mantra in 1922, when he was known as A.C. Dey and a house holder[3]. By profession he used to be a pharmacist. After the retirement from his job he became a full time devotee, left the house to live in Vrndavana, where he made many friends, acquaintances and disciples, some of them were quite wealthy and influential. He also started to write about Sri Krsna and the HKM and to translate many Vaisnava literature into English. At this stage he thought seriously, about the request his spiritual master made, forty-three years ago, to bring the HKM to the West. He was favoured by one of his disciples, the owner of a merchant ship company. He was given free passage in a cargo ship named 'Jalduta' by the Scindia Steamship Company. The voyage was arduous from Calcutta to Boston, USA, for a seventy years old lonely

---

[1]   News Letter by the Gaudiya Mission, London, 1991 p. 2.

[2]   News Letter by the Gaudiya Mission, London, 1991, p. 3.

[3]   Chant and Be Happy: by A.C. Bhaktivdanta Swami Prabhupada, 1985, p. 50.

Indian holy man. The survivor of the previous two attacks of coronary heart disease, did not feel any tiredness, rather the pleasure of the thought of fulfilling the desire of his spiritual master, and bringing the Krsnabhakti of thousands years, only known by the Indians, to the people of America, generated lots of enthusiasm. On his arrival at the Commonwealth Pier, on September 17, 1965, he wrote in his diary the following words[1].

"Absorbed in material life, they (Americans) think themselves are very happy and satisfied and therefore they do not have any taste for the transcendental message of Vasudeva (Krsna) . . . . But I know your causeless mercy can make everything possible, because you are the most expert mystic . . . . How will I make them understand this message of Krsna consciousness? Oh Lord, I am simply praying for your mercy, so that I will be able to convince them about your message . . . I am seeking your benediction . . . . I have no devotion, nor do I have any knowledge, but I have strong faith in the holy name of Krsna".

After landing in American with Indian rupees equivalent to eight dollar, he spent first year in the United States with a family in Butler, Pennsylvania, with an Indian yoga teacher in Manhattan, and later with the help of a friend, rented a small room in upper Manhattan. By the summer of 1966, he found a larger location, more suitable of propagating the desired mahamantra Harekrsna and the ancient science of Krsna consciousness. That summer he had met a young man named Harvey Cohen, who offered him an old Artist's residence in a loft in lower Manhattan.

Here a small group of young Bohemian types of people would join Prabhupada every Monday, Wednesday and Friday for chanting Harekrsna and classes on the Bhagavatagita. At this stage it was not formally announced or not much known, the International Society for Krsna Consciousness (ISKCON), formed with a very small group of supporters.

Swamiji's guests were only very few and their interests included music, drugs, macrobiotics, pacifism and spiritual meditation. Hardly they knew about what they were chanting and what they were singing. They just enjoyed it and liked being in the presence of the man they affectionately called 'Swamiji' (ascetics). These musicians, artists, poets and intellectuals, most of whom have chosen to live outside the mainstream society, felt that

---

[1]   Ibid. p. 50.

by chanting Harekrsna they were taking part in something mystical and unique.

Prabhupada also led the solo chanting: Hare Ksna Hare Krsna Krsna Krsna Hare Hare / Hare Rama Hare Rama Rama Rama Hare Hare.

The melody was always the same a simple four note phrase, the first four notes of the major scale. Prabhupada led the kirtana with small cymbals, he had brought with him from India. He would signal them with one-two-three, one-two-three fashion.

Some of his followers used to clap with him and some used to join in with small finger-cymbals of their own. Others used to sit in a yoga posture, hands outstretched, chanting and meditating on this novel transcendental vibration. Guests would sometimes bring other instruments, including guitars, tambouras, flutes, tambourines and a wide variety of drums[1].

Foundation of ISCKON and its rapid progress

After a few months some of Prabhupada's followers secured him a better place to live in and also for his work. The new Second Avenue location on the hippie filled Lower East side included an apartment for the Prabhupada one floor up and the ground floor for the use of a temple. This was the first designated temple established by the supporter of HKM in the Western World. Since then progress came rapidly in favour of Prabhupada. Within a few weeks, the small sixty by twenty-five feet room, used to be packed with young people three nights a week. Gradually the visitors began to bring tapestries, paintings for the wall, carpet for the floor and amplification equipment for Prabhupada's lectures and kirtanas.

Prabhupada initiated his first disciples in the September, 1966.

This time he had a dozen of students vowed to chant minimum sixteen round a day on their beads. This meant reciting the sixteen word mantra, on their chain of 108 beads, bring a total of 1728 times a day, a meditation that would take them between one and a half to two hours to complete.

The celebrated American poet Allen Ginsberg, accompanying the kirtana on his harmonium (a mini piano like Indian instrument), had by now become a regular attendant at the evening chanting sessions at the

---

[1]   Chant and Be Happy by A.C. Bhaktivedanta Swami Prabhupada, 1985, p. 52.

temple and in near by Topkins Square Park. Allen Ginberg's feeling was like this in his own words.[1].

"I liked the idea that Bhaktivedanta had chosen the Lower Eastside of New York for his practice . . . . I was astounded that he had come with the chanting, because it seemed like a reinforcement from India. I had been running around singing Hare Krsna, but had never understood exactly why or what it meant. I thought it was great that he was here to expound on the Hare Krsna mantra. That would sort of justify my singing. I knew what I was doing, but I did not have any theological background to satisfy further inquiry and here was some who did. So I thought that was absolutely great . . . . If anyone wanted to know the technical intricacies and the ultimate history, I could send them to him. He had a personal, selfless sweetness like total devotion, and that was what conquered me . . . a kind of personal charm, coming from dedication. I always like to be with him."

The chanting of Harekrsna seemed to spread in a magical way. As the time went on, the number of people attracted to it increased in geometrical progression. The mantra seemed to have a life of its own. Whether it was the melody, the beat, the sounds of the words, the look of the devotees or Prabhupada humility or calmness, nearly everyone who then came in touch with the chanting responded favourably. In December 1966 Prabhupada explained in his first record album, the LP that introduced two of the famous Beatles, stars, John Lennon and George Harrison to Hare Krsna "that the chanting of the mantra is not a material sound vibration, but directly comes from the spiritual world"[2].

Prabhupadas kirtana at Topkins Square Park were really spiritual happenings. Hundreds of people from all walks of life took part; some as observers and some as eager participants, chanting, clapping their hands, dancing, and playing musical instruments.

Irvin Halpern, one of many local musicians, who regularly participated, remembers the scene like this.[3]

[1]   Ibid. p. 54.
[2]   Chant and Be Happy by A.C. Baktivedanta Swami Prabhupada, 1985, p. 45-55.
[3]   Ibid: p. 55.

"The park was resounded. The musicians were very careful in listening to the mantras. Many people came here just to tune into the musical gift, the transmission of the drama. 'Hey' they would say, 'listen to this holy monk'.

People were sure they were going to be unusual feats, grandstanding, flashy levitatioins or whatever people expected was going to happen. But when the simplicity of what the Swami was really saying, when you began to sense it whether you were motivated to actually make a lifetime commitment and go this way of life or whether you merely wanted to place it in a place and give certain due respect to it turned you around. And that was interesting too, the different ways in which people regarded the kirtana. Some people thought it was a prelude, and some thought it was the main event. Some people liked the music and some the poetic sound of it".

The New York Times described the kirtana at the Tompkins Square Park with the headlines and comment like this.[1]

"Swami's Flock Chants in Park to Find Ecstasy", sitting under a tree in a Lower East Side park and occasionally dancing, fifty followers of a Hindu Swami repeated a sixteen word chant for two hours yesterday afternoon to the accompaniment of cymbals, tambourines, sticks, drums, bells, and a small reed organ .... Repetition of the chant, Swami A.C. Bhaktivedanta says, is the best way to achieve self-realization in this age of destruction.

. . . Many in the crowd of about hundred persons standing around the chanters found themselves swaying to or clapping to clapping hand in time to the hypnotic rhythmic music. 'It brings a state of ecstasy', said Allen Grinsberg the poet. "The ecstasy of the chant or Mantra Hare Krsna Hare Krsna Krsna Krsna Hare Hare / Hare Rama Hare Rama Rama Rama Hare Hare, has replaced LSD and other drugs for many of the Swami's followers"

At the same time, New York's avantgarde newspaper[2] 'The East Village Other' ran a front page story with a full page photograph of Prabhupada, standing and speaking to large group of people in the park. The headlines read 'Save Earth Now' and just below the picture, the mahamantra was written 'Hare Krsna the sixteen words'.

---

[1] *The New York Times*: 9th October, 1966.
[2] The East Village Others: October, 1966.

The article admired the chanting and described how Prabhupada had succeeded in convincing the world's toughest audience Bohemians, acid heads, potheads, and hippies that he knew the way to go.

The newspaper story described how a visit to the temple at 26 Second Avenue would bring "living, visible, tangible proof" that God is alive and well. The story quoted one of Prabhupada's new disciples: "I started chanting to myself, like the way Swamiji said when I was walking down the street, Hare Krsna . . . over and over, and suddenly everything started looking so beautiful, the kids, the old man and women. even the creeps looked." Finding it superior to the euphoria from any kind of drug, he said, "There is no coming down from this. I can always do this at any time, anywhere. It's always with you"[1]. This gave really good publicity at New York.

Early in 1967, several of Prabhupada's disciples left New York and opened a temple in the heart of San Francisco's Haight Ashbury district, homes for thousands of hippies and 'flower children' from all over the country. Within a short time Prabhupada's temple became a spiritual heaven, for troubled, searching and sometimes desperate young people. Drug overdoses were common, and hundreds confused, dazed, and disenchanted young Americans roamed the street.

Haridasa, the first president of the San Francisco temple remembers what it was like: "The hippies needed all the help they could get and they new it. The Radha Krsna temple was certainly a kind of spiritual heaven. Kids sensed it. They used to run and live in the street. There was no place, where they could go, where people were not going to hurt them.

I think it saved a lot of life; there might have been a lot more casualties if it had not for Hare Krsna. It was like opening a temple in battle field. It was the hardest place to do it, but it was the place where it was most needed.

Although Swamiji had no precedents of dealing with any of this, he applied the chanting with the miraculous results. The chanting was wonderful it worked". Michael Bowen, an artist and one of the leading figures of the Haight Ashbury scene recalled that Prabhupada had "amazing ability to get people off drugs, specially speed, heroine, burntout LSD cases all of that[2]."

---

[1]   Chant and Be Happy: by A.C.B.S. Prabhupada, pp. 57-58.

Everyday at the temple devotees cooked and served over two hundred young people a free, sumptuous, Multicourse lunch of vegetarian food offered to Krsna. Many local merchants helped to make this possible by donating to the cause. An early devotee from San Francisco, Harsarani recalled those days "People who were plain lost, or needed comforting . . . sort of wandered or staggered into the temple. Some of them stayed and became devotee, and some just took prasadam (spiritual food) and left.

Just from medical standpoint, doctor did not know what to do with people on LSD. The police and the free clinic in the area could not handle the over load of people taking LSD. The police saw Swamiji as a certain refuge."

Swamiji would go anywhere to spread the Krsna consciousness. He marked the major spiritual event of the San Francisco hippy era on January 29, 1967[1]. He got the support from the local musical group, voluntary organisation, business companies, such as The Greatful Dead, Moby Grape, Janis Jopkin and Big Brother and the Holding Company, Jefferson Airplane, Quicksilver Messenger Service all the newwave San Francisco bands and had all agreed to appear with Prabhupada at the Avalon Ballrooms Mantra-Rock Dance, a procession from which would go to the local Hare Krsna temple.

Thousands of hippies, anticipating an exciting evening, packed the hall. the LSD pioneer Timothy Leary and Augustus Owsley 11, known for his own brand of LSD, were there too. Prabhupada with a small group of devotee arrived amid uproarious applause and cheering by a crowd that had waited weeks in great anticipation for this moment.

The well known poet Allen Ginsberg introduced Prabhupada and after giving his own account of realization, told the crowd that the chanting of the Hare Krsna mantra in the early morning in the Radha-Krsna temple was an important community service to those who were 'coming down from LSD', because the chanting would 'stabilize their consciousness on reentry'. The chanting started slowly but rythmically, and gradually it spread throughout the ball room, enveloping everyone. Hippies got to their feet, held hands, and began to dance as enormous, pulsing pictures of Krsna were projected around the walls of the ballroom in perfect sync with the beat of the mantra.

---

[1]   Ibid: p. 59.

By the time Prabhupada began to dance with his arm raised, the crowd was completely absorbed in chanting, dancing and playing the small musical instruments they brought for the occasion.

Ginsberg later recalled, "We sang Hare Krsna all evening. It was absolutely great an open thing. It was the height of the Haight-Ashbury spiritual enthusiasm"[1]. As the tempo speeded up, the chanting and dancing became more and more intense, spurred on by a stage full of rock musicians, who were as charmed by the magic of the mahamantra as the amateur musicians had been at the Tompkins Square kirtanas only a few weeks before. When it seemed it could go no further, the changing stopped. Prabhupada offered prayer to his spiritual master into the microphone and ended by saying three times, "all glories to the assembled devotees". The Haight Ashbury neighbourhood buzzed with the Mantra-Rock dance for weeks afterward.

Within a few months of the Mantra-Rock event, devotees in San Francisco, New York and Montreal began to take to the street, their mridangas (clay drums) and kartalas (hand cymbals) to chant the mahamantra as a daily basis.

When the Vietnam war protest movement was reaching its climax, on May 31, 1969, six devotees joined John Lennon and Yoko Ono at Montreal's Queen Elizabeth Hotel-room to play instruments and sing on John and Yoko's famous recording 'Give Peace a Chance'. This song included the mantra. Other important people present on that day were Timmy Leary, Rosemary, Tommy Smothers, Bobby Dylan, Tommy Cooper, Derek Tailor, Norman Mailor and Allen Ginsberg. They were singing "Hare Krsna . . . along with, all we are saying is give peace a chance"[2].

The Hare Krsna devotees had been visiting with Lennon and other important people, several days, discussing world peace and self-realization. Because of this and other wide spread exposure, people all over the world soon began to identify the devotees of chanting Hare Krsna as a harbingers of a more simple, joyful and peaceful way of life. George Harrison was the impetus of the Beatles spiritual quest of the sixties. He produced a hit single. 'The Hare Krsna Mantra' in the September of the same year. Soon after

---

[1] Chant and Be Happy: by A.C.B.S. Prabhupada, pp. 60.

[2] Chant and Be Happy: by A.C.B.S., Prabhupada, pp. 2, 60.

rising to the top ten or top twenty best selling record charts, throughout England, Europe, and parts of Asia, the Hare Krsna chant became a household word especially in England, where the BBC had featured the Hare Krsna chanters (as they were then called), four times in the country's most popular television program, Top of the Pops.

At the anti war demonstration in Washingtono D.C. on November 15, 1969, devotees from all over the United States and Canada chanted the Hare Krsna mantra throughout the day and distributed peace formula, a leaflet based on Prabhupada's teachings from the Vedic scriptures. This leaflet was distributed to mass for many months and influenced thousands of lives.

By 1970, when George Harrison's 'My Sweet Lord' with its beautiful recurring lyrics of Hare Krsna and Hare Rama was the international number one hit song of the day, devotees in dhotis and saris (Indian clothes), chanting the mahamantra with musical instruments, were then a familiar sight in almost every major city throughout the world.

Hare Krsna Movement in the United Kingdom[1]

Since the establishment of ISKCON at New York in 1966, the movement soon became very popular in many countries in the world. In United Kingdom the formal establishment of ISKCON centre was in 1971. But two most popular singers from United Kingdom, had patronized the ISKCON, quite earlier in 1969, when they produced the most popular record of Harekrsna. George Harrison also helped Prabhupada to establish the centre, by providing an enormous estate, on seventeen acres of land, for this accommodation and opening the centre at Lechmore Heath near Watford. The centre was named as Bhaktivedanta Manor.

After the establishment of the Bhaktivedanta Manor ISKCON soon became very popular in U.K., both to the local population and to the Indian Community. Besides this main centre, there were few other recognizable centres also developed at London, Leicester, Liverpool, Manchester and at Lanarkshire in Scotland. In all these centres they have got a temple and

---

[1] Authors own observation and from the ISKCON literature from Bhaktivedanta Manor, 1988.

some full time residential devotees. Besides these centres there are quite few small satellite centres, called 'Namahatta', where there is no temple, but still cater some degree of activities mainly provided by the part time devotees.

The Bhaktivedanta Manor is the main centre of activities and is the most important Hindu establishment in Britain. It is situated in a beautiful and pastures of seventeen acres of land. It is the only Hindu theological college and has a magnificent temple for the worship of Radha-Gokulananda and Ram-Sita.

The Manor's cows provide the sweets and other preparation offered to the Deities. The temple has become famous for distribution of prasad of high quality and flowers from its own garden adorn the deities all year round. The whole establishment is run on the voluntary contribution from the patrons, devotees, well wishers and the visitors. In a pleasant and delightful atmosphere at a London Suburb, it attracts huge number of crowd.

Devotees from the Manor go out daily for 'nagar kirtan', to distribute the society's literature, and to enlighten people in Krsna consciousness.

ISKCON regularly gives presentations at school, colleges and gatherings and many groups visit Bhakktivedanta Manor to learn about the religion and the way of life of a whole time Krsna devotee.

It is like a place of pilgrimage in every Sunday, when people come from distance places to take part in prayer, even sometimes just for a quick visit. On Sundays classes instruct children in the ideals of Indian culture and philosophy. The Manor's theatre group perform dramas to depict the teachings and past times of Lord Krsna. Lectures and study courses are held for the adults. Bhaktivedanta Manor also runs a small Gurukula for about thirty five children.

Because it is an ideal spiritual sanctuary, many families choose to hold important family ceremonies such as weddings, sraddha (religious functions after bereavement) etc. at the Manor. Manor provides the priests to perform all these activities.

It is traditional for Hindus to visit a sacred place for pilgrimage on holy days. Celebrations are held to observe Ramnavami, Janmastami and Diwali. Nowhere else is as popular as Bhaktivedanta Manor to visit on Janmastami, when about more than thirty thousands people come in each year to take view of the Deities. Similar number of people take part in the procession of Rathayatra (pulling the cart containing the statue of Jagannatha).

Time to time crowd becomes so much that it causes traffic problem and hampers the daily life of local people. The participants are mixed of local and Indian origin. Bhaktivedanta Manor functions from 4:30 am to 9:30 pm, every day of the year. There is a large team of dedicated devotees working constantly to keep the centre going.

The HKM is quite popular to the Indian community in Britain. To know the individual favourite reverend, a survey of questionnaire of instant answer was carried out, in England to five thousands of Indians above the age of forty, with male and female almost equal number, similar as was carried out in West Bengal. This survey was carried out in common places, avoiding the religious gatherings.

The result suggested that fifty two per cent were in favour of Krsna, thirteen per cent in favour of Sakti, and thirty five per cent were not sure. It did not make any difference between Krsna and Kali to them. The result was more or less similar as was noted in West Bengal, only difference was that not a significant number was in favour of Siva in Britain.

ISKCON in other Countries

To come back to the activities of ISKCON, which is providing similar services, through many other centres almost in every country, all over the World, no other organization has done so much to introduce the World, to India's spiritual heritage. More and more people are turning to India for spiritual guidance to solve their problems of conflict of thoughts and peace of mind.

ISKCON is at the fore front of this spiritual revolution. Temples have been established in most major cities as oases of spiritual solace from which devotees of ISKCON work selflessly to teach the massage of 'Sanatan dharma'.

Farming communities provide the ideal place to cultivate 'high thinking and simple living' and they practically demonstrate self-sufficiency. Gurukula schools have been set up to provide the perfect balance of spiritual and material education.

Religious colleges are set up to train devotees as priests, teachers and the missionaries of the religion. The devotee serves the community by counseling members of the public on personal problems and how to improve the quality of lives.

Most ISKCON centres operate a programme of relief for the poor under the title 'food for the life'. These programmes have been highly commended by the government officials throughout the World. What makes ISKCON so special is that it attracts dedicated volunteers to give their full service to this vital mission, which is unique.

All these success is the result of the Vision, determination and the tireless energy of a man, A.C. Bhaktivedanta Swami Prabhupada.

He was busy not only in touring and traveling, teaching and preaching, and guiding and managing, but in utilizing every opportunity of free moment, of his valuable time in translating the Vedic literature. Within twelve years he wrote about seventy books. ISKCON now publishes Vedic literature in fifty languages and in just two decades, has sold more than three hundred million books worldwide[1]. These books have created a revolution of thinking in the minds of millions of people. His achievements are extraordinary. No wonder that in 1977, the *times of India* declared him to be the "India's Greatest Spiritual and Philosophical Ambassador in the World".

Vraja, Golak and Vrndavan

What we call Vraja, Golak or Vrndavan were places in a hidden area of deep forest of U.P. in India. Not much known about five hundred years ago, was revived by the thought of Sri-Caitanya and the hard work of his six Goswamins. Till the year 1966, hardly these names, were known outside India. Now along with the Krsna consciousness not only these names are known, in the outside world, but in some countries, some people are really so much amazed and charmed by the history of these places, geographical descriptions, and the delightful thought of the sports ground of Radha-Krsna and other cowherd boys and girls (lila bhumi of Radha-Krsna and Gop-Gopini), that they have ventured to build and create the same atmosphere, by the name Vrndavan, Vraja, or Golak in their own country.

---

[1] Janmastami Publication: Bhaktivedanta Manor, 1992, p. 34.

In 1968 A.C. Bhaktivedanta Swami founded the New Vrndavan at West Virginia, U.S.A. with a modest start in a forest. Now spanning more than four thousands acres of land, it is beehive of activity with some twenty work shops and studios, a school, a press, two hundred cow dairy farm and one of the state's most gorgeous and famous architectural wonders 'Prabhupada's Palace of Gold'.

The New Vrndavan community vaulted to international acclaim in 1979, with the opening of the Palace of Gold, which blends the richness and beauty of Indian architectural design with American technological advances.

The Palace, a creation of marble, onyx, stained glass, goldleaf, crystal and teak, has attracted an estimated 2.5 million people in five years since it opened. As one reporter put it, "the Palace of Gold has to be seen to be believed". One visitor called it "the Hare Krsna temple equivalent of the Sistine Chapel" and the news media had doubted it, "the Taj Mahal of the West"[1].

Many such New Vrndavanas, Gokulas or Golakas, small or large are founded in many countries, such as Villa Vrndavana at Florence in Italy, New Vraja Mandala at Santa Clarain Spain, New Nandagram at Bambra and New Govardhana at Murwillumbah in Australia, Vrajabhumi at Teresopolis, Nova Vrajadhama at Caruaru and Gaur Vrndavana at Parati in Brazil, Bhaktilata Purin in Argentina, Nueva Mathura in Colombia, Nueva Mayapur in Ecuador and Govinda Kunja in Indonesia. Possibly there are many others which are not enlisted. Many vegetarian restaurants by the name Govinda's or Gopal's, Prasad are established in most of the countries where there are ISKCON establishment.

Never in the past, Indian philosophy, religious practice along with the culture and food habit, had been so widely accepted, all over the world, before the advent of ISKCON. The international organizing body has been controlling the coordination, administration and the publicity very efficiently. Although it is the same philosophy, but is being practised by different people in different environment, in different countries. So it is not unexpected that some sort of dilution and adjustment of the thought and practice would not occur, according to the local need.

---

[1] Back to Godhead ISKON Publication, Vol. 19, No. 12, pp. 27-29.

It may also be possible that some difference might be existing between the different groups or may emerge in future, but the central theme and the core message will be carried foreward. On watching the religious map of the world to-day, it is conceivable that the baul song is true[1]:

> *Krsna name jagat jay bhasiya,*
> *balak briddha ak haiye,*
> *Horir name mon majiye,*
> *katajan aj uthila matiya.*

> *Purba paschim nai bhedabhed,*
> *sada kalor naiko prabhed,*
> *garla samaj jat kula bhangiya.*

It means that the world is being over flown, with the name of Krsna. Adult and children, too many of them are so excited to sing together, the name of Krsna.

Without making any discrimination between east and west, white and black, it has founded as new society, by breaking the superstitious restrictions of the family and the caste barrier.

Western intellectual's view on Harekrsna Movement

Steven J. Gelberg (SJG) a prominent western scholar on Hindu religion and an exponent of HKM in the west, had some interviews with a few very prominent persons in history of religion, sometime ago, which give some idea of the view of the western intellectuals on Harekrsna movement[2].

In response to a question about his views on the Harekrsna movement, in relation to its roots in Indian religious and cultural tradition, A.L. Basham (ALB), Ex-Professor and Chairman of the Department of Asian Civilizations at The Australian National University in Canberra answered like this "The caste system stereotype, the evils of caste came also from

---

[1] The Composition of the Author and well accepted in 'Gita Jananti', functio, Calcutta, 1994.

[2] Harekrsna Harekrsna: by S.J. Gelberg, pp. 172, 174, 181-82.

the British rulers of India who, in the last fifty years or so of their power, did their utmost to prove that they were there for India's good. One of the arguments that I remember hearing against India's Independence was that India was so divided by caste that it could never stand on its own two feet, while the caste system existed because the system destroyed the unity of the nation. You hear the same thing being said even by Indian reformers to these days. The British in India, in any case or many of them liked to propagate this idea that the caste system is very evil thing in Indian life."

SJG: In the light of the fact that Westerners tend to stereotype Hinduism as non-theistic, or non-monotheistic, it is quite significant that the Krsna consciousness movement has introduced the theistic side of Hinduism, sankirtan, and the bhakti tradition for the first time to the Westerners.

ALB: Yes, that is certainly true. From the point of view of spreading knowledge of Indian religion, you have done a great deal in the Western world.

You have done much more than the swamis of Ramakrishna Mission and others, because they propagate a form of Hinduism, in which the devotional, theistic aspect is almost entirely cut out and ignored. Yours-you-see, is the straight forward Hinduism of the common man, the best form of it.

I am sure, if nothing else, you have a great educational function in explaining and exemplifying these things, by living example to the people of the western world.

Q: You mentioned that you had taken part in a Caitanya kirtan (Namyajna) at Calcutta. Can you describe that experience?

ALB: Over the years, I have observed several Caitanya kirtans, but I remember one in particular. It was about thirty years ago. I got off a train in Sealdah station, in Calcutta, just about sunset, and noticed that there was a Caitanya kirtan taking place in one corner of the station yard. Whenever I come across a kirtan in progress, I always stop, watch and listen, but often I am in a hurry and have other things to do, and so I can only wait a minute or two. This time I was in no hurry. I had plenty of time to spare. The devotees had erected a decorative tent in which they had set up the statue of Krsna and numerous brightly coloured pictures of Krsna and Caitanya and the various saints of the order. The whole scene was lit up with bright lights and decorated with many flowers and various other decorations. Not very many people were there at first, but as I stood by watching and looking, more and more people came along and got involved.

They were chanting 'Hare Krsna, Hare Rama' as you do. They kept on chanting and chanting and chanting, until after a while, a few of them began to dance and then nearly everybody was dancing. I don't think I got as far as dancing, but I found that I was certainly joining in the chanting and I was really carried away. I was there for at least two hours. It was a wonderful experience.

As I think you know, on a theoretical and logical level I am not able to fully accept your doctrine of the historicity of Krsna and so on, but nevertheless I do see the emotional and spiritual force of the Caitanya movement.

That evening outside Sealdah Station is something which I never forget the intense experience of exhilaration and relief, and the feeling of security and safety and inner happiness which came from it. I feel that this is a very good form of religious worship. Irrespective of truth or falsehood of what they believe in, it does people enormous good. I'm afraid I tend to take a rather pragmatic view of religion.

The Hare Krsna movement is something unique in the West, at least in the history of the last two thousand years. And for that reason, because of its strangeness and unexpectedness, it tends to make the earnest Christians feel a bit nervous. But they ought not to. They ought to recognize you for what you are: a movement with doctrines and ideas very close to their own, with much the same aims and rather an ally than a foe.

Dr. Harvey Cox (HC), Victor S. Thomas Professor of Divinity and Chairman of the Department of Applied Theology at Harvard Divinity School. One of the most prominent and influential Protestant theologian of our time[1].

---

[1]   Hare krsna Harekrsna: by S.J. Gelberj, pp. 25-26.

Q: Did you find your visit to Vrndavana in any way a source of personal spiritual nourishment?

HC: I've found all of my contacts with people of other religious traditions to be a rich source of deepening and strengthening of my own spirituality. But I must say that I always remember my stay in Vrndavana as a very important modal moment in my own spiritual growth.

Q: How so?

HC: Well, you experience Krsna in Vrndavana. That's what they say, and it's true. The spirit of Krsna devotion hangs so thick, so to speak, that you can almost breathe in it. You cannot help getting some feeling for it. What I really began to appreciate there, was the multiple forms that love of God takes. I was deeply influenced by the Vaisnava perception of the infinitely variable forms that God's love for us and our love for God take, and how wrong it is, how shortsighted it is, to limit that relationship to a particular form or phase of love. It's difficult to try to summarize this sort of keep impressions, but that was the insight I came away with. That insight has in some ways enlarged my feeling for the omnipresence of God in the world that God in some sense present in all things. The continuum between immanence and transcendence in Indian culture is unbroken, whereas we in the West have more of the dualistic frame. I felt some kind of effective deepening while I was in Vrndavana.

I was also impressed by certain quality of life in Vrndavana, especially in the Goswami family and their relationship with us as guests. I was especially moved by their combination of devotion of Krsna and their openness to life to everyone.

Dr. Thomas J. Hopkins (TJH), Professor and Chairman of Religious Studies at Franklin and Marshall College, in Lancaster, Pennsylvania[1].

---

[1]   Harekrishna Harekrishna: by S.J. Gelberg, pp. 151, 152.

SJG: I'd like to focus on the Krsna conscious movement itself, as a contemporary social reality. Earlier, you were describing the movement in its beginning, when it was functioning within the social milieu of the 60's counter-culture, and you explained how the movement provided answers and direction to many young people who had been involved in the culture. What is that appeal about the movement that doesn't depend upon the particular social environment for that appeal to work?

TJH: I think that appeal is the same appeal it had all along. People always need some kind of guidance, some kind of direction, some kind of standard to live up to, and some kind of structure to give their lives meaning.

You speak as if the condition of the world that gave rise to counter-culture has suddenly disappeared and we're now in a new age in which the world and society are a great place again, where there are no abuses of authority and no injustice.

Dr. Larry D. Shinn (LDS), Professor of Religion at Oberlin College, Ohio.

(The interview took place after Dr. Shinn had an intensive three-week study of several Krisna communities in America)[1].

SJG: As you know, authoritarian social structures are found with in most religious traditions at least monastic, community oriented dimensions of religious traditions. Its not something which is a unique characteristic of marginal religious movements.

LDS: Yes, of course. That's why almost anything I'm saying now about authoritarian religious social structure in the Hare Krsna movement would be equally applicable to a Catholic or Buddhist monastery, or a variety of yoga ashrams in India. So, of course, this is not something which is a 'cult' feature. And that's why I said early on that I'm treating this movement very much as an authentic

---

[1]   Harekrishna Karekrishna: by S.J. Gelberg, pp. 69, 70.

religious tradition, one which has taken some interesting turns as it has come to the West.

SJG: Are there any other significant reasons why people join the Hare Krsna movement?

LDS: People join the Hare Krsna movement, it seems to me, for a wide variety of reasons. But the central one is that its basic ideas the self as spirit soul, vegetarianism, the necessity for ethical guide lines made sense and were attractive. But from my point of view, commitment is always as much emotionally as it is intellectually motivated, Krsna consciousness 'felt good'. Many devotees say that 'it just seemed right', or 'I felt like I was home' or 'it seemed to me that I had never experienced such peace before', 'I could just tell that the devotees were happy' 'I felt exuberant, blissful'.

These are the kind of responses people gave for why they joined. And that makes sense to me, because anytime one makes a radical commitment of lifestyle, it will always be at least as much an emotional commitment as it will be an intellectual or a conceptual commitment.

CHAPTER XI

Comments And Observations

Comments

Sri Aurobindo made these following valuable comments on youth and the new world:

The future belongs to the young. It is a young and new world which is now under the process of development and it is the young who must create it. But it is also a world of truth, courage, justice, lofty aspiration and straight forward fulfillment which we seek to create.

(a) For the coward, for the self seeker, for the talker, who goes forward at the beginning and afterwards leaves his fellows in the lurch, there is no place in the future.

(b) A brave frank, clear hearted, courageous and aspiring youth is the only foundation on which the future nation can be built.

So learning from the above teaching of Sri Aurobindo, it seems that unless there are some modification of thoughts and practices in the rational sense, the Saivism and Saktaism, are likely to take the course according to the first comment. According to his second comment, subject to minor changes in the tradition of some sections or better understanding of certain points, the HKM remains today, the most simple, broad based, and universal religion on which the young generation could be proudly adherent to the transfer of philosophy to the generations to come.

Saivism

The origin of the Siva worship could be traced up to the fierce Rigvedic god Rudra with whom merged elements of a non-Aryan fertility deity. He lurks in horrible places, such as battle fields, burning grounds and cross roads etc.

He wears garland of skulls and is surrounded by ghosts, evil spirits and demons. His neck is encircled with a snake, of which he is the lord. His body is covered with ashes. Besides him always stays his trident and usually associated his mount, the bull Nandi. He is a great ascetic, sits on a tiger skin, and through his deep meditation the world is maintained. He is the Mahakal (death and time). If he is upset Mahakal comes.

Not much literature is available about this faith. The priests, the Tantrics who conduct his worship, are very cryptic about the worship and never disclose the mantra. The ingredients for the puja and the process, are full of superstitions, about which, apart from the tradition, not much rational explanations are available from any source, particularly for the time and place. Usually the puja has to be done in a moonless night and at a lonely place such as burning grounds or cross roads in a village etc. Participants are expected to be intoxicated to some degree with ganja, charas or bhang (canabis etc). This also need to be explained; the necessity of intoxication, during the act of devotion. Not much literature is available, nor very much is taught about it, at schools and colleges. There may be some fully devoted Sadhus or Saints who are well versed about this philosophy, but usually they remain in lonely places or at forests and engage themselves in devotion and are not much interested to teach the general mass. The intellectuals are not much influenced or mobilized by this faith. So it is no wonder, if not much is known about the faith of if it is not very much popular.

Saktaism

Sakti worship could be traced up to the epic period about, 400 B.C. 200 A.D. It is mentioned in Ramayana that Ramchandra had to pray for mother goddess, Durga (akal bodhan), before he killed Ravana. In Rigveda the only female god mentioned, was Svarasvati, the then river goddess; much later she became the goddess of knowledge.

Sakti also known in different names, such as Sati, Parvati, Gauri, Kali and Annapurna. In the form of Sakti (Kali), she wears a garland of human head and waste belt with human hands. She stands on the body of Siva, her husband. Worship for Sakti is conducted by the Tantric Priests who are again very secretive and do not disclose all the mantras to the participants, with the understanding that if he discloses the mantras, some sort of harmful curse would descent on him.

The various ingredients for the puja and the rituals are full of superstitions without much rational explanations. Very much strictness is followed about the time, according to a particular position of the moon. Moreover there is a general apprehension that if the puja is organized or conducted improperly, with some error or fault in it, serious harmful consequences will descend upon the organizers, the conductors or the participants and their families. So some people are so much scared that they refrain from organizing this puja, although they have devotion towards Sakti in their heart. There are limited amounts of literature available on Saktaism; which apart from the tradition, fails to explain the necessity of so many ingredients and the rationality of the superstitions associated with it. Most of the mantras are originated from the Puranas (Brhnnandikesvara, Devi Purana and Kalika Purana) which apart from prescribing these, did not explain the reasons for their justification and the philosophy behind it.

The participants are expected to join the priest in uttering some hymns, seeking some objectives, which they may not solicit. For example, "putrang dehi, dhanang dehi, jashang dehi etc. It means please grant me a son, wealth and fame. Those who have many children or those who follow the family planning procedures may not want a son. Some people with religious mind may not wish to have wealth or fame etc, rather prefer to have the grace of the Almighty. So in this sense, really devotional people may not find any urge to join the worship in this situation.

Amongst the numerous ingredients the common ones are the various types of corns, sweets, vegetables, fruits, flowers, drinks (alcohol), meats etc. But the uncommon ones are such as grass (durba), a bit of soil from the lawn of a prostitute's home. Very little explanations are available for these.

During the eighteenth century Tantra was popular among a powerful section of Bengali Zaminders or Rajas who used to recruit bands of club weilding bodyguards. These people associated plunder and murder with the worship of Kali. It is the custom for the professional robbers to worship Kali. The killing of animal in the name of sacrifice (bali, particularly goat), during the act of Sakti worship, had been continuing, till not long ago. Possibly the tradition may still prevail in some parts of rural India.

The worshippers of Sakti are usually non-vegetarian. So the reputation of the act of violence is associated with the name of Sakti worship which may not be justified favourably by the young generation. On the top of these, the use of intoxicants (bhang, canabis etc), during the worship or at the end, demands some reasoning.

It is the time for the devotees to give a serious thought how much importance one should pay on the scripture (Kalika Puran) and also to think whether all these scriptural advices are really for worshipping or for a celebration with a big feast[1].

The theology and philosophy of Sakti managed to have very limited success in influencing and mobilizing the intellectuals to produce enormous amount of literature to teach the general mass. The most popular compositions are limited to songs only. Few poet singers, such as Sadhak Ramprased Sen and Kamalakanta Bhattacharya raised the moral of the sects of some extent.

This sect did not produce many religious leaders. But the two leaders who dominated the last century and major part of the century before, could be claimed from this sect. They are Ramkrishna Paramhangsha and Swami Vivekananda.

Bhaktibadi Ramkrishna regarded by all the Indians, although himself was a votary of Kali, never invited people to be a Sakta nor stressed for worshipping Kali. He rather explained very simple and impressive way that the grace of Almighty could be achieved by devotion with bhakti whichever way one imagine, as Shyama (Kali) or Shyam (Krsna) ('jata mat tata path'). The name of Chaitanya used to bring him 'Samadhi'. At Dakshineswar, the place of his austerities, Kali and Krsna temple, still exist side by side. He never went out for preaching, nor initiated anybody to be a sannyasi. He instructed his chief disciple Vivekananda to keep his boys together.

The principle advice came from Vivekananda, was to show kindness to the people (jibe daya), rather than to join a sect of Kali or Krsna. All

---

[1]   Kalika Puranam, Edited by Panchanan Karkaratna. 59/86-87.

along he explained the glory of Vedanta. In 1883 at Chicago, the keynote of his famous speech was universal tolerance and acceptance. He expressed his deep respect toward all the faiths. To him all the religions were equally effective paths to lead their respective devotees, with diverse tastes and temperaments. So from the advices of Ramkrsna and Vivekananda, not necessarily, many extra people, were attracted toward the Saktaism, rather people gained confidence in their own respective faith.

Even today, it is not uncommon in many Ramkrsna Missions to see Kali and Krsna temple side by side, or a statue or photograph of Krsna in some missionaries living room. The source of information for Sakti worship is the puranas, mainly the 'Kalika' puran. These days very rarely a religious leader or a priest, belonging to any sect, including Sakta and Saiva, is found who utters quotations or references from these puranas. Rather invariably almost all of them, utter quotations, either from 'Gita' or 'Bhagavata Purana', where lies the foundation of Vaisnavism.

Prejudicial outlook have been continuing since many centuries, still prevails in almost all the pujas, including the worship of Sakti.

The priest has to be a Brahmin caste learned or ignorant. Vast learned men from the other castes are not allowed to conduct the worship. In some areas the lower castes are not allowed to enter the temple even.

In the male dominated society, the women are deprived of their social and religious rights. The woman cannot be a priest in the worship of Sakti. In certain times, the woman are not supposed to take part in the puja and sometimes are not allowed to enter the temple even. So as a result, the Brahmins with conservative mind, who are very minority group of the Hindu society, excluding their women (fifty percent), even smaller minority of people are controlling the worship of Sakti. It is easily understandable, how much critically these will be judged and accepted by the young generation in this changeable world. Only time will tell how long will this continue.

Vaisnavism

The worship of Vishnu could be traced up to the Rigveda as a solar deity of less importance. He became prominent during the period of Brahmanas. During 400 B.C. two deities were very prominent, Vishnu and Siva. By the period of Purana A.D. 300-1200, Vishnu expanded his scope and dominance by the doctrine of nine Avataras (p. 26), up to Buddha. For the non-Vaisnavas the tenth 'Kalki Avatara', is yet to come. For the Vasinavas Sri-Caitanya was the tenth Avatara.

Highly intelligent with extraordinary personality, incarnation of God or not (p. 74-80), vast learned Caitanya, assessed and recognized the tremendous amount of social and religious injustice to the major section of population, could foresee the disintegration of the social fabrics of the Hindu society, founded the Harekrsna movement, to break down the caste barrier, to bring the social justice and, to simply the devotion, in a universal religion for all.

The movement was very popular at its start and possibly is still popular than any other sect within the Hindu community. People for all castes and social status joined the movement in large number. The movement has managed to influence and mobilize the intellectuals of all categories, in a very large number, which has helped to produce huge and incomparable amount of literature for its continuous publicity.

This movement had everything to go for it at its start. It brought revolution, and possibly saved the Hindu society from disintegration. But after a century the momentum of the progress was relatively slow for various reasons, till the second-half of last century, when it was resurrected at the beginning of the independence movement.

But the real resurrection of the movement occurred in 1966, when ISCON was founded. This is the golden era of the movement. Now enthusiasm generated in the mind of many people to restudy the philosophy of Caitanya and adopt in life. The movement is now all over the World with unequalled momentum.

No doubt this is the majority sect in India and rapidly proliferating religion in the outside world. The Indians who used to consider the Vaisnavas as the platform of Nada and Nedi, due to the liberal lifestyle of the male and female, of the Sahajiya group of Buddhist, absorbed as Vaisnavas, started to revaluate, their conception about the HKM. But to convince, still many Indians, certain points need to be explained.

If by uttering the name Hari or Krsna, one can be free from all the past misdeed or sin, as was Jagai andMadhai at the beginning of the movement, then what is the role of the Guru?

The guru system demands a rational explanation. Generally it is explained, on many occasions by the preachers, that the role of guru is just like a teacher, we need at our school. This is acceptable that one need teacher or guru to increase the knowledge.

But this interpretation should not be exploited in the way that one should worship guru before worshipping the God or that guru worship is essential to achieve God. If the guru or his mantra (customary in guru system), is considered so superior then what is the necessity of chanting Hare Krsna. It wants a rational explanation. It is possible that the importance of the guru system was injected into HKM, by the traditional gurus for the establishment of their superiority and partially the continuance of the Brahminical influence.

Similarly, the role of Mohantas are also quite explorable. If a Mohanta is expected to be respected as the senior most person or most experienced in the community then it is acceptable. But if his role is interpreted like a guru, that to achieve the grace of god is only possible through him (practice in places) then it requires a rational explanation.

These movement was originally founded for the abolition of the caste systems and also for the extermination of the traditional family right as the Brahmins had. Some Vaisnava Adhikaris or gurus, although do not openly observe caste system, but have been trying to establish some sort of class system and transferring their traditional guruship or right to their sons. These are questionable for the movement.

Observations

In this world, everything is being changed, in every sphere of life. It is known on careful study, the history of religion, that the methods of worshipping and devotion have been changing over the centuries.

In a period when people like to think and judge carefully, the rationality of the object before accepting it, there is no scope to put forward ideas and traditions depending on the ancient emotional impulse only, without reasoning it. Now the time has come for the strong supporters, intellectuals and the theologians to come forward with deep research and good explanation, to support and rationalize or to discard in a loud voice, the old and the superstitious ideas. This has become necessary to help the young generation, to understand the religion better and to be attracted towards it. In absence of these, the misunderstanding and the confusion about the religious faith will continue amidst of which the young generation may be misguided and discontent about the Hindu religion.

Some quotations from "Kalika Puran", which are self expanatory. These are written in Bengali Alphabets, the Sanskrit scripts with its Bengali translation. The ingredients of some pujas are explained there. After reading, the readers may not have much problems to make up their mind to justify how inappropriate or unacceptable such ingredients (violents acts like killing, man and many animals and eating them) in a religious place of worshipping.

একোনষষ্টিতমোহধ্যায়ঃ

আম্রদাড়িমকর্করদ্রাক্ষাদিবিবিধৈঃ ফলৈঃ।
ভক্ষ্যভোজ্যাদিভিঃ সর্বৈর্মৎস্যৈর্মাংসৈস্তথৌদনৈঃ।।৮৬

গন্ধৈঃ পুষ্পৈস্তথা ধূপদীপৈশ্চ সুমনোহরৈঃ।
বাসোভির্ভূষণৈশ্চৈব ভবানীসাধকো জপেৎ।।৮৭

নটনর্তকসৈ্জৈশ্চ বেশ্যাভিশ্চৈব ভৈরব।
নৃত্যগীতৈঃ সমুদিতো জাগরং কারয়েন্নিশি।।৮৮

ভোজয়েৎ ব্রাহ্মণাংশ্চাপি জ্ঞাতীনপি দ্বিজাতিভিঃ।
পবিত্রারোপণে বৃত্তে দক্ষিণামুপদাপয়েৎ।।৮৯

হিরণ্যং গাং তিলঘৃতং বাসো বা শাকমেব বা।
ইমং মন্ত্র ততং পশ্চাৎ সাধকঃ সমুদীরয়েৎ।।৯০

মণিবিদ্রুমমালাভি-র্মন্দারকুসুমাদিভিঃ।
ইয়ং সাংবৎসরী পূজা ত্বাস্তু পরমেশ্বরি।।৯১

ততো বিসর্জয়েদ্দেবীং পূজাভিঃ প্রতিপত্তিভিঃ।
এবং কৃতে পবিত্রাণাং দানে দেব্যা যথাবিধি।।৯২

সংবৎসরস্য যা পূজা সম্পূর্ণা বৎসরাদ্ভবেৎ।
কল্পকোটিশতং যাবদ্দেবীগেহে বসেন্নরঃ।।৯৩

তত্রাপি সুখসৌভাগ্যসমৃদ্ধিরতুলা ভবৎ।।৯৪

নানাবিধ নৈবেদ্য, পেয়, অনেক প্রকার পিষ্টক, মোদক, কুষ্মাণ্ড, নারিকেল, খর্জ্জুর, পনস, আম্র, দাড়িম্ব, কর্কন্ধু, দ্রাক্ষাদি বিবিধ ফল, সকল প্রকার ভক্ষ্য ও ভোজ্য, মদ্য, মাংস, ওদন, গন্ধ পুষ্প, মনোহর ধূপ, দীপ বসন ও ভূষণ—এই সকল উপচার দ্বারা সাধক দেবীর পূজা করিবে। ৮৫-৮৭

এবং রাত্রিকালে নট, নর্তক ও বেশ্যা দ্বারা নৃত্য করাইয়া আনন্দিত হইয়া জাগরণ করিবে। ৮৮

দ্বিজাতিগণের সহিত ব্রাহ্মণ, জ্ঞাতি কুটুম্বদিগকে করাইবে। পবিত্রারোহণ সম্পন্ন হইলে সুবর্ণ, গো, ধেনু, তিল, বসন বা অশোক বৃক্ষ দক্ষিণারূপ দান করিবে। অনন্তর, সাধক, বক্ষ্যমাণ মন্ত্র পাঠ করিবে। ৮৯

মণি, বিদ্রুম মালা দ্বারা এবং মন্দার পুষ্প দ্বারা তোমার এই বাৎসরিক পূজা হইতে থাকুক। ৯১

তাহার পর পূজা এবং প্রতিপত্তিপূর্ব্বক দেবীর বিসর্জ্জন করিবে। এইরূপে যথাবিধি

দেবীর পবিত্র-দান সম্পন্ন হইলে বাৎসরিক পূজা সম্পূর্ণ হয়। এই কার্য্যের অনুষ্ঠান করিয়া মনুষ্য একশত কোটি কল্প দেবীর গৃহে বাস করে এবং সেই স্থানে তাহার অতুল-সুখ সৌভাগ্য ও সমৃদ্ধি লাভ হয়। ৯২–৯৪

সপ্তষষ্টিতমোহ্ধ্যায়ঃ

ক্রমস্তু বলিদানস্য স্বরূপং রুধিরাদিতঃ।
যথা স্যাৎ প্রীতয়ে সম্যক্ তদ্বাং বক্ষ্যামি পুত্রকৌ।। ১
বৈষ্ণবীতন্ত্রকরোক্তঃ ক্রমঃ সর্ব্বত্র সর্ব্বদা।
সাধ্যৈকবলিদানস্য গ্রাহাং সর্ব্বসুরস্য চ।। ২
পক্ষিণঃ কচ্ছপা গ্রাহা মৎস্যা নববিধা মৃগাঃ।
মহিষো গোধিকা গাবশ্ছাগো ক্রুক্রশ্চ শূকরঃ।। ৩
খড়্গশ্চ কৃষ্ণসারশ্চ গোধিকা শরভো হরিঃ।
শার্দ্দূলশ্চ নরশ্চৈব স্বগাত্রন্নরুধিরং তথা।। ৪
চণ্ডিকাভৈরবাদীনাং বলয়ঃ পরিকীর্ত্তিতাঃ।। ৫
বলিভিঃ সাধ্যতে মূর্ত্তির্বলিভিঃ সাধ্যতে দিবম্।
বলিদানেন সততং জয়েচ্ছত্রূন্নৃপান্ নৃপঃ।। ৬
মৎস্যানাং কচ্ছপানান্তু রুধিরৈঃ সততং শিবা।
মাসৈকং তৃপ্তিমাপ্রেতি গ্রাহৈর্ম্মাসাংস্ত স্ত্রীনাথ।। ৭
মৃগাণাং শোণিতেদেবী নরাণামপি শোণিতঃ।
অষ্টৌ মাসানবাপ্রেতি তৃপ্তিং কল্যাণদা চ সা।। ৮
গোধিকানাং গোরুধিরৈর্ব্বার্ষিকীং তৃপ্তিমাপ্নুয়াৎ।। ৯

বলিদান-বিধি

ভগবান্ বলিলেন,—হে পুত্রদ্বয়! বলিদানের ক্রম এবং স্বরূপ, অর্থাৎ যে প্রকার রুধিরাদি দ্বারা দেবীর সম্পূর্ণ প্রীতি হয়, তোমাদিগের নিকট কীর্ত্তন করিতেছি। ১

সাধকগণ সকল প্রকার বলিদানেই বৈষ্ণবীতন্ত্রকল্পকথিত ক্রম সর্ব্বদা গ্রহণ করিবে।২

পক্ষী সকল, কচ্ছপ, গ্রাহ, মৎস্য, নয় প্রকার মৃগ মহিষ, অজ, আবিক, গো, ছাগ, রুরু, শূকর, খড়্গ, কৃষ্ণসার, গোধিকা, শরভ, সিংহ, শার্দ্দূল, মনুষ্য এবং স্বীয় গাত্রের রুধির, ইহারা চণ্ডিকা দেবী ও ভৈরবাদির বলিরূপে কীর্ত্তিতে হইয়াছে। ৩–৫

বলি দ্বারা মুক্তি সাধিত হয়, বলি দ্বারা স্বর্গ সাধিত হয় এবং বলিদান দ্বারা নৃপতিগণ সত্রু নৃপতিদিগকে পরাজয় করিয়া থাকেন। ৬

মৎস্য ও কচ্ছপের রুধির দ্বারা শিবা নিয়ত এক মাস তৃপ্তি লাভ করেন এবং গ্রাহদিগের রুধিরাদি দ্বারা তিন মাস তৃপ্তি লাভ করেন। ৭

দেবী মৃগ এবং মনুষ্যশোণিত দ্বারা আট মাস তৃপ্তি লাভ করেন এবং সর্বদা কল্যান প্রদান করেন। ৮

গো এবং গোধিকার রুধিরে দেবীর সাংবাৎসরিক তৃপ্তি হয়।৯

ষষ্টিতমোহধ্যায়ঃ

পক্ষ্যাদিবলিজাতীয়েস্তথা নানাবিধেমৃগৈঃ।
পূজয়েচ্চে জগদ্ধাত্রীং মাংসশোণিতকর্দমৈঃ ।।৫০

রাত্রৌ স্কন্দবিশাখস্য কৃত্বা পিষ্টকপুত্রিকাম্।
পূজয়েচ্ছত্রুনাশায় দুর্গায়াঃ প্রীতয়ে তথা।।৫১

হোমঞ্চ সতিলেরাজ্যে-র্মাংসেরপি তথা চরেৎ।
উগ্রচণ্ডাদিকাঃ পূজ্যা-স্তথাষ্টৌ যোগিনীঃ শুভাঃ।।৫২

যোগিন্যশ্চ চতুঃষষ্টিস্তথা বৈ কোটিযোগিনীঃ।
নবদুর্গাস্তথা পূজ্যা দেব্যাং সন্নিহিতাঃ শুভাঃ।।৫৩

জয়ন্ত্যাদিগন্ধপুষ্পেস্তা দেবা মূর্ত্তয়ো যতঃ।
দেব্যাঃ সর্ব্বাণি চাস্ত্রাণি ভূষণানি তথৈব চ।।৫৪

অস্ত্রপ্রত্যস্ত্রযুক্তানি বাহনং সিংহমের চ।
মহিষাসুরমর্দ্দিন্যাঃ পূজয়েদ্ভুতয়ে সদা।।৫৫

পুর। কল্পে মহাদেবী মনোঃ স্বায়ম্ভুবেহন্তরে।
নৃণাং কৃতযুগস্যাদৌ সর্ব্বদেবৈঃ স্তুতা সদা।।৫৬

মহিষাসুরনাশায় জগতাং হিতকাম্যয়া।
যোগনিদ্রা মহামায়া জগদ্ধাত্রী জগন্ময়ী।।৫৭

ভূজৈঃ যোড়শভির্যুক্তা ভদ্রকালীতি বিশ্রুতা।
ক্ষীরোদস্যোত্তরে তীরে বিব্রতী বিপুলাং ভুবম্।।৫৮

নারোগবোধ মাংসেন ত্রিসহস্রঞ্চ বৎসরান্।
তৃপ্তিমাপ্নোতি কামাখ্যা ভৈরবী মম রূপধৃক্।।

শর্করা, লবলী, নরসক, ছাগল, মহিষ, মেঘ, নিজের শোণিত, পক্ষী আদি পশু, নয় প্রকার মৃগ—এই সকল উপকরণ দ্বারা নিখিল জগতের ধাত্রী মহামায়ার পূজা করিবে, এবং এত পরিমাণে বলিদান করিবে, যাহাতে মাংস ও শোণিতের কর্দম হয়। ৪৭-৫০

শত্রু নাশ-নিমিত্ত এবং দুর্গার প্রীতি ইচ্ছা করিয়া পিষ্টকের পুতুল নির্ম্মাণ করিয়া রাত্রে স্কন্দ ও

বিশাখের পূজা করিবে। ৫১

তিল ও মাংসের সহিত আজ্য দ্বারা হোম করিবে এবং উগ্রচণ্ডাদি শুভদায়িনী অষ্ট যোগিনীর পূজা করিবে। ৫২

চতুঃষষ্টি যোগিনী এবং কোটি যোগিনীরও পূজা করিবে। সর্ব্বদা দেবীর সন্নিহিত শুভদায়িনী জয়ন্তী প্রভৃতি নবদুর্গার গন্ধ পুষ্প দ্বারা পূজা করিবে, যেহেতু তাঁহার দেবীর মূর্ত্তিভেদ-মাত্র। ৫৩-৫৪

মহিষাসুরমর্দ্দিনী দেবীর সমুদয় অস্ত্র এবং অঙ্গ ও প্রত্যঙ্গে স্থিত সমুদয় ভূষণ এবং বাহন সিংহকেও ভূতির নিমিত্ত সর্ব্বদা পূজা করিবে। ৫৫

পূর্ব্বকল্পে স্বায়ম্ভুব মনুর অধিকারে মনুষ্যদিগের ত্রেতাযুগের আদিতে মহিষাসুরের বিনাশ এবং জগতের নিমিত্ত যোগনিদ্রা জগদ্ধাত্রী জগন্ময়ী মহাদেবী মহামায়া—সমুদয় দেবগণকর্ত্তৃক সংস্তুত হইয়াছিলেন। ৫৬-৫৭

অন্তর তিনি ক্ষীরোদ সমুদ্রের উত্তরতীরে অতিবিপুল শরীর ধারণ করিয়া ষোড়শভুজারূপে আবির্ভূত হইয়া ভদ্রকালী নামে আবির্ভূত হন। ৫৮

মনুষ্যমাংস দ্বারা কামাখ্যা দেবী এবং আমার রূপধারী ভৈরব তিন হাজার বৎসর তৃপ্তি লাভ করেন।

CHAPTER XII

Conclusion

1. What is known as Hindu religion today, is not a single religious belief. It is developed gradually from what was known as 'Sanatana' dharma from the prehistoric era, by assimilating and absorbing all the ancient religious belief of the people of Indian subcontinent both Aryan and non-Aryan origin (p. 13). The single name Hinduism was given by the outside invader to the aggregation of all the religious beliefs, without knowing or analyzing in detail, in about 2500 B.C. Hence there are so many Gods and goddesses and so much of variations in worships in this religion. Over the centuries due to the change of religious thought and society, for at least last ten centuries, all over the India and worshippers consolidated around the three main different sects, Vaisnavites, Saivaites and Saktas, along with some regional, local, or cult of less importance, such as Sitala, Manasa, Lakshmi, Swaraswati, Santoshi Ma etc.

2. The origin of class system in the Indian society could be traced up to the Vedic period (1200-1400 B.C.). This classification was based according to the qualification, ability, and profession of a person. According to this classification there were four 'Varnas', Brahmina, Kshatriya, Vaisya and Sudra; learned or adviser to the ruler, the protector or warrior, business community and ancillary workers respectively (p. 7, 8).

    Gradually ignoring the qualification, according to the right of birth only, the conception of 'jati' developed (p.89). These gradually developed into many jaties, as many as three thousoands. In sixteenth century, when Partuguese came to India they introduced the term caste to this class division, without making any distinction between Varna and Jati. (p. 10).

Due to the development of the erroneous interpretation of the class or caste system, certain undesired affairs happened to the Hindu community, such as (p. 11-20):

a. The Brahmins the upper caste dominated the Hindu society.
b. The majority of the Hindus were lower caste who were deprived of their religious right and they suffered from religious and social injustice and tyranny.
c. Some of the lower caste found the oppression unbearable within the Hindu community and were attracted by the liberal view of the other religions, such as the Muhammadan proselytisation, the strong preaching force of the Christianism and also by the already existing Buddhist religion.
d. The liberal minded Brahmins found difficult to practice religion due to very strict Smriti rule and Navyanyaya, introduced by the domineering conservative Brahmins.
e. Due to all the reasons stated, the fabrics of the Hindu society were weakening and were about to break down and even its existence, was threatened.

Some religious and social leaders such as Ramanuja, Nimberka, Madhva and many others who recognized these discrepancies in the society and wanted to remove these but did not say anything about the abolition of caste system. Kabir wanted to remove the caste system but had very limited success.

Guru Nanak recognized these religious and social unfairness and wanted to change these in Western part of India. He tried to simplify the religion and introduced certain new rules and regulations, what he thought were rational. But he ended up in setting up a new religion known as 'Sikh religion'.

Caitanya was contemporary of Guru Nanak recognized these social and religious discrepancies. He was a talented person, an unparalleled scholar and very well versed about Hindu religion, to such an extent that he got the title 'pandita' (teacher) at the age of sixteen years only.

He assessed the situation, initiated by Isvarpuri and Bharati and dedicated himself for the religious reform of the society. He was primarily helped by Advaita, Nityananda, Gadadhar and Srivasa who were liberal minded Brahmins, anxiously waiting for a change in the religious pattern. He was later helped by first six Goswamins, of which Rupa, Sanatana and Jiva were, the main. He also got support from King Pratap Rudra, Roy Ramananda and many other influential and powerful people.

He designed and formulated the simple way of practicing religion. He also realized that the religion should be broadly based with equal right for every body regardless of their caste. Caitanya wanted to bring the people down from the top, and lift the people from the bottom level of status, to a middle ground for a uniform society with the equal right for everybody. He tried to apply the simplest interpretation of the religious scriptures. His philosophy was based on Upanishads, Bhagavata and other Puranas and Bhagavatagita. This philosophy in fact is the devotional form of Vedanta.

He discarded various complicated religious practices such as various complicated Pujas and yajnas, etc. instead advised people to chant the name of God with premabhakti in heart. This way of practicing religion had been mentioned in 'Kalisantaran Upanishad,' 'Vrhanaradiya Purana' and in 'Padma Purana'. In these scriptures it was mentioned only, but there is no evidence that any religious leader had advised to practice religion in this way, before Caitanya.

From the very beginning, although there were resistance from certain corners, the HKM of Caitanya have been accepted by the general mass of people regardless of their caste, irrespective their wealth and social status, with enthusiasm. It was so popular even in his life time, many people regarded him as an incarnation of God.

This study suggests this HKM has three prominent phase in its history, when people not only joined the movement, but also tried to stress on publicity for the others to accept it. These were at the beginning in early sixteenth century, late nineteenth and early twentieth century during the independent movement of India, and the last forty years. This study also suggests other comparable religious sects Sakta and Saiva no way nearer to it, in popularity.

The Reasons for the Popularity of the Harekrsna Movement:

1. It is very simple to practice and very broadly based. There being no caste bar, it became very popular to them, to raise their status, by getting chance to come in contact with people of higher status.

2. Liberal minded Brahmins who found difficult to practice strict Brahminical religion became the follower of HKM.

3. This approach was rational and could be easily explained in term of bhakti. The movement from the beginning, along with the general mass, got the support of the intelligent group of people, such as politicians, historian, writers, poets, and singers who have been publicizing, the movement by lecturing, writing, singing etc. The HKM or Vaisnavism has the wealth of enormous amount of Vaisnava literature, for reading, discussion, and teaching at Schools, Colleges and Universities, which can never be matched not only by Saktas or Saiva sects, but by any other religious belief in India.

4. The foundation of the faith is based mainly on Gita and Bhagavata Purana, along with other Puranas, for the doctrines of all the Avataras. Gita itself is an enormous source and along with other scriptures, generates so abundance of philosophical thought that the preachers and theologians ever can finish on discussing them.

5. From the period of Brahamanas the Vaisnavism started gaining popularity. Since then the faith had many leaders and theologians who had not only whole heartedly supported, but in a calculated and concerted way, managed very successfully to expand, publicize, produce literature to support it and for the future generations to follow it. In this way all the Avataras along with the production of associated literature (Puranas), were incorporated into the fold of Vaisnavism. All these Avataras might well, had been the local prominent deities, Aryan and non-Aryans. Due to their incorporation into the fold of Vaisnavism, it became the biggest and incomparable religious empire within the Hinduism. Since then this faith was fortunate to have many leaders and reformers with renovated thought and ideas to support it.

6. The songs and musics are popular everywhere. In Vaisnavism one way of praying is through singing not only namasankirtana, but by various types of other devotional songs, such as boul, pada vali kirtana, lila kirtana, pala kirtana etc. This also attracted people towards this movement.

This study suggests with confident that since John Lenon and George Harrison produced the hit album on Hare Krsna in 1969 at the early days of ISKCON, it became so popular within a very short spell of time (p. 195, 200).

The Reasons for the Less Popularity of Saktas and Saivas, Compared to Harekrsna Movement:

1. These religious views had been in practice for at least fifteen centuries, but never had a very strong leader to generate interests to the general mass.

2. Ramkrsna Paramhamsha was a worshipper of Kali (Sakta), but he never strongly recommended to worship Kali, rather preached "Jata mat tata pat", means, Godhead can be achieved whichever way one seek for him or her, so long one has 'premabhakti' in heart. So many people instead becoming a strong supporter of Kali remain as Vaisnava with

some adoration for Kali in heart. Vivekananda always expressed his regards towards all the religious faith, and stressed on the service of humanity, rather than inviting people to join as Sakta.

3. The practices of worship or puja are quite complicated process to organize it. Many people suffer from the superstition that if there is any error in performing these pujas particularly for kali, she might be offended and might cause harm to the worshipper, so they refrain from it.

4. The rigidity about the timing of the puja, neither it is convenient for many people, nor there is a good reason for it, particularly when one thinks that Ramkrsna used to visualize Kali, whenever he wanted to, many times at the 'Panchavativan' and mother Kali came to help sadhak Ramprasad to mend his fence, as his daughter.

5. They may have silent supporters, but none of these sects really, neither even mobilized the general mass nor the intellectuals to produce enough literature for discussion or teaching at School, College or University for the continuous publicity unlike the HKM.

6. The basis of foundation of Saktaism is mainly the Puranas which apart from prescribing the ingredients and the system of worshiping, did not discuss the deeper philosophy behind it; so also the 'Purohitdarpan'. More-over from the descriptions of the 'Kalika Puran' about the food arrangement for the puja and killings of various animal (bali), including human and eating their meat, it is not easy for one to understand, whether these were really necessary for praying or for the celebration with a big feast. Possibly the later assumption is right. In the course of time some devotional spirit has been added to the celebration. The Sakta scriptures lack in depth of philosophy, possibly this is the reason why many quotations are not heard from the preacher of this sect.

The Effect of the Hare Krsna movement

It had brought back the confidence and stability within the Hindu community which was badly shaken in fifteenth and early sixteenth centuries.

Proselytisation of lower caste Hindu to other religion had been stopped.

Many lower caste people who left Hindu religion, had come back, particularly thousands of Buddhists in Orissa and Bengal came back to accept Vaisnavism.

The presence of Vaisnavism is regarded, as a watch dog by some Brahminical leaders and adopt comparatively liberal attitude and some areas they have established an understanding with the local Vaisnavas.

The HKM has increased the sphere of Krsna worship all over the world through ISKCON by establishing hundreds of Krsna temples in almost every country of the world.

It has been proved by the circumstantial evidence beyond doubt that HKM is the most popular religious belief within the Hinduism, particularly in India.

The caste barrier has not been fully broken down yet, but whatever amount have been done is mainly through the Harekrsna movement. Incidental finding, not particularly related to the HKM is that caste system have been almost forgotten among the nonresident Indians who had a chance to visualize themselves through the mirror of the Western societies. It may take longer for the resident Indians to be changed in the similar way.

Lord Chaitanya and his Associates Perform Sankirtana

The Pastime Incarnations of Godhead

The Dance at Rasa Lila, in Vrindavana

Lord Krsna Chastses The Kaliya Serpent

Lord Krsna Lift Govadhana Hill

Visnu on The Bed of Ananta Nag

Sri Sri Laksmi-Narayana in Vaikuntha

APPENDIX

List of ISKCON Centres

Within a few years there were numerous temples and centres were established all over the world.

In 1979, Dr. A.L. Basham, the world's leading authority on Indian History wrote on HKM, "It arose out of nothing in less than twenty years and has become known all over the West. This I feel is the sign of the times and an important fact in the history of the Western world"[1].

In fact hardly there is any other example in the history of religion, which could be matched for such a rapid proliferation, and achieving popularity by the establishment of the numerous centres all over the world, within such a short spell of twenty years time.

It is worthwhile at this stage to have a look at the check list of the important ISKCON centres in the different countries of the world[2].

AFRICA
NIGERA

Abeokuta, Anugu, Benin City, Ibaden, Jos, Kaduna, Lagos, Port Harcourt, Warri.

---

[1] Chant and be Happy : by A.C.B.S. Prabhupada, pp X111
[2] Back to Godhead : Journal of ISKCON, Vol.39, No.5 2005.

OTHER COUNTRIES

Accra, Ghana
Abidjan, Ivory Coast.
Kisumu & Mombasa, Kenya
Freetown, Sierra Leon.
Cape Town, Durban & Lenasia, South Africa.
Marondera, Zimbabwe.
Phoenix & Vrindaban, Mauritius.

ASIA
INDIA

Agartala in Tripura, Ahmedabad two Temples, Allahabad in U.P., Bangalore, Belgaum, Bharatpur, Bhubabaneshwar, Chandigarh, Chenni three Temples, Coimbatore, Dvaraka, Gangaput, Ghaziabad, Guntur, Hanumkonda, Hyderabad, Imphal, Jaipur, Karupur, Katra, Kolkata four Temples. Kolur, Kurkshetra two Temples, Lucknow, Ludhiana, Madurai, Mayapur, Moirang, Mumbai three Temples, Nagpur, New Delhi, Pandharpur, Vrindavan two Temples.

MALAYASIA

Alor Setar, Bukit Mertajam, Butterworth, Ipoh, Kuala Lumpur, Lunas, Penang, Sungei Petani, Talping, Teluk Intan, Kuching.

RUSSIA

Almetyevsk, Archangelsk, Astrahan, Berezniki, Cherkessk, Ekaterinberg, Essentuki, Habarovsk, Ijevsk, Irkutsk, Kazan, Krasnoder, Kurjinovo, Moskva, Moskva-Begovaya, Murmnsk, Nalchik, Novorossiysk, Novosibirsk, Omsk, Penza, Perm, Petrograd, Petrozavodsk, Portvino, Rostov, Samara, Simbirsk, Sochi, Stavropo, Tumen, Ulan-ude, Ulyanovsk, Vladimir, Vladvosto, Yaroslavi, Yujno-sahalinsk, Bishkek in Kyrgyzstan and Almaty in Kazakhstan, Dushanbe in Tajikistan, Ashgabat in Turkmenistan, Mirabad Tumani in Uzbekistan.

OTHER COUNTRIES

BANGLADESH
Chittagong, Dhaka and Jessore two Temples.
HONG KONG
Kowtoon
INDONESIA
Bali, Jakarta, and Yogyakarta.
JAPAN
Tokyo
NEPAL
Kathmandu
PHILIPPINES
Makati City,

EUROPE

CROATIA
Osijek, Pula, Rijeka and Split.
GERMANY
Heidelberg, Munich, Koln-Gemberg, Abentheuer, Jandelsbrunn, Hamburg, Berlin, Wiesbaden and Schoena.
HUNGARY
Budapest, Eger, Kecskmet, Pcs, Debrecen and Somogyvmos.
ITALY
Bergamo, Vicenza, Florence and Milano.
SPAIN
Barcelona, Churriana, Madrid, and Brhuega.
SWEDEN
Bromma, Grodinge, Stockholm, Knivsta, Lund, Malmo, Jarna and Goteborg.
SWITZERLAND
Muttenz, Zrich, Locarno and Dole.
UKRAIN
Chernigov, Dnepropetrovsk, Kijev, Lvov, Nilayev, Odessa, Rovno, Simferopol, Ternopol and Vinniza.

UNITED KINGDOM and IRELAND

Belfast, Birmingham, Coventry, Leicester, Derrylin, Liverpool, London four Temples, Manchester, Newcastle upon Tyne, Oxford, Plymouth, Romford, Karuna Bhavan at Lanarkshire and Swansea and Dublin in Ireland.

OTHER COUNTRIES

AUSTRIA
Wien.

ARMENIA
Yerevan

AZERBAIJAN
Baku

GEORGIA
Tiblisi and Sukhumi

BELGIUM
Antwerpen and Septon-Durbuy.

BELARUS
Gomel, Minsk and Vitevsk.

BULGARIA
Sofia.

CZECH REPUBLIC
Mestecko u Benesova Prague, and Praha.

DENMARK
Vanloese and Kobenhavn

ESTONIA
Tallinn

FINLAND
Helsinki.

FRANCE
Noisy-le-Grand at Paris and Chatenois.

LATVIA
Daugavpils, Liepaya and Riga.

LITHUANIA
Kaunas, Klaipeda, and Vilnius.

MACEDONIA
Skopje.
MOLDOVA
Kishinev.
NETHERLANDS
Amsterdam and Den Haag.
NORWAY
Oslo
POLAND
Czarnow and Wroclaw.
PORTUGAL
Porto
ROMANIA
Iasi and Timisoara
SLOVAKIA
Kokosovce and Presov.
SLOVENIA
Ljublijana.
SERBIA and MONTENEGRO
Beograd-Servia.
CANADA
Calgary, Edmonton, Montreal, Regina, Vancouver, Ottawa, Toranto and Saint John's.
UNITED STATES OF AMERICA
Hartford, Atlanta, Austin, Berkeley, Boise, Boston, Catonsville-Baltimore, Chicago, Miami, Columbus, Detroit, Gainsville, Hillsborough, Houston, Seattle, New York, Philadelphia, Phoenix, Hillsboro, Potomac, Saint Augustine, San Jose/Silicon Valley, Spanish Fork, Tallahassee, Towaco, Dallas, Denver, Honolulu, Laguna Beach, Los Angeles, New Orleans, Saint Louis, San Diego, Tucson, Alachua, Port Royal, Mountsville two Temples and Sandy Ridge, Rural communities: Carriere and Mulberry.

AUSTRALASIA AND AUSTRALIA
Brisbane, Canberra, Melbourne, Perth, Sydney North, Murwillumbah and Adelaide. Rural communities: Bambra and Cessnock

FIJI
Labasa, Lautoka, Rakirakiande Suva

NEW ZEALAND
Christchurch, Wellington, Auckland, Dunedin, Hamilton and Caterton.

LATIN AMERICA
ARGENTINA
Rosario, Bernal Este, Buenos Aires, Mar del Plata, Marcos Paz and Pca. de Buenos Aires.

BRAZIL
Belo Horizonte, Curitiba, Porto Alegre, Ribeirao Preto, Goiania, Recife, Rio de Janeiro, Sao Paulo, Salvador, Caruaru and Pindamonhangaba.

MEXICO
Maxico D.F., Monterrey, Saltillo, Tijuana, Tulancingo, Cerr Azul, Guandaljara, Orizaba and Tijuana.

PERU
Cuzco, Lima three Temples and Arequipa.

OTHER COUNTRIES

BOLIVIA
Cochabamba, La Paz and Santa Cruz.

COSTA RICA
San Jose, Avendia 6 and San Jose Avendia 2.

DOMINICAN REPUBLIC
Santo Domingo

GUATEMALA
Guatemala City

HONDURAS
Tegucigalpa

NICARAGUA

Chinandega

PANAMA

Panama

EL SALVADOR

Nueva San Salvador

TRINIDAD TOBEGO

Debe and Londengville

CHILE

Santiego de Chile

COLOMBIA

Bogota, Cali and Pareira.

ECUADOR

Cuenca and Guayaquil

GUYANA

East Berbice, Essequibo Coast and George Town.

URUGUAY

Montevideo

VENEZUELA

Caracus.

Ivory Coast:

Abidjann

Cameron:

Buea

Sieera Leeone:

Freetown

Uganda:

Kampala

Zimbabwe:

Marondera

Mauritus:

Phoenix

Brazil:

Belem P.A., Belo Horizonte MG, Brasill DF, Curitiba PR, Florianopolis SC, Fortaleza CE, Goiania GO, Manus AM, Pirajui SP, Porto Alegre RS, Recife PE, Rio de Janeiro RJ, Salvador

BA, Santos SP, Sao Paulo SP, Caruaru PE, Morretes PR, Pindamonhangaba.

Mexico:

Guadalajara, Mexico City, Monterrey, Saltillo, Veracruz, Tulancingo, Orrizaba,

Peru:

Arquipa, Cuzco, Lima at Pasaje Solea, Lima at Schell, Lima at AV. Garcilazo de la Vega, Harekrsna Correo de Bella Vista.

Argentina:

Bahia Blanca, Buenos Aires, Mendoza, Rosario, Casilla de Correo (Bhaktilata Puri).

Columbia:

Bogota, Cali, Pereira.

Guyana:

Essquibo Coast, George Town, Seawell Village.

Bolivia:

Cochbamba, Santa Cruz.

Ecuador:

Cuenca, Guayaquil, Quito

Paraguuay:

Guatemala Asuncion

Venezuela:

Caracus

Uruguay:

Montevideo

Costa Rica:

Panama, San Jose

El Salvador:

San Salvador

Chile:

Santiago

Dominican Republic:

Santo Domingo

West Indies:

Trininad, Tobago

Within forty years, all these centres were established.

Bibliography

Chapters I and II

1. Aspect of Bengali History and Society: by Rachael Van M. Baumer, p. 10.
2. Astavimsatitattvani: by Raghunandana, Sudranhikacharatattvam', Edited, by Benimadhav De, Calcutta, pp. 441, and also, Suddhitattva', pp 356.
3. Bangabasi: the Dailyl News Paper, review Article by Sasadhar Tarkacudamani, Bhadra (September) 7, 1885.
4. Bani Chakravorti: Op. Cited, pp. 147-48, 237, 249-51.
5. Bengali District Gazeteers: Mymensingh, E.A. Sacshe (1617),
6. Caitanya Bhagavata: by Vrndavana Dasa, Edited by Sukumar
7. Caste System: by Dr. B.R. Ambedkar
8. Dharmapujabidhana: pp. 219 220.
9. Fundamentals of Sociology: by P. Gisberg, 1973, p. 377, 514,
10. History of Bengal(DaccaUniversity), ed: by R.C. Mjumder, 1, PP 630-633.
11. Indian and Far Eastern Religious Tradition: by Robert D. Baird and Alfred Bloom, 1972, p. 132, 10,
12. Kriyakandarvaridhi: by S.C. Mukhapadhyaya, Basumati Press, 2nd Ed. Vol. 1, 'Vaisnavacharaprakarana', 'Saivacharaprakarana'. 'Prayaschittavyavastaprakarana,' Vol III.
13. Origin and Development of Bengali Language: Suniti Kumar Chatterji, 2nd Ed. 1970,
14. Origin and Growth of Caste in India: N.K. Dutta, Vol. I. Calcutta, 1968.
15. Origin and Growth of Caste in India: N.K. Dutta, Vol. 2, Calcutta, 1969.
16. Patterns of Indian Thought: by John B. Chethimattam, 1971.

17. Smritisastre Bangali: by S.C. Bandopadhyay,

18. Sri-Madbhagavata Gita: Chapter 4, Sloka, 13,

19. Sukumar Sen : Part 1, 1, PP 99

20. Sunyapurana: pp. 332-33

21. The Oxford History of India by Vincent A Smith, Edited by Percival Spear, 4th. Edition, 69-70.

22. The Wonder That India Was: by A.L. Basham, 3rd. Edition, 1985, 21.

23. Vaisnavism in Bengal: by Dr. Ramakanta Chakravarty,

Chapters III, IV and V

1. A descriptive Catalogue and Manuscripts of Orissa: by Kedarnath Mahapatra, in Bhubanesvara Meuseum, 1960, pp. XXX,

2. Aryasaptasati, with the Commentry of Ananta Pandita, Nirnayanasagara Press, Bombay, 1934, p. 204.

3. A study of Vaisnavism in Ancient and Medival Bengal: by S. Mukherji, 41-42.

4. Bangladese Nimvarka Sampradayra Vivarana: by Dhananjoyadasa Kathiyababa, Vol. 5, 15-39.

5. Bangla Sahityer Itihas: by Sukumar Sen, 1,1, p. 226.

6. Bhaktiratnavali: by Vishnupuri, Edited and translated into English by A.B. Allahabad, Oriental Publisher, Delhi, 1918.

7. Bhaktisamdarbha: by Jiva Goswami, Edited by Radharamana Goswami and Krsnagopala Goswami, p. 70.

8. Bhaktisutras of Narada and Sandilyasutra: Edited by Nandalal Sinha, Oriental Publishers, Delhi.

9. Brhaddharmapurana: Edited by Panchanan tarkaratna, 4th Ed. 1925.

10. Brhat Tantrasastra: by Basumati Sahitya Mandir, PP, 164, 166, 190-191.

11. Catainyabhagavata: by Vrndavana Das, Edited by Sukumar Sen

12. Catainyacaritamrta: by Krsnadasa Kaviraja, Edited by Sukumar Sen, Sahitya Akademi, 1963.

13. Catainyamangala: Ad. 7 p. 9.

14. Gitgovinda and Its Abhinaya: by Vasudeva Sastri,

15. Hussain Shahi Bengal: by M.R. Tarafdar, p. 248.

16. Indian and Far Eastern Religious Tradition: by R.D. Baird and Alfred Bloom, p. 52-53, 58
17. Kaulikacarandipika: by R. Chattopadhyaya, p. 17.
18. Krsna in History and Legend: by B.B. Majumder, Ch. 1.
19. Literary History of the Pala Period: by Haraprrasad Sastsri, JBORS, V, II, 1919,
20. Manasapujapaddhati: by H.C. Sahittyavinode, pp. 43-44.
21. Mahabharat: by Kashirama Das, Published by Benimadhav Sil, 22.
22. On the Archaism of the Bhagavata Purana: by J.A.B. Van Buitenen, in Milton Singer Edition, 1966, p. 35.
23. Origin and Development of the Bengali Language, 1, p.81.
24. Padavali Kirtaner Itihas: by Svami Prajnananda, Vol. I, Ch. 25.
25. Raghunandana's Indebtness to His Predecessors: by B. Bhattacarya, 1953, XIV.
26. Ramakrishna Kathamrta: Vol. 1, pp. 45-46.
27. Srikrisnakirtana by Badu Chandidasa, p. 235, Verse 4.
28. Sri-Madbhagavata: Edited by S.C. Majumdar.
29. Sri Madbhagavata Gita: by A.C. Bhakibedanta Swami Prabhupada.
30. Tantras in Bengal: by G. Mukhopadhyaya, Vol. 1, 19975, p. 31
31. The Deopara Prasasti of Vijoyasena: Inscriptions of Bengal, III, p. 42.
32. The History of Bengal: Hindu Period, by R.C. Majumder.
33. The Oxford History of India: by Vincent A. Smith, 4th, Ed. 1983.
34. The Wonder That Was India: by A.L. Basham, 1985, p. 332.
35. Vaisnavism in Bengal: by Dr. Ramakanta Chakravarty,
36. Vedic Literature in Civilisation of India Syllabus: by J.A.B. Van Buitenen, Madison, Wis., Univeristy of Wisconsin Press, 1965.
37. West Bengal District Gazeteers, Bankura, Ch. III

Chapters VI and VII

1. Advaitaprakassa: by Isana Nagara, Ch. 12, p. 118.
2. Advaita Siddhi: Edited by Rajendra Nath Ghosh, Vol I.
3. Bhaktirasamtasindhu: by Rupa Goswami, Edited by A.C.B.S. Prabhupada
4. Bangalir Sarasvat Avadan: by D.C. Bhattachaya, p. 94.
5. Caitanya Charcher Pachso Bachhar: by D. Bandopadhyay, (1985)

6. Catainyabhagavata: by Vrndavana Das (Sahitya Akademi, ed)
7. Caitanya Charitamrta: by H.K. Mukhopadhyay
8. Catainyamangala: Sesakhanda: by Jayananda pp. 116-17.
9. Chandogya Upanisad: Vi, XIII, p. 3.
10. Commentary on Catainyacharitmrta: by A.C.B.S. Prabhupada, Adi, part I, p. 140.
11. Commentary on Caitanya charitamrta by Sukumar Sen
12. Complete Works of Swami Vivekananda: Centinary, Vol. III, IV, VI.
13. Description of Hindusthan: by W. Hamilton, Vol. I, p. 208.
14. Jyotirmoy Sri Catainya: by Kalkut, p. 133.
15. Late Medival Temples of Bengal: by D.J. McCutchion, p. 33.
16. Madhyuger Bangla Sahityer Kalakram: by S. Mukhopadhyaya.
17. Padma Purana; Catainyacaritamrta, Madhya, 17 / 133.
18. Religion in Modern India: by R.D. Baird, p. 58.
19. Sajjanatosani: Vol. 2, 1885, pp. 111-13.
20. Santipur Parichaya; by K. Bhattacharya, p. 243-52.
21. Sri Amiya Nimai Charit: by Manatma Sisir Kumar Ghosh.
22. Sri Madbhagavata: by Vasumati Mandir, 1 / 1.
23. Sri Sri Mahasankirtana by Poet Singer, T.K. Sarkar.
24. Sri Sri Ramakrsna Lila Prasanga: by Swami Saradananda.
25. The Science of Self Realiztion: by A.C.B.S. Prabhupada;
26. The Spiritual Heritage of India: by Swami Prabhavananda, 1980.
27. The Teaching and Philosophy of Lord Caitanya: by Srimad B.P. Tirtha Maharaj (1967).
28. Vaisnavism in Bengal: by Dr. R. Chakravarty, p. 53.
29. Vishnu Purana: 1 / 12 / 57.

Chapters VIII, IX, X and XI

1. A Nation in Making: by S.N. Bandopadhyay.
2. A statistical Analysis of Bengal: by Huner, 3.
3. AmarJivan: by Navinchandra Sen, Ed. Sajanikanta Das.
4. Anthropology of Folk Religion: by Milton Singer, ed. Charlse Leslie.
5. Bangalir bishistata: Bangabani, Bhadra, B.S. 1329 (1933).
6. Bangalir Upasak Sampradaya: Bangabani, Kartick, B S 1329 (1935).
7. Bangla Akadami Patrika: Ed. 4, 1971,

8. Bangali Manishay SriCaitanya: by Nirmalnarayan Gupta, 1985.

9. Bangla Bhraman: by Bipinchandra Pal, Vol. 2.

10. Bhakta Charitamala: Published by Guradas Chattopadhyay, 1896.

11. Bangla Samayika Patra: by B. Bandopadhyaya, Vol. I.

12. Bankim Rachanavali: Ed. Jogesh Chandra Bagal, Shitaya Samsad, 1956.

13. Bankura Jelar Purakirti: by A.K. Bandopadhyay

14. Bengal District Ggazeteers: Midnapore.

15. Brhat Banga: by Dinesh Chandra Sen, Vol. 2.

16. Caitanyottara Yuge Gaudiya Vasnavas: by N.G. Goswami

17. Chandimangala: Sahitya Akademi Edition.

18. Charitasudha: by Ramadasa Babaji, Vol. 1, Vol. 2,

19. Dakshin Pascim Banger Silpa: by R. Bandopadhyay, 1929.

20. Description of Hindusthan: by W. Hamilton, Vol. 1.

21. Dharma and Serpent Worship in Bankura District: by Ashutosh Bhattacharya.

22. Gandhi's Work: Vol. 32.

23. Gaudiya Vaisnava Abhidan: Vol. 2.

24. Gaudiya Vaisnavacaryavrnder Granthavalir Vivaran: by Dr. Ramdas Sen, I, 3rd ed. 1937.

25. Gaudiya Vaisnava Itihas: Madhusudan Tattvavacaspati.

26. Gaudiya Vaisnava Jvana: by Haridas Das, Vol. I, Vol. 2,

27. Gaudiya Vaisnava Jivana: by Siddha Caitanya Das, Vol. 2.

28. Hemchandra: by Manmathanath Ghose, Vol. I.

29. Hindu Caste and Sects: by Jogindranath Bhattacharya, 1968.

30. History of Vishnupur Raj: by A. Mallick

31. India: Past and Present: by Shoshee Chunder Dutt.

32. Mahatma Sisir Kumar Ghose; by A.N. Basu, 1976.

33. Nazrul Giti: by Kazi Nazrul Islam.

34. Navin Chandra O Jatiya Abhuthan: Sahitya, Magh B S, 1315 (1921).

35. Obscure Religious Cult: by S.B. Dasgupta.

36. Pallilvichitra: by Ananda Publishers Calcutta, 1982.

37. Paschim Banglar Gramer Nam: by A.K. Bandopadhyay, 1980.

38. Prabahini: Sisir Kumar Ghosh, Poush, B. S. 1321 (1927)

39. Pratahsmaraniyacaritamala: by Yugendranath Vidyabhusan, 2nd ed. 1885.

40. Puthiparicaya: by Panchanan Mandal
41. Ramesvara Racanavali: by Panchanan Chakravarty.
42. Report of the Census of Bengal: by A. Boudilion. Book of W.B. pp 127-129.
43. Religious Movement in Modern India: by B.G. Roy, p.95.
44. Sadhanadipika: byRadhakrsna Goswami
45. Sadhanamrtacandrika: by Siddhakrsnadasa
46. Sahitya Sadhaka Charitamala: by Haraprasad Sastri, Vol. 7.
47. Sahitya Sadhaka Charitamala: by J.N. Tagore, Vol. 6.
48. Sahitya Sadhaka Charitamila: by Sisir Kumar Ghose; Edited by B. Bandopadhyay.
49. Sajjananatosani: 1985, Vol. 2, 1894, Vol. 4, 1892, Vol. 6. 1895, Vol. 7. 1896, Vol. 8. 1897, Vol. 12. 1900-1901.
50. Sakar O Nirakar: Rabindra Rchanavali, Centenary Birthday Ed. Vol. 13, 1911.
51. Sambadpatre Sekaler Katha: Vol. 1, Vol. 2.
52. Sangitakosa: Collected Devotional Songs of Gaudiya Vaisnavas.
53. Selected Papers: by James Long, Ed. M.P. Saha.
54. Social Change in Modern India: by M.N. Srinivas, 1982.
55. Social Mobility of Bengal: by H.R. Sanyal, 1981.
56. Sri Bhaktivinode Thakurer Svalikhita Jivani, pp. 112-114.
57. Srihatter Loka Samgit: by N. Bhowmick and G. Datta.
58. Sri Sri Vishnupriyasahsranama Stotra: by Haridasa Goswami, B S, 1322, (1929)
59. Sri Sri Sadguru Sanga: by Kuladananda Brahmachari, Vol. 2.
60. The Teachings of A.C. Bhaktivedanta Swami Prabhupada: Multiple Books: Published by The Bhaktivedanta Book Trust
61. The Census of 1961: by Das, Raichaudhuri and Raha.
62. Travel of a Hindu: by Bholanath Candra, Vol. 1.
63. The Lecture notes of Deshbandhu C.R. Das, April, 1917, 1918.
64. The Passing of the Empire: Modern Asian Studies, 1975.
65. The Purpose of Avatarhood: by A. Ghose, Centenary Vol. 22.
66. The Speech of Gandhi in Orissa: Published in Young India, 13th April, 1921.
67. Vesasrayavidhih; Bengali Translationby Ramnarayana Vidyaratna, Published by Murshidabad.

68. Vidyapati: in the 3rd edition of Nanaprabandha, 1937.
69. Thakur Bhaktivinode Thakurer Svalikita Jivani, pp. 112-114.
70. Vaisnavism in Bengal; by Dr. R. Chakravarty, 1985.
71. Ward Account: Vol. 3, p. 262.
72. West Bengal Bengal District Gazetteers, Bankura.

Index

G

Ganges 5, 16, 82, 191, 193-4
Gaya 5, 32, 51-2, 57, 146
Gita xv, 10, 29-30, 45, 52, 68, 95, 199, 219, 229, 240, 260-1
Godavari 5
Gopis 32
Goswamins 138, 145, 149-50, 174, 186, 189, 217, 239

H

Hapta Hindu 1
Hari 49, 54-6, 59, 64-5, 71, 80, 82, 84, 118, 123-4, 147-8, 151-5, 157-8, 191, 201
Haridwara 5
Hindi 2-3, 78, 120, 138, 154
Hindu 1-2, 4-5, 8-9, 11-12, 15-16, 18, 20-1, 36-47, 98-9, 109-10, 119-26, 128-31, 141-5, 173-5, 237-9
Hindu Law 9, 20, 42
Hinduism 1, 4-5, 12, 39, 103, 109-10, 122, 130, 142, 220, 237, 241, 243
Hindusthan 1-2, 5, 99, 167, 262-3

I

Indo-Aryan 2-3
Indra 3, 31
Institute of Manu 9

J

Jati 9, 238
Jiva Soul 76, 123, 128, 157
Jurisprudence 9

K

Kacchi 3
Kali 3, 5, 25, 27, 61-2, 64-5, 79-81, 96, 100-1, 107, 109, 155, 174, 227-9, 241-2
Kalpa 50
Kashmiri 3, 84-5
Kaveri 5, 133
Kayestha 18-19, 87-8, 121, 126
Krsnaloka 73
Kshatriya 12, 17, 129, 140, 237
Kurus 3
Kusha 4

L

Lahnda 3
Lakshmi 3, 36, 50, 57, 177, 237
Laws of Manu 9

M

Madhura love 124
Madhurabhava 97
Mahabharata 5, 9-10, 30, 140
Mahadeva 35, 178
Mahotsava 46, 91, 105, 186, 200-1, 203-4
Manasa 5, 26, 35-7, 237
Manasha 3
Manavadharmasastra 9
Mangalchandi 36
Manipur 8, 172
Mantras 18
Marathi 3, 120
Matsyas 3
Maya 64, 66, 68, 76
Mayabadis 59

Mitra   3, 101, 104-5, 111, 159, 171, 176

Moksha 51

Mysians 2

N

Nada 92, 149, 230

Namahatta 215

Namayajna 183, 196, 200-1, 203-4

Namkirtan 46

Namsankirtana 81

Narayana 25, 49, 53, 61, 77-8, 84, 178, 250

Narmada 5

Navadvipa 18, 35, 38, 43, 45-8, 50-7, 60, 77, 89-90, 101-2, 171-2, 188, 190-1, 197, 201-2

Navyanaya 20

Nayanars 4

Nayasastra 119

Nedi 92, 149, 230

O

Oriya 3, 145

P

Panchagavya 4

Panchalas 3

Paramatma xiv, 76-7, 128

Pasandis 42

Persian 1

philistine 20, 42

Philistine 20, 42

Phygyans 2

Pollution 16

Prajapati 7

Pratiloma 15

Premabhakti 58, 62, 70, 78, 88, 99, 125, 197, 203, 239, 241

Proselytisation 243

Punjabi 2

Puranas xiii, 27, 227, 239-42

Puri 5, 20, 42, 45, 48-9, 51, 53, 56, 58-9, 63, 77-8, 99, 124-5, 145-7, 172

Purusa 7

Puskara 5

R

Raja 101, 141, 173

Rajasthani 2

Rama 25, 27-9, 31, 64-6, 101, 107, 169, 172, 177, 201-2, 208, 210, 214, 221

Ramayana 5, 27-9, 53, 139, 226

Rigveda 1-3, 7, 11, 19, 23-4, 27, 226, 229

Rudra 3, 59, 63, 166, 226, 239

S

Sadhanbhakti 70

Sahajiya 92, 103, 126-8, 149, 178, 189, 230

Sai 92, 127

Saiva 27, 32, 35, 53, 100, 130, 143, 163, 171, 176, 183, 196, 229, 240

Saivism 4, 225-6

Sakta 27, 32, 35, 93-4, 100-1, 136, 143, 163, 171, 176, 178-9, 181, 183, 228-9, 240-2

Sakti 3, 5, 95-6, 101, 184, 186, 216, 226-9

Samadhi 25, 228